JADE RAINBOW

玉
虹

JADE RAINBOW

ANCIENT CHINESE POETRY

TRANSLATED BY
KWAN-HUNG CHAN

∞ INFINITY
PUBLISHING

Copyright © 2018 by Kwan-Hung Chan
Library of Congress Control Number: 2018902812

ISBN 978-1-4958-2127-1
ISBN 978-1-4958-2128-8 eBook

This is a work of fiction. Names, characters, places, and incidents either are the product of the author's imagination or are used fictitiously. Any resemblance to actual events or locales or persons, living or dead, is entirely coincidental.

Published April 2018

INFINITY PUBLISHING
1094 New DeHaven Street, Suite 100
West Conshohocken, PA 19428-2713
Toll-free (877) BUY BOOK
Local Phone (610) 941-9999
Fax (610) 941-9959
Info@buybooksontheweb.com
www.buybooksontheweb.com

CONTENTS

Preface 1

1. ZHOU DYNASTY (1122-256 BCE) 5

BOOK OF SONGS (c600 BCE)

Beating Drums 5

Crickets 7

Mayflies 8

My Man 9

Pick Vetches 10

The Seventh Month: Song of Bin 14

2. HAN DYNASTY (206 BCE-220) 19

CAO CAO (155-220)

Ballad of Hao Li...19

XU GAN (171-217)

Boudoir Thoughts 20

WANG CAN (177-217)

Ballad of Expeditions...21

CAO ZHI (192-232)

The Feast Hosted by the Prince 22

Sighing in Lament..23

SHI CHONG (249-300)

    Wang Mingjun...25

3.SIX DYNASTIES (220-589) 27

ZUO SI (250?-305?)

    On History, no.1...27

LIU KUN (217-318)

    The Wind-borne Army...29

    A Second Poem for Lu Chen...31

LU CHEN (284-318)

    In Answer to Wei Ziti..33

TAO YUANMING (365-427)

    Jingke..35

    In Answer to Archivist Guo...36

    On Reading "Geography of Ancient China".........................37

YAN YANZI (384-456)

    Five Gentlemen: Ji Kang,

    Unofficial Political Commentator.......................................38

    Five Gentlemen: Liu Ling, the Adjutant.............................39

    Five Gentlemen:

    Ruan Xian, Chief of Shiping..39

    Five Gentlemen: Xiang Xiu,

    Palace Remonstrance Master..40

    Five Gentlemen: Ruan Ji, the Infantry Man.......................41

XIE HUN (?-412)

    Touring West Pond..42

BAO ZHAO (c414-466)

    Plum flowers Fall...43

    Seeing off Director Fu...43

XIE ZHUANG (421-466)

The Deserted Garden of a House in the North 44

SHEN YUE (441-513)

On the Extremely Limpid River Xinan,
Visible from Top to Bottom, for my Good
Friends in the Capital 45

Seeing off Fan Ancheng 46

Setting out Early for Ding Hill 47

XIE TIAO (464-499)

In Answer to a Poem by Consultant Xie on the
Brazen Birds Terrace 48

On the River 49

Seeing off Fan Yun for Lingling County
at the Shore of Xinting 49

WU JUN (469-520)

Spring 50

In Answer to Liu Yun 51

HE XUN (c472-c519)

For Adjutant Yu, Composed as I
watch Pen City at Twilight 52

Spring Wind...............................53

YU JIANWU (487-551)

In Answer to "Spring Night, a Poem in Reply",
at Imperial Request 53

The Grass of Changxin Palace...............................54

Visiting the Royal Courier Station
of King Wu after the Turmoil 55

YU XIN (513-581)

Crows Caw at Night...............................56

In Answer to an Elegy Written by

Wang, Secretary of the Crown Prince, for Zhou, the Recluse..........57

In Answer to Monk Kan..58

In Answer to the Poem "Sailing

Across a Big River" by King Wen

of the Liang Dynasty, at Imperial Request 58

A Painted Screen, no 59

A Painted Screen, no 60

Paying Homage to the Temple of Laozi 61

Poems in the Style of "Expressing my Mind"

by Ruan Ji, no.1 62

Poems in the Style of "Expressing my Mind"

by Ruan Ji, no.2 62

Poems in the Style of "Expressing my Mind"

by Ruan Ji, no.3 63

Poems in the Style of "Expressing my Mind"

by Ruan Ji, no.4 64

Poems in the Style of "Expressing my Mind"

by Ruan Ji, no.5 65

Poems in the Style of "Expressing my Mind"

by Ruan Ji, no 6 65

Poems in the Style of "Expressing my Mind"

by Ruan Ji, no 7 66

Poems in the Style of "Expressing my Mind"

by Ruan Ji, no 8 67

A Second Poem of Farewell to Secretary Zhou................................68

JIANG ZHONG (519-594)

For Secretary Pei after Meeting

an Envoy from Changan 68

LU SIDAO (531-582)

Ballad of Expeditions...69

A Visit to Daliang 71

XUE DAOHENG (540-606)

Boudoir Complaint (Tune: Xi Xi Yan)...................................72

KONG SHAOAN (577-c622)

Falling Leaves 73

Seeing off Licentiate Xu Yongyuan 74

ANONYMOUS (Six Dynasties)

Midnight Song: Summer...75

Midnight Song: Autumn...75

Midnight Song: Winter...75

FENG XIAOLIAN (Six Dynasties)

Reflections after the Strings of her Pipa Snapped 76

PRINCESS DAYI (Six Dynasties)

Inscribed on a Screen 77

ZHENG GONGCHAO (Six Dynasties)

Seeing off Yu Bao, Imperial Guard..78

ZHU TING (Six Dynasties)

An Elegy for Myself...79

4. SUI DYNASTY (581-618) 81

YANG SU (?-606)

For Xue, Deputy Director, Written in
my Study in the Hills while Sitting Alone, no.1.................81

For Xue, Deputy Director, Written in
my Study in the Hills while Sitting Alone, no.2.................82

For Xue of Bozhou, no.1 83

For Xue of Bozhou, no.2 84

For Xue of Bozhou, no. 3 85

For Xue of Bozhou, no. 4 85

For Xue of Bozhou, no. 5 86

For Xue of Bozhou, no. 6 87

For Xue of Bozhou, no. 7 88

For Xue of Bozhou, no. 8 88

For Xue of Bozhou, no. 9 89

KONG DESHAO (?-621)

An Overnight Stay in a Deserted Village 90

Seeing off Cai Junzhi on his Way to Shu...........................91

ANONYMOUS (Sui Dynasty)

The Crowing Rooster 91

MING YUQING (Sui Dynasty)

Expeditions 92

SUN WANSHOU (Sui Dynasty)

In Reply to a Poem by a Secretay of the

Zhou Dynasty, on Visiting the Site of the Former Capital 93

5. TANG DYNASTY (618-907) 95

ZHANG SHUO (667-730)

Ballad of Ye, Capital of Wei...95

WANG WEI (701-761)

In Answer to Secretary Guo..96

DU FU (712-770)

Ballad of Viewing a Sword Dance

Performed by a Student of Lady Gongsun 98

Facing Snow...99

Recalling my Brothers on a Moonlit Night........................99

WEI YINGWU (732-c792)

Accompanying Censor Yuan on

an Outing in Spring 100

Composed upon Meeting the Poet,

Master Cao, at Night...101

Entertaining Adjutant Li 101

Events on River Huai: to a

Dear Friend in Guangling 102

Facing Snow in Early Spring: to

Former Palace Censor Yuan 103

For Censor Wang 103

For Li Dan 104

For Quanzhen and Yuanchang 105

Hurrying to the Prefect's Dawn

Court: for my Colleagues in Two Counties...................................105

Hurt Feelings at our Former

Residence at Tongde Hermitage 106

In Reply to Former Military Officer of

Changan, Tian Wen, while Serving as

Deputy Magistrate of Luoyang..107

In Response to Granary Chief, Dou

Lu, Inscribed on the

Granary Wall in Public View 107

In Wait for Lu Song, who Wrote

Unconvincingly that he could not

Come Because the Day was Late and

he had no Horse, I Send this Poem in Reply................................108

In Yangzhou, Unexpectedly Meeting

Former Assistant to the Magistrate

Lu Geng of Luoyang 109

Li Wuxi Sees off Li, Assistant to the

Magistrate, on his Return to West Terrace 110

Looking out Together from a
Pavilion of Tongde Temple 110

Meeting Li Qiwu, the Fourth,
at Daliang Pavilion 112

A Note to Lu Zhi 113

On a Leave of Absence, Lu, the
Twenty-Second, Writes me, Claiming
he is Ill in Bed. Also, Surprised that Li,
the Second, has not Visited me in Such
a Long Time, I Reply with a Poem
to Tease Li, the Second. 114

On a Moonlit Night, I met Xu,
the Eleventh, at his Thatched Hut 114

On Floating Clouds and Parting
Manners while Seeing off Zheng Shucheng 115

On Tripod Gate, while Seeing off
Lu Geng to his New Assignment 116

Passing Shaolin Hermitage: To
Friends and Relatives in the Capital...........................117

Recalling my Secluded Residence
by River Feng 117

Recalling Yuan, the Second, in Spring 118

Respectfully Asking to Resign as
the Deputy Magistrate of Luoyang 119

Seeing off Candidate Tan..120

Seeing off County Chief Lin to Yuci...........................120

Seeing off Cui, Assistant to the
Magistrate, to Mianchi 121

Seeing off Deputy Magistrate Han
of Luoyang on his Trip East.......................................122

Seeing off my Brotherly Friend...123

Seeing off Wang, Assistant to
the Magistrate, to Fencheng 123

Seeing off Zhang, Assistant Censor,
for South of Yangzi to Care for his Parents 124

Seeing off Zheng Changyuan 125

To my Cousins on an Early Fall Night...126

To Secretary Yang...126

Touring Xiangshan Springs at Longmen.....................................127

Visiting South Pavilion in Spring 128

Watching Rain in my Leave of Absence:
To my Colleagues in the County Government 128

Written in Luoyang during the Guangde Period.........................129

ZHANG JI (c766-830)

The Cowherd 130

The Old Peasant 131

To an Old Friend Missing in Tibet...132

HAN YU (768-824)

Inscribed on the Gate Tower of the
Temple for the Deity of the Mountains at
Hengshan where I Paid a Visit and Stayed Overnight.................133

LIU YUXI (772-842)

In Reply to the Poem of Letian at
our First Meeting in Yangzhou 135

Recalling the Past at Xisai Hill..135

LIU ZHONGYUAN (773-819)

To Four Prefects: Zhang, Ting, Feng
and Lian, from the City Tower in Liuzhou 136

YUAN ZHEN (779-831)

Lianchang Palace..139

SHI JIANWU (780-821)

The Immortal Returns Home 143

LI HE (790-816)

Ballad of Spring Longings 144

While Recovering from a Drinking
Bout in the Elder Zhang's Mansion
in Luzhou, I Met a Mail Courier on
the River and Sent this Poem to my
Fourteenth Cousin 145

DU MU (803-852)

Confession 147

Drinking Alone 147

Expressing my Mind 148

Given in Farewell, no.1 148

Given in Farewell, no.2 148

Inscribed on Chanzhi Temple
of Yangzhou before I Departed for Xuanzhou.......................149

Inscribed on the City Tower of Qian 149

Inscribed on the Wei Family
Pavilion on a Spring Night 150

Leaving my Family 150

A Limpid Brook in Cizhou..151

A Message for Myself...151

Mister Chunshen 152

Not Accepting Wine..152

On my Way at the End of Spring 153

Palace Ladies as Attendants of Mausoleums..........................153

Palace Ladies Leaving the Palace, no.1 154

Penning my Thoughts 154

A Poem for Myself...155

A Quatrain on a Pond in
the Back of Qian County 155

Rain 156

Reading Collected Poems
of Han Yu and Du Fu..156

Recalling my Past, no.1 157

Recalling my Past, no.2 157

Recalling my Past, no.3 158

Recalling my Past at South of the River 158

Seeing off the Assistant Censor
of Rongzhou for his New Post 159

Shen Xiaxian 160

Sighing for Flowers...160

Sleeping Drunk 160

Spring in South of the River 161

Viewing Changan in fall...161

Visiting Jinbi Cave of Linquan
Temple at Cizhou 162

Written at the Feast Hosted
by the Minister of War 162

ZHAO GU (806-852)

Passing the Former Residence
of Guo Ziyi in Fenyang 163

WEN TINGYUN (812-870)

Morning Trip at Shangshan 164

Visiting the Grave of Chen Lin 164

LI SHANGYIN (813-859)

Administrator Du of the
Department of Appointments 165

For Administrator Du the
Thirteenth of the Department
of Appointments 166
Spring Wind...166

NIE YIZHONG (837-884)
A Peasant Family 167

LI YU (937-978)
Flirtation (Tune: Yi Hu Zhu) 168

LIU KAI (947-1000)
At the Borders 168

5. SONG DYNASTY (960-1279) 171

WANG YUCHENG (954-1001)
Sailing on River Wusong 171
A Trip to a Village 172

LIU YUN (971-1031)
King Wu of Han 173

YANG YI (974-1020)
King Wu of Han 173

LIU YONG (987-1279)
Hangzhou (Tune: Wang Hai Chao).................................175
Lucky Encounter (Tune: Yu Hu Die) 176

YAN SHU (991-1055)
Addressing my Mind...178

OUYANG XIU (1007-1072)
Composed in a Dream 178
The Hand-print of Princess
Chonghui of the Tang Dynasty 179
In Answer to Wang Jiefu's
Poem: "Song of Concubine Ming" 180

Night Mooring at Yellow Creek.....................................181

SU XUN (1009-1066)

In Answer to a Poem of Han Weigong on the Ninth Day.............179

ZENG GONG (1019-1083)

West Tower 183

WANG ANSHI (1021-1086)

Climbing Baogong Pagoda 183

Concubine Ming...184

WANG ANSHI (1021-1086)

Thinking of Wang Fengyuan 186

WANG ANGUO (1028-1074)

Inscribed on the Pavilion of Prince Teng...........................186

WANG LING (1032-1059)

The Bitter Heat in a Dry Spell....................................187

SU SHI (1036-1110)

After Staying over at Weizhou due
to Heavy Snow on New Year's Eve,
I Resumed my Journey on New Year's
Day with Early Sunrise and Got Caught
up with Snow Falling again Midway................................188

For Zhao Huizi while Passing the
Lianshui Administrative
District (Tune: Die Lian Hua)....................................189

Hengcui Pavilion of Fa Hui Temple................................190

Inscribed on the Wall of the City
Hall where a Full Cell of Prisoners
Delayed my Returning Home at
Dusk on New Year's Eve 191

Inscribed on Zhuxi Temple on my Return to Yixing.................192

Lament of a Peasant Woman of Wu.................................193

My Philosophy (Tune: Man Ting Fang)............................194

Night Sailing at Sea on the
Twentieth Day of the Sixth Month.............................195

A Painting of the River on a
Spring Night by Monk Huichong, no.1 196

A Painting of the River on a
Spring Night by Monk Huichong, no.2 196

Rising at Night in a Boat..197

Visiting Jixiang Temple alone at the Winter Solstice.......198

Visiting Temples during the Dragon Boat Festival 198

Written to Accompany a Painting
of Autumn, Drawn by Li Shinan.............................199

HUANG TINGJIAN (1045-1105)

For Ziyou, Following the Rhymes
and Rhyming Pattern Used by Yuanming....................200

In Taiping District, a Singing Girl
called Yang Shu, Played the Qin
and Served Wine (Tune: Hao Shi Jin) 201

Inscribed on Falling Star Temple 202

My Philosophy (Tune: Ding Feng Bo).........................203

On Seeing Plum Blossoms in
Xuanzhou (Tune: Yu Mei Ren) 204

On Snow, a Poem Presented to
Minister Song of Guangping....................................204

Pine Wind Pavilion 205

A Playful Poem Presented to Kong Yifu.....................207

Seeing off Mister Wang, my Brother-in-law.................208

QIN GUAN (1049-1110)

Parting Lament (Tune: Ba Liu Zi) 209

Parting Sorrow (Tune: Man Ting Fang).....................210

A Trip with Wine in Spring (Tune: Hao Shi Jin) 212

ZHANG LEI (1054-1114)

Summer Days..212

ZHOU BANGYAN (1056-1121)

Parting Sorrow (Tune: Yu Lou Chun).............................213

Recalling the Past at Jinling (Tune: Xi He) 214

LI QINGZHAO (1081-1143)

Homesickness (Tune: Pu Sha Man) 216

In Sickness (Tune: Tan Po Huan Xi Sha) 217

Spring Slumber (Tune: Zu Zhong Qing)........................217

ZHU DUNRU (1081-1159)

Composed at West Capital (Tune: Zhe Gu Tian) 218

The Fisherman's Song (Tune: Hao Shi Jin)....................219

Listening to the Pipa (Tune: Jian Zi Mu Lan Hua) 220

LU BENZHONG (1084-1145)

On the Road in Yangshan County

of Lianzhou as I return 221

CHEN YUYI (1090-1139)

On Recollecting my Old Friends

in Luoyang, in a Small Pavilion at

Night (Tune: Lin Jiang Xian) 222

Spring Lament..222

LU YOU (1125-1210)

At Chengtou Station, I Had a Small

Drink before Sleeping..223

In my Study, Fiddling with a Writing

Brush, I Wrote a Casual Poem for my Son Yu...............224

Looking at a Vegetable Garden 225

Mixed Inspiration at South Hall....................................225

My Life Style (Tune: Hao Shi Jin) 226

A New Verse on a Spring Day 227

A Night Walk to the Top of White Deer Spring 228

Not Sleeping 228

The Patriot's Song..229

Quatrains on my Vegetable Garden, no.1 231

Sitting at Night with a Short Drink...231

Spring Outing 232

FAN CHENGDA (1126-1193)

South of the River (Tune: Die Lian Hua) 233

Written in my Carriage during a
Short Rest from my Deep Fatigue
by Willow Pond, on my Way through
Pingxiang County, as the Sun has
just Appeared (Tune: Yan Er Mei) 234

XIN QIJI (1140-1207)

Late Spring (Tune: Zhu Ying Tai Jin) 235

Life in the Village (Tune: Qing Ping Le).................................236

Thoughts in Beigou Pavilion at
Jingkou (Tune: Nan Xiang Zi)...237

JIANG KUI (1155-1220)

Plum Blossoms (Tune: An Xiang)..238

DAI FUGU (1167?-)

An Old Wild Man (Tune: Qing Ping Le) 239

LI JUNMIN (1176-1269)

A Fall Scene of a Stray Wild Goose over a River 240

LIU KEZHUANG (1187-1269)

Current Events in the Year of Wuchen (1208) 241

Enjoying the Moon on the Fifteenth
Night of the Fifth Month (Tune: Qing Ping Le)............................242

Written in Jest for my Fellow
Townsman, Prefectural Judge
Lin (Tune: Yu Lou Chun)...242

YUAN HAOWEN (1190-1257)

Autumn Thoughts...243
On the Twenty-ninth Day in the
Fourth Month of the Year
of Gui Ji (1233), I left the Capital................................244
To my Eyes...245
The Tomb of Two Wild Geese (Tune: Mo Yu E).............246

WU WENYING (1200?-)

Boudoir Complaint (Tune: Huan Xi Sha).......................249
Disappointment (Tune: Feng Ru Song)...........................249
Reflections (Tune: ShuangYe Fei)...................................250

LIU CHENWENG (1232-1297)

Spring Moon (Tune: Bao Ding Xian)..............................251

WANG YISUN (1240-1290)

The Cicada: an Elegy for the Kings
of the Southern Song Dynasty (Tune: Qi Tian Le).........254
The New Moon (Tune: Mei Wu)......................................255

ZHANG YAN (1248-1329?)

In Memory of my Northern
Sojourn (Tune: Ruan Lang Gui)......................................257
A Short Warm Spell like
Spring (Tune: Man Ting Fang)..258
Spring Inspiration at West
Lake (Tune: Gao Yang Tai)..259

ZHAO MENGFU (1254-1322)

Quatrains, no.1 260
Quatrains, no.2 261

YANG ZAI (1271-1323)

A Trip to North Hill of West Lake in Late Spring.........................261

LUO YUZI (Song Dynasty)

Watching Leaves...262

YANG PU (Song Dynasty)

My Straw Cloak 263

6. YUAN DYNASTY (1280-1367).................. 265

GUAN YUNSHI (1286-1324)

The Quilt of Reed Flowers..265

YANG WEIZHENG (1296-1370)

Inscribed on a Painting on "Signs of Spring" 266

ZHANG YINING (1301-1370)

The Fishing Terrace of Yan Ling 267

SONG LIAN (1310-1382)

Song of Yue 268

GAO QI (1336-1374)

The Evening Parties under
Candlelight of King Ming 269

Looking at the Big River after
Climbing Yuhua Terrace of Jinling..271

7. MING DYNASTY (1368-1644) 273

LI MENGYANG (1472-1529)

General Shi on the Battlefield...274

The Painting of Two Eagles with
Horn-like Feathers by Lin Liang..278

HE JINGMING (1483-1521)

Ballad on the End of the Year 280

YANG SHEN (1488-1559)

The Temple of Zhuge Liang 282

Willows...283

XUE HUI (1489-1541)

The Terrace of King Zhao..284

XIE ZHEN (1495-1575)

Inspiration in the Wilds 284

HUANGPU PANG (1498-1583)

Under Moonlight, in Answer to my

Elder Brother, Zijun, Expressing my

Concern for our Brothers 285

GAO SHUSI (1501-1537)

On the Road in Dingxing County on Cold Food Day 286

TANG SHUNZI (1507-1560)

A Report to my Friends in the Capital

after Resuming my Post in the Government 287

HUANG JISHUI (1509-1574)

Drinking Wine with Friends 288

LI PANLONG (1514-1570)

Mourning for Adjutant Wang, no.1..288

Mourning for Adjutant Wang, no.2..289

Opening up my Mind at the End of the Year 289

Reaching the Peak of Mount Taihua in Late Fall........................290

Seeing off Yuan Mei for the Pass 291

WANG SHIZHENG (1526-1590)

Accompanying Attending Censor

Yin on a Hike to the Peak of Lingyin Hill 291

An Elegy for Sun Taichu at his Grave 292

Visiting Taibai Tower..293

ZHANG JIAYIN (1527-1588)

Climbing the City Tower of Hangu Pass.............................294

LI LIUFANG (1575-1629)

The Seventh Night at the West Gate of Nanjing.........................294

XU WEIHE (c1580-1637)

Meeting Old Li at a Wine Shop 295

Wilted Flowers of a Courier Station 296

QIAN QIANYI (1582-1664)

Eight Poems on Autumn Inspiration

in Jinling, Following the Rhymes Used

by Du Fu, in a Poem of a Similar Title,

Written on the First Day of the Seventh Month,

in the Year of Jihai (1659), no 296

Eight Poems on Autumn Inspiration

in Jinling, Following the Rhymes Used

by Du Fu, in a Poem of a Similar Title,

Written on the First Day of the Seventh Month,

in the Year of Jihai (1659), no 297

Mixed Thoughts at West Lake 298

Receiving Spirits...298

Seeing off Li Sheng in Mid-Spring

on his Return to Changgan from Wumen 299

KUANG LU (1604-1650)

A wine Shop of Lake Dongting 300

CHEN ZILONG (1608-1647)

Crossing River Yi...301

Mixed Thoughts on an Autumn Day, no.1 301

Reflections on Looking

East from Qiantang County 302

WU WEIYE (1609-1671)

Delayed by Snow..303

Feelings at Wujiang County 304

Listening to the Music on the Qin
Played by a Daoist Priestess, Bian Yujing 306

Reading the Poems of my Contemporary,
Written as an Envoy to the North, in Jile
Temple of Xiaxiang County..307

Yuanyuan 312

FANG YIZHI (1611-1671)

My Exile Alone...316

HUANG ZHOUXING (1611-1689)

Visiting Guozuo Temple and Climbing
Yuhua Terrace with Mister Du on a Fall Day 317

QIAN BINGDENG (1612-1693)

Visiting Wang Chenchu at Yangzhou, no.1 318

Visiting Wang Chenchu at Yangzhou, no.2 319

GU YANWU (1613-1682)

Nanjing..320

On the Sea 320

A Sacrificial Poem for Two Men of
Integrity in Fenzhou: Wu Yan
and Pan Chengzhang...321

GONG DINGZHI (1615-1673)

On a Forthcoming Visit to Jinling
on the Third Day of the Third Month 322

WU JIAJI (1618-1684)

For Lin Maozi at a Farewell Feast 323

ZHANG HUANGYAN (1620-1664)

Leaving my Hometown in the Eighth Month of the Year of
Jiachen (1664)...324

FEI MI (1625-1701)

Chaotian Gorge..325

MOU TONG (1627-1697)

Crossing the River..326

ZHU YIZHUN (1629-1709)

Mister Jade Belt...328

XIA WANCHUN (1631-1647)

For Zitui, Recalling Shao Jingshuo on a Boat 331

Jing Wei: the Legendary Bird that
Carried Pebbles to Fill the Sea 332

WANG SHIZHEN (1634-1711)

Mourning for my Wife..332

Written on a Re-visit at the
Peak of Swallow Ridge in a Dawn Rain 333

WANG YANHONG (?-1642)

Untitled...334

HAN QIA (1644-?)

Moonlit Passes and Hills 334

MENG YANG (Ming Dynasty)

Climbing Yueyang Tower 335

ZHANG MEIZHONG (Ming Dynasty)

Tiger Mound in Mid-spring...336

YUAN KAI (Ming Dynasty)

The White Swallow 337

8. QING DYNASTY (1644-1911) 339

LI E (1692-1752)

Inscribed on the wall of a Lake Tower 339

YAN SUICHENG (1694-?)

Dragon Spring Pass 340

QIAN ZHAI (1708-1793)

Viewing Mount Lu about Six

to Seven Miles from Donglin Temple 341

YUAN MEI (1716-1798)

Chan Yuan 341

One Scroll 342

Sitting at Night 342

Watching the Hills of Guilin on

a Trip to Xixia Temple with Jin Peien, the Eleventh 344

JIANG SHIQUAN (1725-1785)

The Corridor with the Sound of Clogs 346

LI JIAN (1747-1799)

A Small Garden 347

HUANG JINGREN (1749-1783)

Autumn Thoughts in the Capital, no 1 348

Autumn Thoughts in the Capital, no 2 348

Ballad on Watching Tidal Bores,

a Successive Piece 350

Ballad on Youth 351

Written while Drunk in a Feast at

Taibai Tower, Hosted by Mister Sihe 352

SHU WEI (1765-1815)

The Birthday of Flowers, Written on

the Way to Weitang 354

Empty Valley 354

A Random Poem on a Snowy Night..............................355

Watching Evening Clouds on Yuping Hill..................355

Willow Flowers 356

Willows..356

Yongzhou 357

CHEN WENSHU (1771-1843)

Summer Days..357

CHENG ENZHE (1785-1837)

Current Events on Crossing River Huai.......................358

GONG ZHIZHEN (1792-1841)

Falling Blooms at the West Outskirts...........................359

My Autumn Mood...361

WEI YUAN (1794-1857)

A Casual Verse on a Fall Day at my

Office in Gaoyouzhou 362

HE SHAOJI (1799-1873)

River Ningqiang..363

LU YITONG (1805-1863)

Bright Moon 363

More Reflections 364

YAO XIE (1805-1844)

Weeping for the Incorruptible Zhang Jiliang 365

ZHENG ZHEN (1806-1864)

Stone Steps of Gateway-to-the-Clouds 366

WANG KAIYUN (1833-1916)

Yuanming Garden 370

SHEN ZENGZHI (1850-1922)

A Random Poem at West Lake 377

KANG YOUWEI (1858-1927)

Climbing Yue King Terrace in Fall...............................378

Expressing my Mind while Sick
in Bed in Su Village, no.1 379
Expressing my Mind while Sick
in Bed in Su Village, no.2..381
Farewell to my Friends as
I Leave the Capital, no.1 380
Farewell to my Friends as I
Leave the Capital, No.2...381

TAN SITONG (1865-1898)
Inscribed on a Painting of
Eagles by Huizhong of Song....................................382
Inscribed on the Wall of my Prison..........................382
Tong Pass 383

ZHANG BINGLIN (1868-1936)
For Zhou Rong in Prison 384
Four Poems on Dangerous Times, no.1 384
Four Poems on Dangerous Times, no 2 385

JIN TIANYU (1874-1947)
Yellow Crane Tower...385

QIU JIN (1875-1907)
Before Wine 386
Begonias...387
Feeling Angry...387
In Response to a Poem Written
by Mister Ishii, a Japanese,
Using his Rhymes...388
Swallows...389

CHEN ZENGSHOU (1878-1949)
Miscellaneous Poems on the Lake, no.1.....................389
Miscellaneous Poems on the Lake, no.3.....................390

Waterfall-Watching Pavilion 390

SU MANSHU (1884-1918)

For Xuanxuan at our Stay
in a Villa of Pingyuan 391

An Inscription on a Painting to
Say Goodbye to Tang Guodun, no.1 392

An Inscription on a Painting to
Say Goodbye to Tang Guodun, no.2 392

Sitting Indoors by Lake Mochou 393

Ten Poems of my Activities, no.1 393

LIN WEN (1885-1911)

Spring Prospect 394

JIANG SHI (Qing Dynasty)

From Jiangshan to Pucheng, I Passed
Several Hills after Snow and Wrote
Nine Quatrains in my Sedan Chair, no.1 395

PREFACE

The waterfall, a massive expanse of water dropping from a height, catches the imagination of writers and painters of all time. In the poem "The Northern Chill", Li He 李賀 (790-816) called it a jade rainbow, a term not used by Chinese poets before his time, including Xie Lingyun 謝靈運 (385-433), a famed nature poet, known for his descriptions of craggy cliffs and cascading streams. I have chosen the title to honor the originality of Li He.

Some poets of the Song Dynasty called the waterfall a white rainbow. It was also used to describe any aqueous, foamy mass, semi-circular in shape, found in billows on waters or tides on shores.

The sources of poems translated in this book are various, with some emphasis on poems from the Six Dynasties (250-859) and the Qing Dynasty (1644-1911) which have been under-represented in many books of translation.

Many poets of the Qing Dynasty do not receive the high level of recognition accorded to those in the Tang and Song Dynasties. This is especially true of Shu Wei 舒位

(1765-1816) who was considered a peer of the top Tang and Song poets but relatively unknown.

Shu Wei lived a full life as a poet, critic, playwright, calligrapher and painter. His accomplishments earned him the small fame as one of the three prominent, younger poets of the Qianlong era (1736-1795). The other two are Wang Xian 王縣(1760-1817) and Sun Yuanxiang 孫原湘 (1760-1829), all under the shadow of the three outstanding, senior poets of the Qianlong era: Yuan Mei 袁枚 (1716-1791), Zhao Yi 趙翼 (1727-1814) and Jiang Shiquan 蔣士銓 (1725-1785)

Many literary critics give the highest praise to Shu Wei for his creativity, forcefulness and diction. His preference of historical topics and references from the classics lends seriousness and substance to his lines. However, some of his poems, with the liberal use of synecdoche and symbolism are not easily understood. His detractors call his poetic style eclectic and flippant.

With effortless ease, Shu Wei could produce poems of different styles and topics. Some of his verses on ghostly, supernatural and fantastic themes, can instill a feeling of apprehensiveness and bewilderment in his readers and remind us of the idiosyncrasy of Li He.

Shu Wei died in abject poverty. To his friends, he declined to be called another Li He but wanted to be remembered as another Du Mu 杜牧 (803-852)

This may come as a surprise. For centuries, Du Mu has been known as a second-rate poet with off-shaped wings. This is the result of a quatrain of satire that Li Shangyin 李商隱 (813-859) composed on him in 849, entitled "Administrator Du of the Department of Appointments", in which he was ridiculed for writing poems mainly on farewell to spring and people.

An examination of the complete essays and poems of Du Mu shows that he wrote relatively few verses on spring. In the poem "On my Way at the End of Spring", he expressed spring lament in the capacity of a detained, homesick wanderer, not a mere sentimentalist. As for verses of farewell to people, his output was neither exclusive nor excessive. His quatrain "Given in Farewell" about leaving a thirteen-year-old top courtesan of Yangzhou, is a classic.

In 849, Li Shangyin also wrote a poem in praise of Du Mu, entitled "For Administrator Du the Thirteenth of the Department of Appointments", calling his writing as significant as the memorial for General Yang Hu 楊祜 (221-278) at the Monument of Tears 墮淚碑

Because of the inconsistency and controversy created by Li Shangyin on the achievements of Du Mu, I have included the verses involved in this book for reference. Light-hearted poems of satire always appeal to the average public but fall short of the rigorous academic standards expected in meaningful evaluations.

A master of erudition skilled in the use of parallelism and historical anecdotes, Shu Wei could also appreciate verses in simple language on everyday life with great impact. He cast his vote for Du Mu. Along the same vein, international readers are drawn to the poems of Wei Yingwu 韋應物 (737-792), composed without any layer of allusion.

407 classical Chinese poems written by 150 poets, dating from 600 BCE to the nineteenth century, are included. The poets are presented in chronological order.

The books "Gu Shi Guan Zhi" 古詩觀止and "Xin Yi Gu Shi Yuan"新譯古詩源, among others in Chinese, inspired me on this project. Also, friends and relatives have encouraged me and I would like to thank them for their support.

1

ZHOU DYNASTY (1122-256 BCE)

BOOK OF SONGS (c600 BCE)
詩經

擊鼓

擊鼓其鏜，踴躍用兵。土國城漕，我
獨南行。從孫子仲，平陳與宋。不我
以歸，愛心有忡。爰居爰處，爰喪其
馬。于以求之，于林之下

死生契闊，與子成說。執子之手，
與子偕老。于嗟闊兮，不我活兮。
于嗟洵兮，不我信兮。

Beating Drums

Beat the drums and bang the gongs.
Send soldiers off in a joyous tone.
From a city state with a canal,

I go south alone.
For wars in Chen and Song,
Sun Zizhong I follow.
I may not return.
My worries make me feel low.
Thereupon in action my horse is killed.
According to a plan, I camp down to rest.
I look for my horse
That lies in a forest.

The living and the dead are wide apart.
In my words, my lover was told:
"I want to hold your hands
And together we grow old".
I sigh for a distant separation
And the fact that I may die.
Something like this is real and certain.
Other people's disbelief makes me sigh.

蟋蟀

蟋蟀在堂，歲聿其莫。今我不樂，
日月其除。無已大康，職思其居。
好樂無荒，良士瞿瞿。

蟋蟀在堂，歲聿其逝。今我不樂，
日月其邁。無已大康，職思其外。
好樂無荒，良士蹶蹶。

蟋蟀在堂， 役車其休。 今我不樂，
日月其慆。 無已大康， 職思其憂。
好樂無荒，良士休休。

Crickets

Crickets are in the hall.
It is late in the year.
Should merrymaking stop now,
Time will disappear.
Indulge not.
Let household duties be in your main thought.
Enjoy within rite and reason.
Of nature's unknowns, the good man is in fear.

Crickets are in the hall.
The year will go out of sight.
Should merrymaking stop now,
Leaving us will be each day and night.
Indulge not.
Let field work be in your main thought.
Enjoy within rite and reason.
The good man is diligent and bright.

Crickets are in the hall.
Farm carts have been put away.
Should merrymaking stop now,
Gone will be each night and day.
Indulge not.
Let future worries be in your main thought.

Enjoy within rite and reason.
At ease the good man can stay.

蜉蝣

蜉蝣之羽，衣裳楚楚；心之憂矣，於我
歸處。蜉蝣之翼，采采衣服；心之憂
矣，於我歸息。蜉蝣掘閱，麻衣如雪；
心之憂矣，於我歸說。

Mayflies

The wings of mayflies
Resemble pretty robes that shine.
I worry for my transitory lover.
Let him return to the house of mine.

The wings of mayflies
Resemble colorful robes that shine.
I worry for my transitory lover.
Let him rest in the house of mine.

Mayflies dig holes.
Their hempen, snow-white wings can shine.
I worry for my transitory lover.
Let him reside in the house of mine.

伯兮

伯兮朅兮，邦之桀兮。伯也執殳，為王前驅。
自伯之東，首如飛蓬。豈無膏沐，誰適為容。
其雨其雨，杲杲出日。願言思伯，甘心首疾。
焉得諼草？言樹之背。願言思伯，使我心痗。

My Man

How majestic and forceful is my man!
A hero of the land,
You serve the king as a vanguard,
With a pole in your hand.

Ever since you headed east,
Like a tumbleweed, my hair flies.
I can wash and oil my hair,
But a trim look is for whose eyes?

The sun is shining bright
When people hope for rain.
I think of my man,
With my heart and head in pain.

Where can I get daylilies
That grow at the back of trees.
With a troubled heart, I miss my man.
The plant should put me at ease.

采薇

采薇采薇 ， 薇亦作止 。 曰歸曰歸 ，
歲亦莫止 。 靡室靡家 ， 玁狁之故 ；
不遑啓居 ， 玁狁之故 。

采薇采薇 ， 薇亦柔止 。 曰歸曰歸 ，
心亦憂止 。 憂心烈烈 ， 載飢載渴 。
我戍未定 ， 靡使歸聘 。

采薇采薇 ， 薇亦剛止 。 曰歸曰歸 ，
歲亦陽止 。 王事靡盬 ， 不遑啓處 。
憂心孔疚 ， 我行不來 。

彼爾維何 ？ 維常之華 。 彼路斯何 ？
君子之車 。 戎車既駕 ， 四牡業業 。
啓敢定居 ， 一月三捷 。

駕彼四牡 ， 四牡騤騤 。 君子所依 ，
小人所腓 。 四牡翼翼 ， 象弭魚服 。
豈不日戒 ？ 玁狁孔棘 。

昔我往矣 ， 楊柳依依 ； 今我來思 ，
雨雪霏霏 。 行道遲遲 ， 載渴載飢 。
我心傷悲 ， 莫知我哀 ！

Pick Vetches

Pick vetches, pick vetches.
Vetches have grown above the soil already.
Go home, go home.
The year is ending already.

I own no house or home,
Because of the Huns.
I can neither sit on my heels nor kneel,
Because of the Huns.

Pick vetches, pick vetches.
Vetches are tender already.
Go home, go home.
My heart is anxious already,
Burning like fire,
As if from hunger and thirst.
My duties at the borders are not done.
To send regards to my family, I can ask none.

Pick vetches, pick vetches.
Vetches are strong already.
Go home, go home.
The tenth month, like spring, comes already.
The king's assignments are not over.
I can neither sit on my heels nor kneel.
My worried heart suffers great pain.
I cannot go home again.

What is that in bloom?
It is the crab-apple.
Whose chariot is that?
It belongs to the general.
His chariot is ready,
With four sturdy stallions.
How dare I sit on my heels or kneel
When we score three victories in a month?

The four stallions of the chariot
Show strength and fight.
The general relies on them.
Behind them, we soldiers take cover.
Their strides and gaits are steady.
We carry fish-skin quivers and ivory-tipped bows.
How can we not be on guard every day?
The Huns attack us without delay.

When I left home,
Willows were swaying.
Now as I return,
Like rain, a big snowfall is spraying.
Roads stretch afar.
In thirst and hunger, I go.
Who understands my grief?
My heart hurts in sorrow.

七月
豳風

I

七月流火。九月授衣。一之日觱發。二
之日栗烈。無衣無褐。何以卒歲。三
之日于耜。四之日舉趾。同我婦子。
饁彼南畝。田畯至喜。

七月流火。九月授衣。春日載陽。有
鳴倉庚。女執懿筐。遵彼微行。爰求
柔桑。春日遲遲。采蘩祁祁。女心
傷悲。殆及公子同歸。

七月流火。八月萑葦。蠶月條桑，
取彼斧斨。以伐遠揚。猗彼女桑。
七月鳴鵙。八月載績。載玄載黃。
我朱孔陽。為公子裳。

四月秀葽。五月鳴蜩。八月其穫。十
月隕蘀。一之日于貉。取彼狐貍。為
公子裘。二之月其同。載纘武功。
言私其豵。獻豜于公。

II

五月斯螽動股，六月莎雞振羽。七月在
野。八月在宇。九月在戶。十月蟋蟀。入
我床下。穹之室熏鼠。塞向墐戶。嗟我婦
子。曰為改歲。入此室處。

六月食鬱及薁。七月烹葵及菽。八月
剝棗。十月穫稻。爲此春酒。以介眉
壽。七月食瓜。八月斷壺。九月叔苴，
采茶薪樗。食我農夫。

九月築場圃。十月納禾稼。黍稷重穋。
禾麻菽麥。嗟我農夫。我稼既同。上
入執宮功。晝爾于茅。宵爾索綯。亟
其乘屋。其始種百穀。

九月肅霜。十月滌場。朋酒斯饗。曰殺羔
羊。躋彼公堂。稱彼兕觥。萬壽無疆。

The Seventh Month:
Song of Bin

I

In the seventh month, like fire, Antares sinks.
In the ninth, fabric is handed out for making clothes.
The first month comes with a noisy blast.
The second is icy cold.
Without woolen clothing,
In the remaining days of the year, how shall we last?
On days of the third month, we mend the ploughs.
On days of the fourth, we set foot on the plots.
My wife and children
Bring food to the southern lots.
The overseers look glad.

In the seventh month, like fire, Antares sinks.
In the ninth, fabric is handed out for making clothes
Warmth comes with each spring day.
Trills from the orioles go.
Girls carry deep baskets.
On tiny trails, they file and follow,
To pick tender mulberry leaves.
Spring days are slow.
Their hearts are in sorrow,
Fearful to be picked to return with the Lord's son.

In the seventh month, like fire, Antares sinks。
In the eighth, we gather rushes.
In the silkworm month, we trim the mulberries
And lop off branches overgrown.
To one side, the roped, young twigs are led.
In the seventh month, shrikes cry.
In the eighth, we begin weaving.
With threads dyed black and yellow.
I stain them bright red,
For the robe of my lord's son.

In the fourth month, grass makes seeds.
In the fifth, cicadas chirp.
In the eighth, we reap.
In the tenth, leaves drop.
On days of the first month, we catch badgers
And hunt foxes
For the fur coats of my lord's son.
On days of the second month, together we drill
On our hunting skill.
We keep young beasts
And offer bigger ones to the lord.

II

In the fifth month, locusts beat their thighs.
In the sixth, grasshoppers shake their wings.
In the seventh, crickets inhabit the wilds,
In the eighth, under the eaves,
In the ninth, at the door
And in the tenth, under my bed.

Fill the cracks and smoke out rats.
Paste up windows and mud the doors.
With pity, I sigh and say
To my wife and children,
That at the year's end,
They need to go inside to stay.

In the sixth month, we eat wild pears and grapes.
In the seventh, we cook mallows and beans.
In the eighth, we flog down dates.
In the tenth, we harvest rice,
For wine to be ready in spring,
To wish longevity on old people with bushy brows.
In the seventh month, we eat melons.
In the eighth, we snip off gourds.
In the ninth, we take beans and hempseeds,
Pluck sow thistles and cut stink trees for firewood.
From these, farmers earn their livelihood.

In the ninth month, we make ready our plantation
And in the tenth, store the harvest.
We have millets and other crops, early or late,
Like paddy, hemp, beans and wheat.
The farmer sighs and begins to relate:
"After putting away the grains in one place,
Officials assign me to build the palace.
By day, I collect reeds for thatch
And by night twist ropes,
Rushing to climb up to fix the roof.
After the new year, I shall sow seeds."

On days of the second month, noisily we chisel ice.
On days of the third, it is put away in cold sheds.
On days of the fourth, early on, we make a sacrifice
And worship with leeks and lambs.
In the ninth month, it is bleak and frosty.
In the tenth, we clean the plantation.
We share wine in a feast
And kill a young lamb.
We go up to the common hall,
Raise cups of rhino horns
And say "May the Lord Live Forever".

2

HAN DYNASTY
(206 BCE-220)

CAO CAO (155-220)
曹操

蒿里行

關東有義士，興兵討群凶。初期會盟津，
乃心在咸陽。軍合力不齊，躊躇而雁行。
勢利使人爭，嗣還自相殘。淮南弟稱
號，刻璽於北方。鎧甲生蟣虱，萬姓以
死亡。白首露於野，千里元雞鳴。生民
百遺一，念之斷人腸。

Ballad of Hao Li

To form an army to quell usurpers,
Upright Guandong governors thought it was right.
They first met at Mengjin to plot,
To rid the rebels at Xianyang on site.

Soon the allies split and acted hesitant,
Like lines of leaderless wild geese in flight.
They tried to kill one another.
Power and gain made them fight.
The commander of the allies chose a king,
With an engraved seal in the north, out of sight.
Lice and fleas grew from armors.
Death for the citizens was their common plight.
No rooster was heard for a thousand miles.
Exposed in the wilds were bones turned white.
It breaks my heart to think of the people
And their chance of survival being so slight.

XU GAN (171-217)
許幹

室思

浮雲何洋洋，願因通我詞。飄颻不可
寄，徙倚徒相思。人離皆復會，君獨無
反期。自君之出矣，明鏡暗不治。思君
如流水，何有窮已時，

Boudoir Thoughts

How widespread are floating clouds!
To send my letters, I wish they could have a way.
Pacing and leaning, I am lovesick and helpless,

With feelings that drifting clouds cannot convey.
People apart all reunite.
Only you chose to stay away.
Ever since my man left me,
Dark and dusty my bright mirrors stay.
Like flowing waters, my thoughts for him
Will not end any day.

WANG CAN (177-217)
王粲

從軍行

衆軍征遐路，討彼東南夷。方舟順廣川，
薄暮未安坻。白日半西山，桑梓有餘暉。
蟋蟀夾岸鳴，孤鳥翩翩飛。征夫心多懷，
惻淒令吾悲。下船登高防，草露沾我衣，
回身赴床寢，此愁當告誰？身服干戈事，
豈得念所私？即戎有授命，茲理不可違。

Ballad of Expeditions

Expeditionary forces go afar,
To rid southeastern barbarians in warfare.
Our boats sail down wide streams,
Not yet safely docked by early twilight.
Bright sunshine fills half of western hills
And on my hometown, casts its residual light.

Crickets of both banks chirp.
A lone bird is freely gliding in flight.
As a soldier, I am sunk in thoughts,
Feeling sad for what I would have to bear.
Dewy grasses wet my clothes
As I leave my boat for land at a height.
Returning to sleep in bed, I wonder
With whom this worry should I share?
In my army uniform for battles,
Why should I mind my private affair?
I cannot forsake my duties by law and reason
When soldiery duties have been assigned to my care.

CAO ZHI (192-232)
曹植

公讌詩

公子敬愛客，終宴不知疲。清夜遊西園，
飛蓋相追隨。明月澄清景，列宿正參差。
秋蘭被長阪，朱華冒綠池。潛魚躍清波，
好鳥鳴高枝。神飆接舟轂，輕輦隨風移。
飄颻放志意，千秋長若斯。

The Feast Hosted by the Prince

The prince is not tired at the end of feasts.
Entertaining his guests with respect is his delight.

Fast carriages follow one another,
On a trip to West Garden on a quiet night.
Stars look dissimilar and random.
The scenery is aglow under bright moonlight.
Fall orchids cover the whole long slope.
From the green pond, red flowers come in sight.
Submerged fish spring up with clear waves.
Pretty birds sing on twigs at a height.
Scarlet wheels ride on divine gales.
Moving in the wind, carriages look light.
I let my mind follow where I see right.
To be like this for a thousand years, I am alright.

吁嗟篇

吁嗟此轉蓬，　居世何獨然！　長去本根逝，
宿夜無休閑。　東西經七陌，　南北越九阡。
卒遇回風起，　吹我入雲間。　自謂終天路，
忽然下沉泉。　驚飆接我出，　故歸彼中田。
當南而更北，　謂東而反西。　宕宕當何依？
忽亡而復存。　飄飄周八澤，　連翩歷五山。
流轉無恆處，　誰知吾苦艱？　願為中林草，
秋隨野火燔。　糜火豈不痛？　願與株荄連。

Sighing in Lament

Sigh in lament for a tumbleweed like me.
How lonely a life can I get!
Long uprooted and gone,

Day and night, I have no rest.
On nine lanes from south to north,
Or seven paths from east to west,
A sudden whirlwind picks me up
And into clouds, I am blown.
I shall end up in the sky, I say.
Suddenly to an abyss, my sinking body is sent.
A frightening gale takes me out
And puts me to the fields on return.
The direction changes from south to north.
Then from east to west, I am carried away.
What should this free, draggled mass follow?
Instant death become rebirth again.
Circling eight marshes as I waver,
I pass three hills in relay.
In constant displacement,
I face bitter hardship understood by none.
I wish to be the grass of a forest
That in a wildfire of fall may burn.
In a big fire, how can I not feel pain?
Linked to my kin and kind, I just want to stay.

SHI CHONG (249-300)
石崇

王明君辭

我本漢家子，將適單于庭。辭訣未及終，
前驅已抗旌。僕禦涕流離，轅馬為悲鳴。
哀郁傷五內，泣淚沾朱纓。行行日已遠，
遂造匈奴城。延我于窮廬，加我閼氏名。

殊類非所安，雖貴非所榮。父子見淩辱，
對之慚且驚。殺身良不易，默默以苟生。
苟生亦何聊，積思常憤盈。願假飛鴻翼，
棄之以遐征。飛鴻不我顧，佇立以屏營。
昔為匣中玉，今為糞上英。朝華不足歡，
甘與秋草并。傳語後世人，遠嫁難爲情。

Wang Mingjun

For my marriage to Chief Danyu,
I arrived as a Han kingdom's dame.
Before I finished saying goodbye,
Vanguards had raised a banner.
Servants and drivers wept bitterly.
Horses for my carriage neighed in grief.
Tears wet my red tassels.
My guts tore in the sedan without relief.
After traveling for days afar,
To the Xiongnu's city I came.

Led into a domed tent,
I was called Lady Yu by name.

Ill at ease among strangers,
I took no pride in my fame.
Wedded to both the chief and then his son,
I felt awed and undignified in this manner.
To kill myself was not easy.
I silently lived without aim.
How boring is life without aim!
An angry woman deep in thought, I became.
Wish I could use the wings of a wild swan
And travel leisurely as I leave.
Wild swans do not care about me.
I stood in wait for what I wanted to achieve.
I was a piece of jade in a chest
But now a flower with animal waste beneath,
I take no joy being a bloom in the prime of my life.
As fall grass, I am willing to be the same.
Let me pass my words to people of later generations.
A marriage to a distant land is one with shame.

3

SIX DYNASTIES
(220-589)

ZUO SI (250?-305?)
左思

詠史，其一

弱冠弄柔翰，　卓犖觀群書。　著論准過秦，
作賦擬子虛。　邊城苦鳴鏑，　羽檄飛京都。
雖非甲冑士，　疇昔覽穰苴。

長嘯激清風，　志若無東吳。　鉛刀貴一割，
夢想騁良圖。　左眄澄江湘，　右盼定羌胡。
功成不受爵，　長揖歸田廬。

On History, no.1

At twenty, I reached adulthood with a ceremony
And read many books with sharp, deep insight.
I follow "Guo Qin Lun" composed by Jia Yi
And "Zi Xu Fu" of Sima Xiangru when I write.
Urgent dispatches for help fly to the capital.
At the border, enemy arrowheads whiz loud and
    tight.
Not a warrior myself,
I once studied military classics to learn to fight.

In the clear wind, I make a long, big howl.
My wish is to wipe off East Wu if I might.
Like a blunt knife, my limited talents are untried.
My dream is to gallop on a planned warpath that
    works alright.
I eye East Wu on the left
And the Qiang barbarians on the right.
In success, I shall not accept any title bestowed
But return to my hut and fields, each day and night.

LIU KUN (217-318)
劉琨

扶風歌

朝發廣莫門，暮宿丹水山。左手彎繁弱，
右手揮龍淵。顧瞻望宮闕，俯仰禦飛軒。
據鞍長嘆息，淚下如流泉。繫馬長松
下，發鞍高岳頭。烈烈悲風起，冷冷澗
水流。揮手長相謝，哽咽不能言。浮雲
為我結，歸鳥為我旋。

去家日已遠，安知存與亡？慷慨窮林中，
抱膝獨摧藏。糜鹿遊我前，猿猴戲我側。
資糧既乏盡，薇蕨安可食？

攬轡命徒侶，吟嘯絕岩中。君子道微矣，
夫子故有窮。維昔李騫期，寄在匈奴庭。
忠信反獲罪，漢武不見明。

我 欲 竟 此 曲 ， 此 曲 悲 且 長 。 棄 置
勿重陳，重陳令心傷。

The Wind-borne Army

At dawn I set out by Guangmo Gate
And rest on Danshui Hill at twilight.
Carrying the famed bow, Fanruo, on my left,
I have a rare sword, Longyuan, on my right.
I look back at the palace gate
And upwards at eaves that seem to take wing.
On my saddle, I sigh for a long time,
With tears like a flowing spring.
To a tall pine, I tie my horse
And hang the saddle on a crag at a height.
While the cold spring water runs,
A rising cheerless wind starts to show its might.
I remember the hand-waving of our long goodbye
And how choked up for words we got.
Floating clouds cease to scud overhead.
Homing birds circle above my head.

It gets farther from home each day.
I am not sure whether I may live or die.
Getting emotional in the leafless grove,
I embrace my knees and sigh.

Deer roam before me.
Gibbons and monkeys play by my side.
My provisions are gone.
How can I eat what ferns and brackens can provide?

I order my soldiers to get in motion
And howl at a cliff all the way.
The Way of Life for a gentleman can be challenged.
Confucius met setbacks in his day.
General Li Qianqi defected
And settled in the Xiongnu court long ago.
He meant to be loyal and truthful,
But King Wu of Han failed to know.

I want to end this tune.
The tune is sad and long.
Let me discard it and stop repeating.
Repeating breaks hearts through the song.

重贈盧諶

握中有玄璧，本自荊山璆。維彼太公望，
昔在渭濱叟。鄧生何感激，千里來相求。
白登幸曲逆，鴻門賴留侯。重耳任五賢，
小白相射鉤。苟能隆二伯，安問黨與讎！

中夜撫枕歎，想與數子遊。吾衰久矣夫，
何其不夢周？誰云聖達節，知命故不憂。
宣尼悲獲麟，西狩涕孔丘。功業未及

建，夕陽忽西流。時哉不我與，去乎若
雲浮。朱實隕勁風，繁英落素秋。狹路
傾華蓋，駭駟摧雙輈。

何意百煉鋼，化爲繞指柔。

A Second Poem for Lu Chen

You resemble a jade disc in my hand,
Carved from a stone of Jing Hill with its glow,
And the old fisherman who watched by River Wei,
An elder statesman whom a Zhou king met long ago.
I feel gratified like King Guangwu of Han,
Assisted by General Deng Yu far away.
You helped me like what the "Qu Yi Marquis" did
 at Baideng Hill,
With the rescuer's wit at the Hong Gate Feast of
 another day.
You have the wisdom of the Five Sages under
 Chong E.
Xiao Bai forgave a shooter and you are as forgiving.
If both kings were benefited,
Why ask about any bonding or misgiving?

Without the chance to learn from the sages,
I touch my pillow and sigh at midnight.
For long, I have grown old and weak.
In my dream, why has not the righteous duke of
 Zhou come in sight?
Who says a saint and a good judge for propriety

Would reach the age of fifty and be worry-free?
Sad over a captured unicorn in a west hunting trip,
Confucius wept over the moral decline he could
    foresee.
Suddenly the setting sun has flown west,
Before any achievements can be done.
Time waits not for me.
Like floating clouds, away it has run.
Red fruits drop in the blast.
In bleak autumn, numerous flowers wilt.
Frightened horses break double shafts
On narrow roads where grand carriages tilt.

Who would expect a strong human will, like steel
    refined,
Could be bent around a finger, softly entwined?

LU CHEN (284-318)
盧諶

答魏子悌

崇臺非一幹，珍裘非一腋。多士成大業，
群賢濟弘績。遇蒙時來會，聊齊朝彥蹟。
顧此腹背羽，愧彼排虛翮。寄身蔭四岳，
托好憑三益。傾蓋雖終朝，大分邁疇昔。
在危每同險，處安不異易。

俱涉晉昌艱， 共更飛狐厄。 恩由契濶生，
義隨周旋積。 豈謂鄉曲譽， 謬充本州役。
乖離令我感， 悲欣使情惕。 理以精神通，
匪曰形骸隔。 妙詩申篤好， 清義賁幽頤。
恨無隨侯珠， 以酬荊文璧。

In Answer to Wei Ziti

A high terrace rests not on a log,
Nor a rare fur coat comes from one fox alone.
Many people complete a huge project.
Collective brains help get big jobs done.
Let us all review the court's good deeds.
By fate, into each other we have run.
My closeness to you, like back and belly feathers,
Shames me for flapping in vain with work undone.
Under the patronage of Liu Kun, like the four hills,
And the help of wise, upright friends, I got my
    battles won.
Our friendship grows stronger than before,
With discussions going on all day, once begun.
We face danger together.
In peaceful times, you are easygoing to everyone.

At Jinchang county, we both experienced hardship,
And at Feihu Pass, got overrun.
Gratitude arises from occasions of union and parting.
Loyalty is built on relationships, one to one.
I accepted an offer to work in my home state.
For any praise from any villager, I received none.

Sorrow and joy may give me fear and caution.
I feel affected if parted from someone.
Understanding relies on the linkage of minds,
Even though I may be physically far from anyone.
With lofty precepts nourished from seclusion,
Your wonderful poem is deeply refined in tone.
For lack of a comparable piece in answer to yours,
To feel regretful, I am prone.

TAO YUANMING (365-427)
陶淵明

詠荊軻

燕丹善養士，志在報強嬴。招集百夫良，
歲暮得荊卿。君子死知己，提劍出燕京。
素驥鳴廣陌，慷慨送我行。雄髮指危
冠，猛氣衝長纓。飲餞易水上，四座列
群英。漸離擊悲筑，宋意唱高聲。蕭蕭
哀風逝，淡淡寒波生。

商音更流涕，羽奏壯士驚。心知去不歸，
且有後世名。登車何時顧，飛蓋入秦庭。
淩厲越萬里，逶迤過千城。圖窮事自至，
豪主正怔營。惜哉劍術疏，奇功遂不成。
其人雖已沒，千載有餘情。

Jingke

Prince Dan of Yan treated knights-errant well.
Revenging a strong tyrant was his aim.
From a group of a hundred good fighters,
At the year's end, Jingke came.
He held his sword and left the capital.
For the son of a king, he was willing to die.
White horses neigh on wide trails.
With noble generosity, the prince bade him goodbye.
His forceful energy jilted his long chin-strap.
He bristled and precariously askew his hat went.
By River Yi, at his farewell feast,
A full house of heroes joined the event.
Sadly, Jianli played his zhu.
The dying wind was cheerless and bleak.
Songyi sang with a high pitch.
The rising waves were weak.

Slow tunes made him weep.
Fast beats brought fright to the hero's heart.
Jingke knew he could not return.
With a name in history, he was to part.
Without looking back, he climbed onto a carriage
That took him to the Qin palace fast.
Relentlessly he covered myriad miles,
On long, winding roads of many towns he passed.
The unrolled scroll revealed his dagger.
The nervous and scared Qin king failed to react.
To our regret, Jingke's swordsmanship faltered,
To complete the wonderful act.

Although underground his body has lain,
For centuries, his valor will remain.

和郭主簿

靄靄堂前林，中夏貯清陰。凱風因時來，
回飆開我襟。息交遊閒業，臥起弄書琴。
園蔬有餘滋，舊穀猶儲今。營己良有極，
過足非所欽。春秋作美酒。酒熟吾自斟。
弱子戲我側，學語未成音。此事真復樂，
聊用忘華簪。遙遙望白雲，懷古一何深。

In Answer to Archivist Guo

In mid-summer, there is plenty of cool shade,
With trees before the hall in their prime.
A whirlwind loosens my lapel,
With a south wind coming on time.
Retired from my official duties,
I rise to read and take out my qin to play.
Vegetables from my garden are nourishing.
Grains from last year are still stored today.
My day-to-day needs are limited,
Indulgences of life do not come my way.
I grind rice for fine wine
And fill myself cups of aged brew.
A toddler frolics by my side,
Having learned to speak a word or two.
These things, real and joyous,

Make me forget about wealth and might.
With my eyes on white clouds afar,
My mind holds dear to ancient recluses' insight.

讀山海經

孟夏草木長，繞屋樹扶疏。群鳥欣有托，
吾亦愛吾廬。既耕亦已種，時還讀我書。
窮巷隔深轍，頗回故人車。歡然酌春
酒，摘我園中蔬。微雨從東來，好風與
之俱。泛覽周王傳，流觀山海圖。俯仰
終宇宙，不樂復何如！

On Reading "Geography of Ancient China"

In early summer, plants thrive.
Around my hut, luxuriantly trees grow.
Birds happily perch on twigs for support.
I love my hut also.
Time and again, I read my books
After I get to till the land and sow.
I live way off the beaten tracks.
For return visits, my friends and their carriages go.
I pluck vegetables from my garden
And drink spring wine with gusto.
A drizzle comes from the east,
Accompanied by good winds that follow.
"Biography of King Zhou" and "Geography of
    ancient China"

Are titles of my reading portfolio.
What can be greater joy than this
When my mind explores the universe, high and low?

YAN YANZI (384-456)
顏延之

五君詠：嵇中散康

中散不偶世，本自餐霞人。形解驗默仙，
吐論知凝神。立俗迕流議，尋山洽隱淪。
鸞翮有時鎩，龍性誰能馴。

Five Gentlemen: Ji Kang,
Unofficial Political Commentator

By nature an immortal, feeding on cloud and dew,
From others, the unofficial political commentator
   abstained.
Quietly he freed himself from his form to be a fairy.
Through his book, calmness and concentration
   can be obtained.
He stood against trite customs and conventions.
The chance to be near recluses in the hills, he sought
   and gained.
Sometimes feathers on wings of phoenixes may
   break,
But his dragon-like haughtiness could not be
   restrained.

五君詠：劉參軍伶

劉伶善閉關，懷情滅聞見，鼓鐘不足歡，
榮色豈能眩！韜精日沉飲，誰知非荒宴？
頌酒雖短章，深衷自此見。

Five Gentlemen: Liu Ling, the Adjutant

Liu Ling kept to himself well.
From others, he was concealed.
Bell and drum gave him no delight.
To dazzling flowers, how could he feel appealed?
Hiding his talent, he got drunk every day.
From excessive feasts, he was not to be peeled.
Although his "Ode to Wine" is short,
His deep thoughts through the poem can be revealed.

五君詠：阮始平咸

仲容青雲器，實稟生民秀。達音何用深，
識微在金奏。郭奕已心醉，山公非虛覯。
屢薦不入官，一麾乃出守。

Five Gentlemen: Ruan Xian, Chief of Shiping

A man of inborn excellence,
On lofty ideals, Zhongrong showed his bent.
Why need detailed theories on notes and rhythms?

They came out through his instrument.
His music got Guo Yi carried away.
Shan Tao did not bypass his real talent.
Once solicited, he stayed on as the magistrate,
After refusing several job offers sent.

五君詠：向常侍秀

向秀甘澹薄，深心托豪素。探道好淵玄，
觀書鄙章句。交呂既鴻軒，攀嵇亦鳳舉。
流連河裡遊，惻愴山陽賦。

Five Gentlemen: Xiang Xiu,
Palace Remonstrance Master

Xiang Xiu willed against worldly desires.
Through paper and pen, his deep thoughts were
    expressed.
He despised annotations of words and phrases in
    texts,
Preferring hidden philosophies in his quest.
He befriended Lu An, lofty like a wild swan
And Ji Kang, uplifting like a phoenix, not to be
    repressed.
In recalling their meetings at Henei and Shanyang,
His exposition on their executions got his grief
    addressed.

五君詠: 阮步兵籍

阮公雖淪蹟， 識密鑒亦洞。 沉醉似埋照，
寓辭類托諷。 長嘯若懷人， 越禮自驚眾。
物故不可論， 途窮能無慟？

Five Gentlemen: Ruan Ji, the Infantry Man

Though Mister Ruan hid his tracks,
He possessed sharp, deep insight.
He wrote to satire society and others.
Drunk, he retreated from any spotlight.
He made a long whistle and left a shallow recluse,
Acting against traditions, to everyone's fright.
We cannot comment on him in his time, but also
    weep,
Astray before a forked road of life, in a sad plight.

XIE HUN (?-412)
謝混

遊西池

悟彼蟋蟀唱， 信此勞者歌。 有來豈不疾，
良遊常蹉跎。 逍遙越城肆， 願言屢經過。
回阡被陵闕， 高臺眺飛霞。 惠風蕩繁囿，
白雲屯曾阿。 景昃鳴禽集， 水木湛清華。
褰裳順蘭沚， 徒倚引芳柯。 美人愁歲月，
遲暮獨如何？ 無爲牽所思， 南榮戒其多。

Touring West Pond

Awaken to the shortness of life,
I chant what my mind wants to say.
All too soon, good times come to an end.
Fine trips often get in delay.
I hope to revisit this place often,
A city that puts me at ease on my way.
On a winding trail by palaces,
I reach a high terrace to view clouds flying away.
Layered white clouds stop at high peaks.
A breeze makes the garden's many trees sway.
At sundown, fowls gather and call.
Flowering trees get reflected on limpid waters.
I wade to an islet with orchids.
For the fragrance, I linger to stay.
A beauty will wane in years.
How do the aged deal with loneliness, come the day?
Let us be free from excessive worldly ties.
On this, Nanrong was warned before his breakaway.

BAO ZHAO (c414-466)
鮑照

梅花落

中庭雜樹多，偏為梅咨嗟，問君何
獨然，念其霜中能作花，露中能作

實。搖蕩春風媚春日，念爾零落逐寒
風，徒有霜華無霜質。

Plum flowers Fall

In the central courtyard, many different trees grow.
The highest esteem on plum trees I hold.
Why do I let my unique preference show?
For their ability to flower in the frost
And seed in the dew.
On breezy spring days, other trees flirt and sway.
In the cold wind, their petals become scattered and
    lost.
In a frost, charming blooms lack the grit to stay.

贈傅都曹別

輕鴻戲江潭，　孤雁集洲沚。　邂逅兩相親，
緣念共無已。　風雨好東西，　一隔頓萬里。
追憶惝宿時，　聲容滿心耳。　落日川渚寒，
愁雲繞天起。　短翮不能翔，　徘徊煙霧里。

Seeing off Director Fu

I am a lone wild goose on islets and sandbanks.
You are a wild swan on rivers and ponds, playful
    and light.
After our bonding since we met,
Endless yearnings in parting form our common
    plight.

Ten thousand miles separate us amid wind and rain,
East and west, at a different site.
As I recall our togetherness,
To my ears and heart come fully your voice and
    sight.
Cheerless clouds rise to encircle the sky.
Streams and sand bars get chilled in the sunless
    twilight.
In the mist, I pace to and fro,
Being short-winged and unable to take flight.

XIE ZHUANG (421-466)
謝莊

北宅秘園

夕天霽晚氣，輕霞澄暮陰。微風清幽
幌，餘日照青林。收光漸窗歇，窮園自
荒深。綠池翻素景，秋槐響寒音。伊人
儻同夢，絃酒共棲尋。

The Deserted Garden of a House in the North

Things look sharp under light clouds at dusk.
The sky is clear after rain at the end of the day.
The last sunbeams remain on green groves.
A breeze makes drapes in chambers sway.
Gradually the sun disappears from windows.

The poor garden appears neglected all the way.
Locust trees in chilly autumn make noise.
Moonlight in the green pond ripples in play.
If my friends share my love for this place,
Over wine and music, we can gather here and stay.

SHEN YUE (441-513)
沈約

新安江至清淺深見底貽京邑遊好

眷言訪舟客，茲川信可珍。洞澈隨清淺，
皎鏡無冬春。千仞寫喬樹，百丈見游鱗。
滄浪有時濁，清濟涸無津。豈若乘斯去，
俯映石磷磷。紛吾隔囂滓，寧假濯衣巾？
願以潺湲水，沾君纓上塵。

On the Extremely Limpid River Xinan, Visible from Top to Bottom, for my Good Friends in the Capital

This river is truly a gem,
In retrospect, for any guest sailing here.
It is limpid and visible at any depth,
In winter or spring, like a mirror, clean and bright.
Tall trees cast their reflected images.
Fish from a great depth come in sight.
Transparent River Ji is already dry.
At times, dark waters may not be clear.

45

Let me glide down the river
And watch submerged rocks with reflected light.
I left the din and dust of officialdom.
Would I not want to wash my robe on site?
I wish I could use the water of this running stream
To dust the chin-straps of your official headgear.

別范安成

生平少年日，分手易前期。及爾同衰暮，
非復別離時。勿言一樽酒，明日難重持。
夢中不識路，何以慰相思。

Seeing off Fan Ancheng

On younger days for both you and me,
Meeting again was easy.
Now that we are both old and weak,
A reunion may never be.
Mention not the cup of wine
That by tomorrow will come with difficulty.
We do not know the road to meet in a dream.
How can we set our mutual yearnings free?

早發定山

夙齡愛遠壑，晚蒞見奇山。標峰彩虹外，
置嶺白雲間。傾壁忽斜豎，絕頂復孤圓。
歸海流漫漫，出浦水濺濺。野棠開未落，
山櫻發欲燃。忘歸屬蘭杜，懷祿寄芳荃。
眷言採三秀，徘徊望九仙。

Setting out Early for Ding Hill

At an old age, I come to see strange hills.
In my youth, I loved to tour valleys far away.
Sharp peaks show beyond rainbows.
Among white clouds, ridges stay.
Steep cliffs suddenly stand aslant.
A single crag at the top becomes round again.
The river freely flows into the sea,
With the water at the shore making a spray.
Wild pear flowers still stay on trees.
Blooms of mountain cherries glow, as if they might
    burn.
Orchids and herbs make me forget to return.
Fragrant grasses, not riches, endear my heart.
I want to linger to watch the nine fairies
And pick thrice-blooming lingzhis, with affection I
    say.

XIE TIAO (464-499)
謝朓

同謝諮議詠銅雀臺

繐帷飄井幹，罇酒若平生。鬱鬱西陵樹，
詎聞鼓吹聲。芳襟染淚跡。嬋娟空復情。
玉座猶寂莫，況乃妾身輕。

In Answer to a Poem by Consultant Xie on the Brazen Birds Terrace

Hempen tents flutter on the terrace,
With set cups of wine the dead king used to know.
He cannot hear any drum or flute music.
Luxuriantly, trees of West Mausoleum grow.
With tear stains on her fragrant robe,
In vain, a pretty lady attendant weeps with sorrow.
Even a dead monarch who sat on the jade throne
   feels lonely,
Let alone a woman whose social class is low.

江上曲

易陽春草出，踟躕日已暮。蓮葉尚田
田，淇水不可渡。願子淹桂舟，時同千
里路。千里既相許，桂舟復客與。江上
可採菱，清歌共南楚。

On the River

Spring grass sprouts on the north of River Yi, as we
  play
And linger until late in the day.
Lotus leaves spread and spread.
To our re-union, the unnavigable River Qi causes
  delay.
I hope to sail with him for myriad miles
If my lover would stop and let his cassia boat stay.
Then leisurely on the boat,
We can fulfill our mutual wish to sail away,
Sing refreshing love songs of Chu
And pick caltrops of the river on our way.

新亭渚別范零陵雲

洞庭張樂地，瀟湘帝子遊。雲去蒼梧野，水還江漢流。停驂我悵望，輟棹子夷猶。廣平聽方籍，茂陵將見求。心事俱已矣，江上徒離憂。

Seeing off Fan Yun for Lingling
County at the Shore of Xinting

You will leave for Dongting Hill with its music
And Xiaoxiang visited by princesses years ago.
Like clouds, you depart for the wilds of Cangwu
  Hill.

I return like a river in its flow.
Depressed, I watch while stopping my carriage.
Dropping your oars, you hesitate to go.
Like that of Guangping's chief, your name will
    be widely heard.
Like Xiangru at Maoling, I wait for recognition and
    lie low.
I have expressed my mind
And by the river, fail to curb my parting sorrow.

WU JUN (469-520)
吳均

春詠

春從何處來？ 拂水復驚梅。 雲障青鎖闥，
風吹丞露臺。 美人隔千里， 蘿幃閉不開。
無由得共語， 空對相思杯。

Spring

From where does spring come?
Plum trees flower; ponds ripple on the surface.
Clouds block green palace doors.
Winds blow on the Dew Collecting Terrace.
Distance blocks me from a pretty lady.
Her gauze drapes are shut to my face,
Unable to talk to her,
I drink with yearnings for someone without a trace.

答柳惲

清晨發隴西，日暮飛狐谷。秋月照層
嶺，寒風掃高木。霧露夜侵衣，關山曉
催軸。君去欲何之，參差問原陸。一見
終無緣，懷悲空滿目。

In Answer to Liu Yun

At dawn, you will depart from Longxi,
Reaching Feihugu by twilight.
The autumn moon shines on layered ridges.
A cold wind sweeps fall trees with might.
You cover hills and passes in haste by morn,
With your robe seeped by dew at night.
Why do you want to leave us,
Covering plains and terraces at a height?
By fate, I shall miss seeing you again,
Save the sad void in full sight.

HE XUN (c472-c519)
何遜

日夕望江山贈魚司馬

溢城帶溢水，溢水縈如帶。日夕望高城，
耿耿青雲外。城中多宴賞，絲竹常繁會。
管聲已流悅，弦聲復淒切。歌黛慘如愁，
舞腰凝欲絕。仲秋黃葉下，長風征騷屑。

51

早雁出雲歸， 故燕辭檐別。 畫悲在異
縣， 夜夢還洛内。 洛内何悠悠， 起望西
南樓。 的的帆向浦， 團團月映洲。 誰能
一羽化， 輕舉逐飛浮。

For Adjutant Yu, Composed as I
watch Pen City at Twilight

River Pen girdles Pen City,
Like a belt, coiling around.
I watch the grand city at twilight,
Beyond blue clouds, far away.
Feasts in celebration number many in the city,
Often with music in the background.
Pipe tunes give delight.
Sharp string notes bring sorrow.
Dancers appear stiff and dead.
Singers with black brows make a grievous sight.
In mid-autumn, yellow leaves fall,
With a howling wind on its way.
Swallows leave their former nests on beams.
Through dawn clouds, homing wild geese take
    flight.
By day, I am a sad wanderer.
Dreaming of returning to the capital at night.
How distant the roads are to the capital!
In the southwest, I watch from a tower at a height.
Vividly, sails head towards the shore.
Islets under the fall moon look bright.
Who can become fairies with feathered wings,
Flying afloat with bodies so light?

詠春風

可聞不可見，能重復能輕。鏡前
飄落粉，琴上響餘聲。

Spring Wind

It can be heard but not seen,
Weak but then again strong.
Before a mirror, it makes her face powder waver.
From her qin are borne the trailing notes of a song.

YU JIANWU (487-551)
庾肩吾

奉和春夜應令

春牖對芳洲，珠簾新上鈎。燒香知夜漏，
刻燭驗更籌。天禽下北閣，織女入西樓。
月皎疑非夜，林疏似更秋。水光懸蕩壁，
山翠下添流。詎假西園讌，無勞飛蓋遊。

In Answer to "Spring Night, a Poem in Reply", at Imperial Request

Through pearl blinds newly hooked up and hung,
Fragrant isles in spring through windows come in
    sight.
Burning incense, clepsydras and marked candles

Verify that the night watches are right.
With the Tianqin star behind North Pavilion
And the Weaving Maid star within West Tower,
    time flies at night.
I think of autumn under sparse trees
And daytime when the moon is bright.
The shimmering river gets reflected on cliffs.
Green hills add colors to the flow from a height.
Why need feasts in West Garden
Or rides on fast carriages for our delight?

詠長信宮中草

委翠似知節，含芳如有情。全由
履跡少，併欲上階生。

The Grass of Changxin Palace

The fragrant green grass, politely prostrate,
Seems to have emotion to show.
Rarely visited and walked on,
It wants to climb the steps to grow.

亂後行經吳禦亭

禦亭一回望，風塵千里昏。青袍異春草，
白馬即吳門。獯戎鯁伊洛，雜種亂輾轅。

輦道同關塞，　王城似太原。　休明鼎尚重，
秉禮國猶存。　殷牖爻雖頤，　堯城吏轉尊。
泣血悲東走，　橫戈念北奔。　方憑七廟略，
誓雪五陵冤。　人事今如此，　天道共誰論？

Visiting the Royal Courier Station
of King Wu after the Turmoil

From the Royal Courier Station as I look back,
For myriad miles, wind and dust darken our land.
On white horses, green-robed rebels, like spring
　　grass, came.
In the Wu empire, with their lives our people paid.
Like the Xunyongs, they cut off Rivers Yi and Luo.
The bastards shook up Huanyuan Hill.
The capital became a battleground like ancient
　　Taiyuan.
Imperial highways resembled passes under blockade.
Any rule of virtue justifies a long mandate.
States based on rites and ceremonies survive still.
Prison guards turned against King Wu, like Yao.
Political projections through divinations of Yin are
　　hard to understand.
Your helpers hurried north with their halberds
And weeping blood, sadly came to your aid.
With a scheme based on our established sovereignty,
There was a vow of revenge for our ancestry to
　　fulfill.
Human affairs in politics have come to this.
Who can argue with Heaven's will?

YU XIN (513-581)
庾信

烏夜啼

促柱繁絃非子夜，歌聲舞態異前溪。禦史
府中何處宿，洛陽城頭那得棲！彈琴蜀郡
卓家女，織錦秦川竇氏妻。詎不自驚長淚
落，到頭啼烏恆夜啼。

Crows Caw at Night

Their cawing is unlike "Front Brook" composed for
    dancing

And sadder than "Midnight" performed with many
    strings set tight.

In the mansion of the Imperial Censor, where do
    they live?

For perching on the city wall of Luoyang, where is
    the site?

Dou's wife of Qinzhou wove a palindrome in
    brocade for her loyal husband.

Cho's daughter of Shu County played a parting tune
    for her unfaithful lover.

How can I not weep in fear continuously

When crows caw the whole night?

和王少保遙傷周處士

冥漠爾遊岱，淒涼予向秦。雖言異生死，
同是不歸人。昔予仕冠蓋，值子避風塵。
望氣求真隱，伺關待逸民。忽聞泉石
友，芝桂不防身。悵然張仲蔚，悲哉鄭
子真。三山猶有鶴，五柳更應春。遂令
從渭水，投弔往江濱。

In Answer to an Elegy Written by Wang, Secretary of the Crown Prince, for Zhou, the Recluse

Your soul in the void traveled to Mount Dai.
I am detained in the land of Qin in sorrow.
Though the living and the dead are different,
No hope of returning is true for you and me also.
When I worked as a government official,
A haven from life's wind and dust, you could follow.
Watch the energy around a true recluse.
The gate-keeper waited to spot Laozi years ago.
Herbs and cassias cannot let a recluse live forever.
Of your sudden death, I came to know.
Zhang Zhongwei and Zheng Zizhen, past recluses,
Left sad memories that make me feel low.
You live now on Three Hills with cranes.
By your former house, every spring willows grow.
To send my elegy as a tribute to you,
To the shore of River Wei I shall go.

和侃法師

客 遊 經 歲 月 ， 羈 旅 故 情 多 。 近 學
衡陽雁，秋分俱渡河。

In Answer to Monk Kan

You have left home traveling for years.
To a detained wanderer, homeland is a strong call.
Recently you follow wild geese going south,
Across the Yellow River for Hengyang, in fall.

奉和泛江

春江下白帝， 畫舸向黃牛。 錦纜回沙磧，
蘭橈避荻洲。 濕花隨水泛， 空巢逐樹流。
建平船柹下， 荊門戰艦浮。 岸社多喬木，
山城足迴樓。 日落江風靜， 龍吟迴上游。

In Answer to the Poem "Sailing Across a Big River" by King Wen of the Liang Dynasty, at Imperial Request

In spring, your navy sailed towards Baidi City.
Painted ships sped towards Yellow Ox Beachhead.
Exquisite ropes avoided the sandy shores.
Small boats stayed clear of the rushes that spread.
Damp rush flowers followed the flow.
By trees adrift, empty nests were led.

Wood shards from ships at Jianping came down.
Battleships at Jingmen got moored head to head.
Many tall trees grow near ancestral halls.
From towers of hillside towns, one can see far ahead.
Your Majesty's orders can reach upstream.
At sunset, above the river, the wind is dead.

詠畫屏風詩，其一

昨夜鳥聲春，驚鳴動四鄰。今朝梅樹下，
定有詠花人。流星浮酒泛，粟瑱繞杯屑。
何勞一片雨，喚作陽臺神。

A Painted Screen, no

Birdsongs beckoned spring last night,
Putting my neighbors all over in fright.
Under a plum tree this morning,
Someone chanting on plum flowers must be in sight.
Her sparkling eyes float on a full cup of wine.
Her corn-like jade earrings trace the rim in her
    drunken delight.
Who needs a goddess of Yang Terrace in the rain
When the lady on the screen looks right?

詠畫屏風詩，其二

三危上鳳翼，九阪度龍鱗。路高山裡樹，
雲低馬上人。懸崖泉溜響，深谷鳥聲春。
住馬來相問，應知有姓秦。

A Painted Screen, no

Like dragon scales, the slopes like Jiuban appear.
On phoenix wings, tall hills like Sanwei can go.
Trails on high grounds top hillside trees.
Men on horseback move like clouds hanging low.
Springs cascading from cliffs sound sharp.
Birdsongs in spring start from deep valleys below.
Stay your horse and talk to the locals.
There must be refugees from Qin, I know.

至老子廟應詔

虛無推馭辨，寥廓本乘蜺。三門臨苦縣，
九井對靈谿。盛丹須竹節，量藥用刀圭。
石似臨邛芋，芝如封禪泥。毟毛新鵠
小，盤根古樹低。野戍孤煙起，春山百
鳥啼。路有三千別，途經七聖迷。唯當
別關吏，直向流沙西。

Paying Homage to the Temple of Laozi

You push your cart all over the void,
Following the rainbow in the wild sky.
Your temple with three doors stands in Ku County.
Nine wells joined by a brook form a tie.
Bamboo nodes store your cinnabar concoction.
On Dao Gui as your measuring device, you rely.
Stones are boiled soft like taros of Linqiong.
The hue of the soil of Mount Tai's altar is what your
    herbs go by.
A young swan between molts appears small.
Buttress roots make an old tree look not as high.
One column of smoke rises by barracks in the wilds.
On hills in spring, a hundred birds cry.
On the road where seven saints in the past got lost,
You have to cover three thousand miles that lie.
You head straight towards the desert in the west,
After bidding the gate-keeper goodbye.

擬詠懷，其一

疇昔國士遇，生平知己恩。直言珠可
吐，寧知炭可吞？一顧重尺璧，千金輕
一言。悲傷劉孺子，淒愴史皇孫。無因
同武騎，歸守霸陵園。

Poems in the Style of "Expressing my Mind" by Ruan Ji, no.1

As the top national scholar named by the Liang king,
I owe my life and a debt to his favor shown.
There was talk that my writings shone like pearls.
About me as his avenger, I would not have known.
As a diplomat like Lan Xiangru with his big disc,
I value highly what I say.
I am sad that the child emperor of Liu
And the grandson of King Wu were put away.
Unlike Sima Xiangru, Mounted Military Attendant,
I fail to return to guard his mausoleum today.

擬詠懷，其二

榆關斷音信，漢使絕經過。胡笳落淚曲，羌笛斷腸歌。纖腰減束素，別淚損橫波。恨心終不歇，紅顏無復多。枯木期填海，青山望斷河。

Poems in the Style of "Expressing my Mind" by Ruan Ji, no.2

Isolated beyond the northern borders,
I get no visits from my empire's envoys again.
Songs from Tartar reed pipes or Qiang flutes
Make me shed tears of pain.
Parting tears hurt my eyes.

Like thin white silk, my slim waist will remain.
Youth stays no more.
My regrets will never wane.
Like attempts to fill up the sea or block a river,
My wish to return is in vain.

擬詠懷，其三

搖落秋為氣，淒涼多怨情。啼枯湘水竹，
哭壞杞梁城。天亡遭憤戰，日蹙值愁兵。
直虹朝映壘，長星夜落營。楚歌饒恨曲，
南風多死聲。眼前一杯酒，誰論身後名！

Poems in the Style of "Expressing my Mind" by Ruan Ji, no.3

Autumn is the season for falling leaves,
Often with feelings in complaint and sorrow.
Ladies of River Xiang wept and wilted bamboos.
Tears for Qi Liang, the dead soldier, wrecked the
    city years ago.
In face of a lost kingdom,
Soldiers in defeat feel low.
A meteor at night fell onto our camp.
At dawn, by our barracks rose an ill-fated rainbow.
Songs of Chu deal mainly with regret.
The tempo of southern tunes is deadly slow.
Officials of the Liang Dynasty set eyes on pleasure.
Any wish for historical fame was let go.

擬詠懷，其四

橫流遘屯慝，上慘結重氛。苦市聞妖
獸，頹山起怪雲。綠林多散卒，清波有
敗軍。智士今安用，忠臣且未聞。惜無
萬金產，東求滄海君。

Poems in the Style of "Expressing my Mind" by Ruan Ji, no.4

With dark, disastrous omens from the sky
And turmoil from beacon fires, we were beset.
Strange clouds fell like collapsed hills on our tents.
Weird beasts cried in the market.
Like troops at Qingbo, our army met defeat,
But resisters like those of Lulin Hill, we could get.
Now how do we recruit and use the wise?
Loyal ministers have kept quiet.
For an avenger through Canghai Jun in the east,
I lack ten thousand pieces of gold, to my regret.

擬詠懷，其五

日夜荒城上，蒼茫餘落暉。都護樓蘭
返，將軍疏勒歸。馬有風塵色，人多關
塞衣。陣雲平不動，秋蓬卷欲飛。聞道
樓船戰，今年不解圍。

Poems in the Style of "Expressing my Mind" by Ruan Ji, no.5

Sunset wanes in the endless, misty sky,
Above the city wall of a deserted town at twilight.
The commander came back from Loulan,
With the general from Shulei at a different site.
War horses look dusty after countless wars.
Soldiers in uniform are ready to fight.
Unmoving clouds signal impending wars.
Armies roll out like fall tumbleweeds in flight.
I heard of sea battles from the south.
This year, no relief is in sight.

擬詠懷，其六

蕭條亭障遠，淒愴風塵多。關門臨白狄，
城影入黃河。秋風別蘇武，寒水送荊軻。
誰言氣蓋世，晨起帳中歌！

Poems in the Style of "Expressing my Mind" by Ruan Ji, no 6

The distant sentry-station looks bleak.
Sadly skirmishes often rise overall.
The Baidi tribe stays close to the Pass.
Yellow River gets the shadow of the Great Wall.
Would that I be Jingke leaving by a cold river
Or Su Wu bidden goodbye in the winds of fall!

Rising at dawn in his tent, Xiang Yu sang in defeat,
Though named the greatest hegemonic king of all.

擬詠懷，其七

步兵未飲酒，中散未彈琴。索索無真
氣，昏昏有俗心。涸鮒常思水，驚飛每
失林。風雲能變色，松竹且悲吟。由來
不得意，何必往長岑。

Poems in the Style of "Expressing my Mind" by Ruan Ji, no 7

A poet like Zhongshan, I do not play the qin.
Unlike Ruan Ji, the foot soldier, I do not drink wine.
My befuddled mind sticks to worldly thoughts.
Unenergetic and undisciplined, I feel out of line.
A frightened, stray bird fails to rejoin its group.
For water, fish in a pond drying up often pine.
Loyalists, like pine and bamboo, chant in sorrow.
With new masters, defectors easily align.
All of my life, I do not have my wishes met.
Going home is not a feasible choice of mine.

擬詠懷，其八

悲歌度燕水，弭節出陽關。李陵從此
去，荊卿不復還。故人形影滅，音書兩
俱絕。遙看塞北雲，懸想關山雪。遊子
河梁上，應將蘇武別。

Poems in the Style of "Expressing my Mind" by Ruan Ji, no 8

With a sad song, I cross River Yan.
Out of Yang Pass, my steps are slow.
Like Jing Ke, I cannot return.
Like Li Ling, away from home I go.
I cannot see my old friends.
No voice or letters from them can come by.
I watch distant clouds beyond the borders.
Under snow, hills and passes lie.
Downcast and regretful, I know how Li Ling felt
When on the bridge, to Su Wu he said goodbye.

重別周尚書

陽關萬里路，不見一人歸。唯有
河邊雁，秋來南向飛。

A Second Poem of Farewell to Secretary Zhou

It is a long way to Yang Pass.
None can be seen returning home at all.
Only wild geese by the river
Take flight southwards in fall.

JIANG ZHONG (519-594)
江總

遇長安使寄裴尚書

傳聞合浦葉，遠向洛陽飛。北風尚嘶
馬，南冠獨不歸。去雲目徒送，離琴手
自揮。秋蓬失處所，春草屢芳菲。太息
關山月，風塵客子衣。

For Secretary Pei after Meeting
an Envoy from Changan

Fall leaves from distant Hepu
Flew to Luoyang, from hearsay I know.
A wanderer in the south, I get detained alone.
Tartar horses neigh as north winds blow.
I watched as the envoy left like clouds,
Striking my qin for a parting song of sorrow.
Like tumbleweeds in fall, I feel uprooted.
Again and again, fragrant spring grasses grow.
Sighing under moonlight by passes and hills,
I feel like a guest under wind and dust as I go.

LU SIDAO (531-582)
盧思道

從軍行

朔方烽火照甘泉，長安飛將出祁連。犀渠
玉劍良家子，白馬金羈俠少年。平明偃月
屯右地，薄暮魚麗逐左賢。谷中石虎經銜
箭，山上金人曾祭天。

天涯一去無窮已，薊門迢遞三千里。朝見
馬嶺黃沙合，夕望龍城陣雲起。庭中奇樹
已堪攀，塞外征人殊未還。白雪初下天山
外，浮雲直上五原間。

關山萬里不可越，誰能坐對芳菲月？流水
本自斷有腸，堅冰舊來傷馬骨。邊庭節物
與華異，冬霰秋霜春不歇。長風蕭蕭渡水
來，歸雁連連映天沒。

從軍行，軍行萬里出龍庭。單于渭橋今已
拜，將軍何處覓功名？

Ballad of Expeditions

North beacon fires make Ganquan Palace bright.
At Changan, generals from Qilin Hill come in sight.
Our fine sons with jade swords and rhino shields,
On white steeds with gold saddles, show fight.
At dusk, the Yuli formation chased off our foe.
By dawn, the Yanyue formation stood in the right.

Shooting a tiger-like rock and winning gold war
  trophies,
Our Han generals demonstrate their might.

Treks continue once expeditions go all the way.
Jimen stands three thousand miles away.
They eye the yellow sands of Maling Pass by morn
And war clouds of Longcheng at the end of the day.
Rare trees in her courtyard have grown tall
Before soldiers beyond the pass can return at all.
Like floating clouds, they march straight to Wuyuan.
Beyond Tianshan, snow has just begun to fall.

She cannot meet him beyond hills and passes.
Who wants to sit before moonlit flowers alone?
His sobs are like flowing water from a broken heart.
Hard ice has cut and hurt him to the bone.
There, seasons and things differ from our own.
Winter sleet and fall frost persist in spring.
Endless returning wild geese go off the sunlit sky.
Over waters, a whistling wind keeps blowing.

Ballad of expeditions.
Over myriad miles, they captured Longting.
At Wei Bridge, foreign chiefs already bowed to the
  Han king.
For military fame, where will our generals be going?

遊梁城

揚鑣歷汴浦，廻扈入梁墟。漢藩文雅地，
清塵曖有餘。賓遊多任俠，臺苑盛簪
裾。　　歎息徐公劍，悲涼鄒子書。亭高落
照盡，原野泫寒初。鳥散空城夕，煙銷古
樹疏。東越嚴子陵，西蜀馬相如。修名
竊所慕，長謠獨課虛。

A Visit to Daliang

Along River Bien, in a horse-drawn carriage,
To the ruins of Daliang, on a detour I go.
This highly civilized capital of the Han Dynasty
Practiced benevolent rule, warm and mellow.
The elite at the royal compounds looked elegant.
Each guest behaved like a hero.
Praising its past is like offering a sword after death
Or clearing one's name after being jailed in sorrow.
The plains in the wild got their first harsh cold front.
On the bank, sunset has shed its last glow.
Birds above this deserted city scatter at dusk.
Old trees look sparse when the mist is clear.
Yan Ziling of Yue of East Han
And Sima Xiangru in Shu of West Han, years ago,
Earned their fame which I admire.
I chant on end alone, without a grip on my career.

XUE DAOHENG (540-606)
薛道衡

昔昔鹽

垂柳覆金堤， 靡蕪葉復齊。 水溢芙蓉沼，
花飛桃李蹊。 採桑秦氏女， 織錦竇家妻。
關山別蕩子， 風月守空閨。 恆斂千金笑，
長垂雙玉啼。 盤龍隨鏡隱， 彩鳳逐帷低。
飛魂同夜鵲， 倦寢憶晨雞。 暗牖懸蛛網，
空梁落燕泥。 前年過代北， 今歲往遼西。
一去無消息， 那能惜馬蹄。

Boudoir Complaint
(Tune: Xi Xi Yan)

Drooping willows cover firm banks.
Blades of angelicas evenly grow.
Peach and pear petals fall to cover a path.
Waters in a lotus marsh overflow.
Qin's daughter, a picker of mulberry leaves, yearned
　　for her husband.
Dou's wife made a palindrome in sorrow.
She saw her husband off for the passes and hills,
Waiting alone indoors in the wind and moonglow.
Her precious smiles are often withheld.
Her two streams of tears, like jade, often show.
She put away her mirror with a coiled dragon.
Her bed curtains with colorful phoenixes hang low.
She feels as lost as a night magpie without a nest.

Helplessly tired, she recalls the dawn rooster's crow.
Cobwebs hang all over her dark windows.
From her open beams falls the soil of the swallow.
This year he travels to Liaoxi County,
Passing Dai County in the north two years ago.
Once gone, no news came from him.
To see me, why cannot he make his horse go?

KONG SHAOAN (577-c622)
孔紹安

落葉

早 秋 驚 落 葉 ， 飄 零 似 客 心 。 翻 飛
未 肯 下 ， 猶 言 惜 故 林 。

Falling Leaves

Leaves falling in early autumn give me fright.
Their restlessness reflect the wanderer's heart.
Adrift and afloat, they delay in settling down.
From their former forests, they say they cannot part.

別徐永元秀才

金 湯 既 失 險 ， 玉 石 乃 同 焚 。 墜 葉 還 相
覆 ， 落 羽 更 爲 群 。 豈 謂 三 秋 節 ， 重 傷 千

里分？促離弦易轉，幽咽水難聞。欲識
相思處，山川間白雲。

Seeing off Licentiate Xu Yongyuan

Invaders let everything burn
After our strong city walls held up in vain.
Like fallen leaves, we helped to cover each other.
Like wounded birds, flocking together we have lain.
How is it that in autumn we shall be parted,
For myriad miles, with deep, hurtful pain.
It is easy to play music in your sudden departure,
But hard to hear the quiet sobs we try to contain.
If you want to know of my yearnings,
Like white clouds amid hills and streams, they never
    wane.

ANONYMOUS (Six Dynasties)
無名氏

子夜曲：夏

青荷蓋綠水，芙蓉葩紅鮮。郎見
欲采我，我心欲懷蓮。

Midnight Song: Summer

Lotus buds look red and fresh.
Green lotus leaves on the water make a cover.
It is his wish to pluck me off.
My heart yearns for seeds embedded by my lover.

子夜曲：秋

涼 秋 開 窗 寢 ， 斜 月 垂 光 照 。 中 宵
無人語，羅幌有雙笑。

Midnight Song: Autumn

The open bedroom window in cool fall
Lets in slanting moonlight.
Through the gauze bed curtains comes the laughter
Of two people, without a word, at midnight.

子夜曲：冬

淵 水 厚 三 尺 ， 素 雪 覆 千 里 。 我 心
如松柏，君情復何似？

Midnight Song: Winter

To three feet thick, the ice can go.
Over a thousand miles is a cover of white snow.

My unchanged heart is like pine and cypress.
How you feel about me, I have yet to know.

FENG XIAOLIAN (Six Dynasties)
馮小憐

感琵琶弦

雖 蒙 今 日 寵 ， 猶 憶 昔 時 憐 。 欲 知
心斷絕，應看膝頭弦。

Reflections after the Strings of
her Pipa Snapped

Although I am favored by a new master today,
I still remember my former king's love for me.
If you want to know about my broken heart,
You should look at the snapped strings on my knee.

PRINCESS DAYI (Six Dynasties)
大義公主

書屏風詩

盛衰等朝暮，世道若浮萍。榮華實難守，
池臺終自平。富貴今何在？空事寫丹青。
杯酒恆無樂，絃歌詎有聲？予本皇家

子，飄流入虜庭。一朝睹成敗，懷抱忽
縱橫。古來共如此，非我獨申名。唯有
明君曲，偏傷遠嫁情。

Inscribed on a Screen

Like floating duckweeds, social values waver.
Ups and downs await us, like night and day.
Ponds and terraces end up flat on the ground.
It is hard for glory and grandeur to stay.
Where are my wealth and class now?
Inscribing on a painted screen whiles the time away.
Cups of wine do not give me joy.
Any musical string I no longer play.
Being of royal birth, I was made a bride
Of the barbarian court, adrift on my way.
Suddenly my mind becomes thoughtful,
Having seen success and failure today.
Since the old days, it has been like this,
Not that I alone have this to say.
To the unique "Song of Mingjun" only,
Can my hurt feeling of being married afar relay.

ZHENG GONGCHAO (Six Dynasties)
鄭公超

送庾羽騎抱

舊宅青山遠，歸路白雲深。遲暮難爲別，
搖落更傷心。空城落日影，迴地浮雲陰。
送君自有淚，不假聽猿吟。

Seeing off Yu Bao, Imperial Guard

Your former home lies far beyond green hills,
Deep within white clouds, by a pathway.
Parting at an old age is hard.
To add to our grief, leaves fall and sway.
Clouds make an overcast from a distant height,
At sunset, shadows of the empty city stay.
I do not need to hear the sad cries of gibbons.
From my eyes, tears of parting naturally break away.

ZHU TING (Six Dynasties)
祖珽

挽歌

昔日驅駟馬，謁帝長楊宮。旌懸白雲外，
騎獵紅塵中。今來向漳浦，素蓋轉悲風。
榮華與歌笑，萬里盡成空。

An Elegy for Myself

Riding a carriage with four horses to the palace,
To see the king, I was granted the right.
My hunting entourage kicked up red dust.
My ceremonial banner hung at the clouds' height.
I come now towards Zhangpu in a sad mood,
In a hearse painted white.
Fame, riches, laughter and songs,
Over myriad miles, vanish outright.

4

SUI DYNASTY
(581-618)

YANG SU (?-606)
楊素

山齋獨坐贈薛內史，其一

居山四望阻，風雲竟朝夕。深溪橫古樹，
空巖臥幽石。日出遠岫明，鳥散空林寂。
蘭亭動幽氣，竹室生虛白。落花入戶飛，
細草當階積。桂酒徒盈樽，故人不在席。
日落山之幽，臨風望羽客。

For Xue, Deputy Director, Written in my Study in the Hills while Sitting Alone, no.1

The hills block my view on all sides at home.
Wind and cloud gather from day until night.
An old tree hangs across a deep creek.

Boulders spread on ridges at a height.
With birds gone, the empty forest is quiet.
The far hills under the sun look bright.
In a bamboo hut, my mind glows in sublimation.
Courtyard orchids exude fragrance ever so slight.
Fine grasses crowd the steps.
Falling petals get indoors in flight.
Cassia wine may fill bottles to the brim,
But old friends are not around to share my delight.
Hills darken after sunset.
In the wind, I watch for a fairy's sight.

山齋獨坐贈薛內史，其二

巘壑澄清景，景清巘壑深。白雲飛暮色，
綠水激清音。澗戶散餘彩，山窗凝宿陰，
花草共縈映，樹石相陵臨。獨坐對陳榻，
無客有鳴琴。寂寂幽山裡，誰知無悶心？

For Xue, Deputy Director, Written in my
Study in the Hills while Sitting Alone, no.2

Hills and valleys look clear and sharp,
Allowing greater depths for the eyes to follow.
White clouds scud with twilight hues.
Green waters bob with distinct notes and tempo.
Waning dusk colors spread by my brook-side door.
Overnight moisture covers my hill-facing window.
Trees and rocks peacefully encroach one another.

Flowers and grass reflect and glow.
I sit against an empty bed.
The secluded hill is quiet so.
There is a qin to be played but there are no guests.
Of my wish to be a recluse, who could know?

贈薛播州，其一

在昔天地閉，品物屬屯蒙。和平替王
道，哀怨結人風。麟傷世已季，龍戰道
將窮。亂海飛群水，貫日引長虹。干戈
異革命，揖讓非至公。

For Xue of Bozhou, no.1

When Heaven and Earth were one,
Everything was muddled in the early days.
Folksongs express the complaint of the people.
A peaceful succession of power shows kingly ways.
The wounded unicorn signaled a waning dynasty.
Feudal lords let benevolent rules suffer from delays.
A long rainbow piercing the sun signals disasters.
The sea is a riot of flying water sprays.
Wars are not revolutions according to Heaven's will.
Polite abdications do not guarantee that justice plays.

贈薛播州，其二

兩河定寶鼎，八水域神州。函關絕無
路，京洛化爲邱。漳滏爾連沼，涇渭予
別流。生郊滿戎馬，涉路起風牛。班荊
疑莫遇，贈縞竟無由。

For Xue of Bozhou, no.2

Two sections of Yellow River and eight tributaries
Saw wars by each contender, to claim his right.
Luoyang, the capital, was in ruins;
Hengu Pass was shut tight.
Now we pursue dissimilar callings,
Like rivers that are warm, cold, muddied or bright.
War-horses fill the outskirts.
Our paths are as different as day and night.
Unsure of a chance-meeting or my gift reaching you,
I feel trapped in a sad plight.

贈薛播州，其三

道昏雖已朗，政故猶未新。刳舟洹水
際，結網大川濱。出遊迎釣叟，入夢訪
幽人。植林雖各樹，開榮豈異春？相逢
一時泰，共幸百年身。

For Xue of Bozhou, no. 3

Though misgovernment has been corrected,
To old policies, the empire still adheres.
Ship-building and weaving nets for fishing
Are responsibilities that the state bears.
Stories of finding an able minister in a fisherman
Or a recluse in a dream of the king come to our ears.
Trees may grow to different heights
But the same floral glory in spring appears.
We met as colleagues at a time of prosperity,
Sharing the luck of a hundred years.

贈薛播州，其四

荏苒積歲時，契闊同遊處。閶闔既趨
朝，承明還宴語。上林陪羽獵，甘泉侍
清曙。迎風含暑氣，飛雨淒寒序。相顧
惜光陰，留情共延佇。

For Xue of Bozhou, no. 4

Time has passed for a long time
As we work and play in a pair.
In palace feasts, we casually talk
Or during court sessions, discuss any state affair.
We accompany the king in hunting
And at morn, wait for an audience to share.
A flying rain and a sad chill come in season,

After hot winds with humid air.
Our friendship stays and meets the test of time
Which is something we both treasure and care.

贈薛播州，其五

滔滔彼江漢，實為南國紀。作牧求明
德，若人應斯美。高臥未襄帷，飛聲已
千里。還望白雲天，日暮秋風起。峴山
君儻遊，淚落應無已。

For Xue of Bozhou, no. 5

The big rivers, Yangzi and Han, flow on and on,
Called "Southland's Leaders" by name.
An ethical supervisor for a province,
You should enjoy good fame.
Your style, away from micro-management,
Earns you wide acclaim.
As I look, the sky, full of white clouds,
Will be under the fall dusk wind's claim.
You will tear endlessly at Mount Xian's epitaph.
To an able governor like you, it means the same.

贈薛播州，其六

漢陰政已成，嶺表人猶蠹。彈冠比方
新，還珠總如故。楚人結去思，越俗歌
來暮。陽烏尚歸飛，別崔還廻顧。君見
南枝巢，應思北風路。

For Xue of Bozhou, no. 6

At Xiangyang, you did your new reforms,
But at Bozhou, public morals are still low.
You offer a new, incorruptible rule.
Like pearls back to Hepu, prosperity returns to grow.
People of Xiangyang recall your wise management.
Your late re-assignment is a complaint citizens echo.
Cranes on leaving look back.
Homing routes allow migratory birds to follow.
At the sight of nests on southern branches,
You should think of paths where north winds blow.

贈薛播州，其七

養病願歸閒，居榮在知足。棲遲茂陵
下，優游滄海曲。故人情可見，今人遵
路矚。荒居接野窮，心物俱非俗。桂樹
芳叢生，山幽竟何欲！

For Xue of Bozhou, no. 7

Sick in bed, I wish to be idle to recuperate.
In good times, one should be content.
I travel in Maoling County leisurely
And by the gray sea, tour according to my bent.
An old friend like you can read my sensibilities.
People today cannot catch my full intent.
Simple huts in the wilds make an endless stretch.
On mundane things, my whole existence is not spent.
Cassia trees and fragrant herbs grow all over.
In the quiet hills, no other wishes meet my intent.

贈薛播州，其八

秋水魚游日，春樹鳥鳴時。濠梁暮共
往，幽谷有相思。千里悲無駕，一見杳
難期。山河散瓊蘂，庭樹下丹滋。物華
不相待，遲暮有餘悲。

For Xue of Bozhou, no. 8

Whether in spring with birds singing
Or fish swimming on a fall day,
We develop our friendship and mutual regard.
In our outings, we enjoy togetherness in play.
Our meeting again will be hard.
You are a thousand miles away.
Red blooms drop from courtyard trees.

Jade-like petals fly all over in a spray.
At sunset, my sadness hangs on.
Like aging, nature cannot wait, with no delay.

贈薛播州，其九

銜悲向南浦，寒色黯沉沉。風起洞庭
險，煙生雲夢深。獨飛時慕侶，寡和乍
孤音。木落悲時暮，時暮感離心。離心
多苦調，詎假雍門琴。

For Xue of Bozhou, no. 9

It was cold, bleak and dark
When you left me for Bozhou in sorrow.
Yunmeng Marsh is shrouded by deep mist.
Lake Dongting is dangerous when winds blow.
Flying alone, I yearn for a companion.
Short of a duet, I sound off in a solo.
Falling leaves remind me of the year's end
Which in turn gives me parting woe.
The music of separation is mostly bitter,
Without the Yongmen qin for its tone and tempo.

KONG DESHAO (?-621)
孔德紹

夜宿荒村

綿綿夕漏深，客恨轉傷心。撫絃無人聽，
對酒時獨斟。故鄉萬里絕，窮愁百慮侵。
秋草思邊馬，遶枝驚夜禽。風度谷餘響，
月斜山半陰。勞歌欲敍意，終是白頭吟。

An Overnight Stay in a Deserted Village

A wanderer laments in grief
As the clepsydra shows it is late at night.
Any listener to my music
Or fellow drinker before me is out of sight.
Shut off from my hometown myriad miles away,
I am sad, worried and uptight.
Border horses think about fall grass.
Night fowls circle branches in fright.
Valleys echo the passing wind.
Half of the hill is shaded under slanting moonlight.
If I try to sing to express myself,
It is all about a white-haired man's sad plight.

送蔡君知入蜀

金陵已去國，銅梁忽背飛。失路
遠相送，他鄉何日歸？

Seeing off Cai Junzhi on his Way to Shu

Jinling is already distant from the capital.
Suddenly for Tongliang Hill, you push further away.
In seeing you off this far, I almost lost my way.
When is your returning day?

ANONYMOUS (Sui Dynasty)
無名氏

雞鳴歌

東方欲明星爛爛，汝南晨雞登壇喚。曲終
漏盡嚴具陳，月沒星稀天下旦。千門萬戶
遞魚鑰，宮中城上飛烏鵲。

The Crowing Rooster

Like Runan roosters, the time-keeper on an altar
    sings.
Stars in the east, pre-dawn sky look bright.
As songs end and clepsydras wane, toilet articles are
    set.
The sunlit sky has scarce stars and no moon in sight.
Fish-shaped keys open myriad doors..
Crows on palace walls take flight.

MING YUQING (Sui Dynasty)
明餘慶

從軍行

三邊烽亂驚，十萬且橫行。風卷常山陣，
笳喧細柳營。劍花寒不落，弓月曉逾明。
會取淮南地。持作朔方城。

Expeditions

Ten thousand troops terrorize our land.
Border beacon fires cause unsettling fright.
The Changshan formation rolls up like wind.
With loud reed pipes and strict rules, we show fight.
Our swords cannot be defrosted.
The bow-shaped moon by dawn gets more bright.
We should reclaim south of River Huai
And build a city in the north on site.

SUN WANSHOU (Sui Dynasty)
孫萬壽

和周記室遊舊京

大夫憫周廟，王子泣殷墟。自然心斷絕，
何關繫慘舒？僕本漳濱士，舊國亦淪胥。
紫陌風塵起，青壇冠蓋疏。臺留子建

92

賦，宮落仲將書。譙周自題柱，商容誰
表閭？聞君懷古曲，同病亦漣洳。方知
周處歎，前後信非虛。

In Reply to a Poem by a Secretay of the Zhou Dynasty, on Visiting the Site of the Former Capital

An official lamented the fallen Zhou Dynasty.
A prince wept for the Yin ruins in blight.
Naturally, they were heart-broken,
Totally shut to mere feelings of grief or delight.
Like the man by River Zhang, I am mostly sick.
My former kingdom of Qi also collapsed outright.
Wind and dust rise on roads of the outskirts.
To pray at the spring altar, few observe the rite.
At Brazen Birds Terrace, Zijian left an exposition.
Palace inscriptions were for Zhongjiang to write.
Who honored Shangrong with commendations on
    the door?
Predictions on a board by Qiaozhou were right.
I read your poem recalling the past
And wept, being in the same plight.
Now I know why Zhou Chu sighed.
Of the grief of dynastic changes, none can make
    light.

5

TANG DYNASTY
(618-907)

ZHANG SHUO (667-730)
張說

鄴都引

君不見魏武草創爭天祿，群雄睚眥皆相馳
逐。盡攜壯士破堅陣，夜接詞人賦華屋。
都邑繚繞西山陽，桑榆汗漫漳河曲。城郭
為墟人代改，但見西園明月在。鄴旁高冢
多貴臣，蛾眉曼綠共灰塵。試上銅臺歌舞
處，惟有秋風愁煞人。

Ballad of Ye, Capital of Wei

Do you not see
King Wu of Wei fought for Heaven's mandate?
Contenders set eyes on the Head of State.

Cao Cao and his men broke up strong formations,
Writing poems at night on a grand estate.
The capital wound around West Hill to the east.
Villagers had come and gone; cities were in blight.
Above West Garden, only the moon shone bright.
By the capital were buried those of the noble caste.
Ladies with green, moth-like brows did not last.
Go up Brazen Birds Terrace with song and dance
And get overwhelmed by the grief of a fall blast.

WANG WEI (701-761)
王維

酬郭給事

洞門高閣藹餘輝，桃李陰陰柳絮飛。禁裡
疏鐘官舍晚，省中啼鳥吏人稀。晨搖玉佩
趨金殿，夕奉天書拜瑣闈。強欲從君無那
老，將田臥病解朝衣。

In Answer to Secretary Guo

By tall pavilions with arched doors, with sunset
    aglow,
Willow fuzz flies, with peach and pear trees in the
    shadow.
The palace bell chimes now and then at dusk.
Few civil officers are on duty as birds crow.

With jade pendants swinging, you rush to the dawn
  court.
To the palace gate, with an edict at night you go.
I shall retire to the fields, being sick and bedridden.
Your footsteps force an old man like me to follow.

DU FU (712-770)
杜甫

觀公孫大娘弟子舞劍行

昔有佳人公孫氏，一舞劍器動四方。觀者
如山色沮喪，天地為之久低昂。霍如羿射
九日落，矯如群帝驂龍翔。來如雷霆收震
怒，罷如江海凝清光。

絳唇珠袖兩寂莫，晚有弟子傳芬芳。臨潁
美人在白帝，妙舞此曲神揚揚。與予問答
既有以，感時撫事增惋傷。

先帝侍女八千人，公孫劍器初第一。五十
年間似反掌，風塵澒洞昏王室。梨園弟
子散如煙，女樂餘姿映寒日。金粟堆南
木已拱，瞿唐石城草蕭瑟。玳筵急管曲
復終，樂極哀來月東出。老夫不知其所
往，足繭荒山轉愁疾。

Ballad of Viewing a Sword Dance Performed by a Student of Lady Gongsun

Lady Gongsun did a sword dance in the past.
Her fame spread afar and reached a great height,
Walls of viewers, like hills, lost their countenance.
The sky and earth shook for a long time at the site.
Dazzling like the nine stars shot down by Yi
And agile like fairies on dragons in flight,
Her dance was a big thunder's wrath until the end
When it resembled rivers and seas, limpid and bright.

Her red lips and pearl sleeves are gone.
Of late, a student of hers carries on her art.
To all in Baidi City, from her wonderful skill,
The energy of this beauty from Linying can impart.
From our talk, after her relationship to Sun is shared,
I recall the past and add regrets to my heart.

Of the former king's eight thousand female staff,
Gongsun with her sword dance was number one.
Fifty years passed like one flip of the palm.
Wind and dust of wars got the kingdom overrun.
Like smoke, students of Pear Garden dispersed,
With aging lady musicians under a cold sun.
South of Jinshu Hill, trees have grown huge.
Weeds of Stone City by Qutang Gorge look bleak.
At the end of fast tunes in a grand feast,
Grief follows ecstasy under the moon in the east.
I linger, as if losing my bearings on a deserted hill,
With corns on my feet, feeling in turn pleased.

對雪

戰哭多新鬼，愁吟獨老翁。亂雲低薄暮，
急雪舞迴風。飄棄樽無綠，爐存火似紅。
數州消息斷，愁坐正書空。

Facing Snow

Many new ghosts wail during wars.
Alone this old man chants in woe.
A whirlwind speeds up snowflakes in a dance.
At twilight, jumbled clouds hang low.
In my drifting life, I lack green brew for my goblets.
The stove remains with a fire emitting a red glow.
News has stopped coming from several states.
Without letters, I sit in sorrow.

月夜憶舍弟

戌鼓斷人行，邊秋一雁聲。露從今夜白，
月是故鄉明。有弟皆分散，無家問死生。
寄書長不達，況乃未休兵。

Recalling my Brothers on a Moonlit Night

A wild goose cries at the border in fall.
Garrison drums stop human traffic outright.
Dewdrops will be white from this night on.
Here as well as at home, the moon is bright.

I have brothers scattered all over,
Not knowing if my family members are alright.
My letters never reached them,
Especially when peace is not yet in sight.

WEI YINGWU (732-c792)
韋應物

陪元侍禦春遊

何處醉春風， 長安西復東。 不因俱罷辭，
豈得此時同。 賒酒宣平里， 尋芳下苑中。
往來楊柳陌。 猶避昔年驄。

Accompanying Censor Yuan on
an Outing in Spring

Where to get drunk in the spring wind, I don't know.
West and east of Changan, we want to go.
We would not meet at the same time
If we had not resigned but held onto our status quo.
Let us buy wine on credit at Xuanping Lane
And seek flowers of Xiayuan, high and low.
We still need to dodge rude officials and fast horses
As we stroll on willow-lined paths, to and fro.

夜偶詩客操公作

塵襟一蕭灑，清夜得禪公。遠自鶴林寺，
了知人世空。驚禽翻暗葉，流水注幽叢。
多謝非玄度，聊將詩興同。

Composed upon Meeting the
Poet, Master Cao, at Night

Once my robe is cleansed from dust,
I get to meet Master Cao on this quiet night.
Coming afar from Helin Temple,
Of the fleeting human life, he has deep insight.
A stream flows past secluded bushes.
Dark leaves flip over with fowls in fright.
My apologies for not being another Zen recluse.
Our mood for poems might reach the same height.

燕李錄事

與君十五侍皇闈，曉拂爐煙下赤墀。花開
漢苑經過處，雪下驪山沐浴時，近臣零落
今誰在，仙駕飄飄不可期。此日相逢思舊
日，一杯成喜亦成悲。

Entertaining Adjutant Li

At fifteen as the king's guards, on red steps,
We walked past incense smoke, at the break of day.

Whether in Han Garden during blossom time
Or at snowy Li Shan for baths, in his stay.
Do not hope to see the dead king rise with the fairies.
Where are his close ministers who withered away?
Each cup of wine is mixed with joy and grief
As I recall the past in our meeting today.

淮上即事寄廣陵親故

前舟已渺渺，欲渡誰相待。秋山起暮鐘，
楚雨連滄海。風波離思滿，宿昔容鬢改。
獨鳥下東南，廣陵何處在？

Events on River Huai: to a Dear Friend in Guangling

The earlier ferry is already faint.
Who would have waited for me?
The evening bell chimes from autumn hills,
In rainy Chu here and at the gray sea.
Too soon I look different, amid wind and wave.
From deep parting thoughts, I am not free.
A lone bird is heading southeast with my letter,
But where in Guangling will you be?

早春對雪寄前殿中元侍郎

掃雪開幽徑，端居望故人。猶殘臘月酒，
更值早梅春。幾日東城陌，何時曲水濱。
聞閑且共嘗，莫待繡衣新。

Facing Snow in Early Spring: to Former Palace Censor Yuan

Suitably retired, I look for old friends
And sweep the snow from my secluded pathway.
I still have some wine for the year's end.
Plum trees blossom on an early spring day.
When shall we follow the trail of East City?
How soon by the winding stream shall we stay?
Together we should enjoy leisure.
Do not wait and let our plans be in delay.

贈王侍禦

心同野鶴與塵遠，詩似冰壺見底清。府縣
同趨昨日事，升沉不改故人情。上陽秋晚
蕭蕭雨，洛水寒來夜夜聲。自歎猶為折腰
吏，可憐聰馬路傍行。

For Censor Wang

Like a wild crane, your heart is way above dust.
Like ice in a vase, your poems are totally clear.

We both ran errands for the prefecture in the past.
Life changes alter not our bond from a yesteryear.
A whistling rain comes to Shangyang in late fall.
The nightly noise of cold River Luo I hear.
I sigh for being junior in rank still.
As a subservient, pitiable official I appear.

贈李儋

絲桐本異質，音響合自然。吾觀造化
意，二物相因緣。誤觸龍鳳嘯，靜聞寒
夜泉。心神自安宅，煩慮頓可捐。何因
知久要，絲白漆亦堅。

For Li Dan

Silk and paulownias are basically different,
But the sound from their union is naturally right.
In my view, it is the Creator's wish
That their bond of coordination will be tight.
Hit the strings for the roar of dragon and phoenix.
Quietly, the notes mimic a spring on a cold night.
My mind and spirit find peace
As troubles and worries are instantly out of sight.
I have known the cause for a long time.
The lacquer does not fade and the silk stays white.

示全真元常

予辭郡符去， 爾為外事牽。 寧知風雪夜，
復此對床眠。 始話南池飲， 更詠西樓篇。
無將一會易， 歲月坐推遷。

For Quanzhen and Yuanchang

You gave up something else to come here.
I resigned and let my official seal be cast.
We lie across beds to talk now,
Unexpectedly on a night with snow and blast.
We recall parties for chanting poems and drinking,
At South Lake and West Tower in the past.
Not for a moment should we change our life-styles.
As we sit, time is moving fast.

趨府候曉呈兩縣僚友

趨府不遑安， 中宵出戶看。 滿天星尚在，
近壁燭仍殘。 立馬頻驚曙， 垂簾卻避寒。
可憐同宦者， 應悟下流難。

Hurrying to the Prefect's Dawn Court: for my Colleagues in Two Counties

I hurry to the Prefect's court without rest
And look outdoors in the middle of the night.
The sky is still full of stars.

By the wall, waning candles are not bright.
Drapes are lowered to ward off cold air.
My horse towards daybreak is often in fright.
To my dear fellow colleagues, let me say:
Awareness of the people's hardships should be your
    insight.

同德精舍舊居傷懷

洛京十載別，　東林訪舊扉。　山河不可望，
存歿意多違。　時遷跡尚在，　同去獨來歸。
還見窗中鴿，　日暮遶庭飛。

Hurt Feelings at our Former Residence
at Tongde Hermitage

I visited my former home at East Grove
After I had left Luoyang ten years ago.
Life and death are mostly against my wish.
I could not view the hill and river without sorrow.
She came here without me; I returned alone.
Her tracks remain; onwards time must go.
At sundown, I see pigeons circling the courtyard,
After taking off from my window.

任洛陽丞答前長安田少府問

相逢且對酒，相問欲何如。數歲猶卑吏，
家人笑著書。告歸應未得，榮官又知疏。
日日生春草，空令憶舊居。

In Reply to Former Military Officer of Changan, Tian Wen, while Serving as Deputy Magistrate of Luoyang

We asked each other about our prospects,
Over wine, finally meeting again.
My family mocks at what I write.
After some years, the title of a petty official I retain.
Your glorious career has known negligence.
An approval to my retirement I need to gain.
Spring grass grows every day.
Yearnings for my former residence are in vain.

酬豆盧倉曹題庫壁見示

掾局勞才子，新詩動洛川。運籌知決勝，
聚米似論邊。宴罷常分騎，晨趨又比肩。
莫嗟年鬢改，郎署定推先。

In Response to Granary Chief, Dou Lu, Inscribed on the Granary Wall in Public View

The clerical office has put your talent to waste.

Your new poems stir River Luo.
I know of your winning, decisive plans.
Stockpiling rice aids the border staff, I presume.
After a feast, we often ride separate ways,
But at dawn, standing side by side we resume.
Sigh not over your changing temple hair each year.
A first priority for promotion from your chief you
    can assume.

期盧嵩枉書稱日暮無馬不赴以詩答

佳期不可失，終願枉衡門。南陌人猶度，
西林日未昏。庭前空倚杖，花裏獨留罇。
莫道無來駕，知君有短軒。

In Wait for Lu Song, who Wrote Unconvincingly that he could not Come Because the Day was Late and he had no Horse, I Send this Poem in Reply

A fine date should not be missed,
To meet a final wish of a visit from you.
People still walk on the south pathway.
Sunlight on West Grove is not through.
I lean on my staff by the gate in vain.
Among flowers is left your cup of brew.
Do not say you lack a horse.
You have a small cart, from what I knew.

揚州偶會前洛陽盧耿主簿

楚塞故人稀，相逢本不期。猶存袖裏字，
忽怪鬢中絲。客舍盈樽酒，江行滿篋詩。
更能連騎出，還似洛橋時。

In Yangzhou, Unexpectedly Meeting Former Assistant to the Magistrate Lu Geng of Luoyang

In Yangzhou, my old friends are rare.
The chance of our meeting here is basically bare.
Your letters are still well kept by me.
How odd to see white in your hair!
Let us fill our cups with wine at the inn
And the voyager's luggage with poems to the fullest
    share.
As we once did on Luoyang Bridge,
May we also ride on horseback again in a pair.

李五席送李主簿歸西臺

請告嚴程盡，西歸道路寒。欲陪鷹隼集，
猶戀鶺鴒單。洛邑人全少，嵩高雪尚殘。
滿臺誰不故，報我在微官。

Li Wuxi Sees off Li, Assistant to the Magistrate, on his Return to West Terrace

The road to the west is cold.
His leave of absence is up, let it be known.
He is to join an Imperial office, like the hawks,
But like a wagtail, cannot leave his brother alone.
Families in Luoyang seldom stay whole.
On high Mount Song, melting snow is still shown.
Who will he not befriend in the whole office there?
Even me, a petty official, quite unknown.

同德寺閣集眺

芳節欲云晏，　遊遨樂相從。　高閣照丹霞，
颻颻含遠風。　寂寥氛氳廓，　超忽神慮空。
旭日霽皇州，　岧嶢見兩宮。　嵩少多秀色，
羣山莫與崇。　三川浩東注，　廛澗亦來同。
陰陽降大和，　宇宙得其中。　舟車滿川陸，
四國靡不通。　舊堵今既葺，　廣田亦已豐。
周覽思自奮，　行當遇時邕。

Looking out Together from a Pavilion of Tongde Temple

The fragrant season may be late.
Traveling in a group brings me delight.
A distant wind blows noisily.
Red clouds make this tall pavilion bright.

An atmosphere of bleakness pervades the open land.
In the void, an immortal may suddenly be in sight.
I see two towering palaces
As the imperial city gets bathed in dawn light.
Songsao Peak shows much verdant growth.
In color, hills around cannot reach the same height.
Three streams grandly flow eastwards,
Joined by two rivers, Chan and Jian, left and right.
Yin and Yang forces fall in place in great harmony,
With our universe at a central site.
We can reach states in all directions.
Boats and carts pack our rivers and land tight.
Farmers with wide fields have prospered,
Now that they have fixed old walls in blight.
This tour takes place in peaceful time.
The view around us can excite.

大梁亭會李四栖梧作

梁王昔愛才，　千古化不泯。　至今蓬池上，
遠集八方賓。　車馬平明合，　城郭滿埃塵。
逢君一相許，　豈要平生親。　入仕三十載，
如何獨未伸。　英聲久籍籍，　臺閣多故人。
置酒發清彈，　相與樂佳辰。　孤亭得長望，
白日下廣津。　富貴良可取，　褐來西入秦。
秋風旦夕起，　安得客梁陳。

Meeting Li Qiwu, the Fourth, at Daliang Pavilion

King Liang loved to play host to talented men
Whose fame for ages does not wane.
Today at Lake Pengchi,
Distant guests from all over have gathered again.
Horse-drawn carriages arrive at dawn.
On city walls, dust has fully lain.
Our friendship, once mutually built up,
Needs no lifetime nurturing to retain.
After thirty years as an official,
You are not the only one with goals yet to attain.
Your good name has long been well known.
In the office, bonding with many old friends you
    maintain.
Let us have wine with music
And a good time here together to entertain.
From this lone pavilion, we can see afar.
Falling into the wide waters, the bright sun is to
    wane.
After you head west for Changan,
Wealth and power will be yours to gain.
As the autumn wind starts to blow any day,
A guest here at Lake Pengchi is not for us to detain.

簡盧陟

可憐白雪曲，　未遇知音人。　恓惶戎旅下，
蹉跎淮海濱。　澗樹含朝雨，　山鳥哢餘春。
我有一瓢酒，　可以慰風塵。

A Note to Lu Zhi

You have not met your patron,
Despite your worth like the lovely song "White
　Snow".
Feeling unachieved by River Huai,
With the army, worriedly you go.
A dawn rain covers trees by the brook.
In late spring, birds of the hills crow.
I have a gourd of wine
To comfort you as wind and dust blow.

假中枉盧二十二書示稱臥疾兼訝李
二久不訪問以詩答書因以戲李二

微官何事勞趨走，　服藥閑眠養不才。花裏
棋盤憎鳥汗，　枕邊書卷訝風開。　故人聞訊
緣同病，　芳月相思阻一盃。　應笑王戎成俗
物，　遙持麈尾獨徘徊。

On a Leave of Absence, Lu, the Twenty-
Second, Writes me, Claiming he is Ill in Bed.
Also, Surprised that Li, the Second, has not
Visited me in Such a Long Time, I Reply
with a Poem to Tease Li, the Second.

My lost talent finds no cure in rest and drugs.
A petty official like me feels spent, always on the go.
I hate bird shit while playing chess in the garden.
A rising wind alarms me as I read by my pillow.
Lu inquired, claiming the same sickness.
To be tardy in my drinking parties under moonlight,
    Li is prone,
Aptly jeered for being vulgar and materialistic, like
    Wang Rong,
Afar holding a fly whisk for power, lingering alone.

月夜會徐十一草堂

空齋無一事，岸幘故人期。暫輟觀書夜，
還題翫月詩。遠鐘高枕後，清露卷簾時。
暗覺新秋近，殘河欲曙遲。

On a Moonlit Night, I met Xu, the
Eleventh, at his Thatched Hut

In my empty study, I had nothing to do
And accepted a casual date to meet an old friend
    like you.

We composed verses on the moon.
For the night, with reading we were through.
As the distant bell chimed for worry-free sleepers,
We made poems until blinds were rolled up with
    dew.
The pre-dawn, waning Milky Way stayed on,
A slight hint of autumn coming anew.

賦得浮雲起離色送鄭述誠

遊子欲言去，浮雲那得知。偏能見行色，
自是獨傷離。晚帶城遙暗，秋生峯尚奇。
還因朔吹斷，疋馬與相隨。

On Floating Clouds and Parting Manners
while Seeing off Zheng Shucheng

Before a wanderer says he is leaving,
How would floating clouds have known?
They can see no other manners of journeying
Than your pain of leaving alone.
They dim the city afar, late in the day.
In fall, as strange peaks, they have grown.
Follow them as companions on horseback,
Even as broken bits, after north winds have blown.

賦得鼎門送盧耿赴任

名因定鼎地，門對鑿龍山。水北樓臺近，
城南車馬還。稍開芳野靜，欲掩暮鐘閑。
去此無嗟屈，前賢尚抱關。

On Tripod Gate, while Seeing off Lu Geng to his New Assignment

The name comes from the placement of a tripod.
The gate faces Carved Dragon Hill.
Towers and terraces stand near the river to the north.
Around south of the city, returning carriages mill.
It is closed as the evening bell stops,
Opening to the wilds, fragrant and tranquil.
Do not sigh in complaint as you depart.
An earlier martyr saving the gate holds his fame still.

經少林精舍寄都邑親友

息駕依松嶺，高閣一攀緣。前瞻路已窮，
既詣喜更延。出巘聽萬籟，入林濯幽泉。
鳴鐘生道心，暮磬空雲煙。獨往雖暫適，
多累終見牽。方思結茅地，歸息期暮年。

Passing Shaolin Hermitage: To Friends and Relatives in the Capital

I tied my horse below a pine ridge
And hiked towards a pavilion at a height.
The trail ahead looked blocked,
But once I arrived, I wanted more for my delight.
From the peak, I heard myriad sounds of nature
And in the groves, bathed in a secluded spring.
The chime of the bell awakened me to the Way.
The dusk musical stone drove cloud and mist out of
    sight.
I finally saw what worried me
Though for now, on this trip alone, I felt alright.
I know my retirement will have to wait at an old age,
When I start thinking of building a hut on site.

憶灃上幽居

一來當復去，猶此厭樊籠。況我林棲子，
朝服坐南宮。唯獨問啼鳥，還如灃水東。

Recalling my Secluded Residence by River Feng

Hopping one way then back again,
A bird already finds its cage a bore.
The boredom for one who resided in the woods,
Now in court attire in South Palace, is much more.

My only interest is to ask song birds:
"How is it still on River Feng's east shore?"

春中憶元二

雨歇萬井春，柔條已含綠。徘徊洛陽陌，
惆悵杜陵曲。遊絲正高下，啼鳥還斷續。
有酒今不同，思君瑩如玉。

Recalling Yuan, the Second, in Spring

Spring comes to myriad households after rain.
Signs of green on tender twigs already show.
I linger on the paths of Luoyang,
Depressed on recalling winding trails of Duling
    years ago.
Gossamer is falling from a height..
On and off birds crow.
I have wine but it is different now,
Without you, in my memory, a lustrous fellow.

任洛陽丞請告

方鑿不受圓，直木不為輪。揉材各有用，
反性生苦辛。折腰非吾事，飲水非吾貧。
休告臥空舘，養病絕囂塵。游魚自成族，
野鳥亦有羣。家園社陵下，千歲心氛氳。

天晴嵩山高，雪後河洛春。喬木猶未芳，
百草日已新。著書復何為，當去東皋耘。

Respectfully Asking to Resign as the Deputy Magistrate of Luoyang

Square holes do not fit round pegs.
Straight wooden beams never make wheels too.
Aptitudes find different usages.
All callings against nature let bitterness brew.
Drinking water is not my style of poverty.
Begging by bending my waist is not what I do.
I can nurse my ills, shunning din and dust.
And lying in an empty hall as my career is through.
Wild birds form flocks,
Just like fish in schools without a cue.
In my family garden of Duling, for ten decades,
To get my mind nurtured and uplifted, I am due.
Let me enjoy high Mount Song under sunlight
And snowy rivers when the year is new.
Tall trees are not yet fragrant.
Each day, a hundred herbs rise anew.
I should be a farmer like Tao Qian in East Paddy,
Besides writing books, a project I pursue.

送別覃孝廉

思親自當去，不第未蹉跎。家住青山下，
門前芳草多。秭歸通遠徼，巫峽注驚波。
州舉年年事，還期復幾何。

Seeing off Candidate Tan

Visiting your parents is a right thing to do.
Failing an examination puts not your efforts in vain.
Before your door are many fragrant herbs.
Your home is at the foot of a green mountain.
Wu Gorge sends fearful waves.
Through a long, far road, access to Zigui you gain.
Provincial examinations are held every year.
It will not be long before you come back again.

送榆次林明府

無嗟千里遠，亦是宰王畿。策馬雨中去，
逢人關外稀。邑傳榆石在，路遶晉山微。
別思方蕭索，新秋一葉飛。

Seeing off County Chief Lin to Yuci

You will still be with the royal domain.
For going myriad miles afar, do not complain.
Fellow travelers are scarce beyond the pass.
Just gallop off in the rain.

Narrow roads wind the hills of Jin.
In your new post, legends of the rock that advised
    the king last.
As parting thoughts make me feel forlorn,
An early autumn leaf flies past.

送澠池崔主簿

邑帶洛陽道，年年應此行。當時匹馬客，
今日縣人迎。暮雨投關郡，春風別帝城。
東西殊不遠，朝夕待佳聲。

Seeing off Cui, Assistant to the Magistrate, to Mianchi

Luoyang road links this place to Mianchi.
There is an annual trip for you, I should say.
A lone traveler on horseback,
You will be welcomed by people there today.
As you advance towards the pass in the evening rain,
A spring wind leaves the capital on its way.
It is not that far between east and west.
Let me wait for the good news of your return night
    and day.

送洛陽韓丞東遊

仙鳥何飄飄，綠衣翠為襟。顧我差池羽，
咬咬懷好音。徘徊洛陽中，遊戲清川潯。
神交不在結，歡愛自中心。駕言忽祖
征，雲路邈且深。朝遊尚同啄，夕息當
異林。出餞宿東郊，列筵屬城陰。舉酒
欲爲樂，憂懷方沉沉。

Seeing off Deputy Magistrate Han
of Luoyang on his Trip East

Like a bird of fairyland, you flutter with ease.
In a kingfisher green robe, you are dressed right.
Though I claim to have a good voice,
My feathered wings are off-shaped, in your sight.
We linger in Luoyang
And in clear streams play.
As soulmates, we need no vowed alliance.
In our hearts, joy and love stay.
Suddenly you talk about a long trip,
Under clouds on land to a remote site.
We may still enjoy each other's company by day,
But rest in different places by night.
We lodge in East Outskirts for your farewell feast,
With none in the city, away from sunlight.
My heart is heavy with worries and grief
As I raise my cup of wine, meant for delight.

送中弟

秋風入疏戶，　離人起晨朝。　山駿多風雨，
西樓更蕭條。　嗟予淮海老，　送子關河遙。
同來不同去，　沉憂寧復消。

Seeing off my Brotherly Friend

A fall wind enters my weak door.
A traveler is up at the break of day.
The west tower is bleaker still.
This hilly town sits on most rainstorms' pathway.
I am seeing you off for distant passes.
Alas, aging by River Huai, I shall stay.
We came here together but you are leaving alone.
How can my deep worries go away?

送汾城王主薄

少年初帶印，　汾上又經過。　芳草歸時徧，
情人故郡多。　禁鐘春雨細，　宮樹野煙和。
相望東橋別，　微風起夕波。

Seeing off Wang, Assistant to the Magistrate, to Fencheng

You have carried an official seal since young
And sailed on River Fen on a former day.
Fragrant herbs will greet you on return

To your old county where many good friends stay.
Farm smoke has diffused among palace trees.
In the spring rain, the imperial bell fades away.
The dusk breeze makes waves
As I see you off on East Bridge on your way.

送張侍禦秘書江左觀省

莫歎都門路，歸無駟馬車。繡衣猶在篋，
芸閣已觀書。沃野收紅稻，長江釣白魚。
晨湌亦可薦，名利欲何如？

Seeing off Zhang, Assistant Censor, for South of Yangzi to Care for his Parents

Do not sigh over the road beyond the capital's gate.
On return, no horse-drawn carriage you can obtain.
You watched your books packed from the library.
In a chest, your official robes have lain.
Catch white fish from River Yangzi.
Harvest rice in red husks from the wild, lush terrain.
Even breakfasts are palatable.
Why wish for fame and gain?

送鄭長源

少年一相見， 飛轡河洛間。 歡遊不知罷，
半路忽言還。 冷冷鵾弦哀， 悄悄冬夜閑。
丈夫雖耿介， 遠別多苦顏。 君行拜高堂，
速駕難久攀。 雞鳴儔侶發， 朔雪滿河關。
須臾在今夕， 罇酌且循環。

Seeing off Zheng Changyuan

Once we met in our youth,
Between two rivers, we galloped away.
We could never end our joyous rides.
Midway, you are leaving, you suddenly say.
From phoenix strings come tunes, chilly and sad.
Wintry nights are listless and quiet.
Though a man should be high minded and stiff
    mannered,
On parting, sad faces we mostly get.
Your trip is to honor your parents.
It is hard to climb your fast carriage and follow.
At the crow of the rooster, you will depart.
Rivers and passes will be full of frosty snow.
Our togetherness tonight is brief.
Plying each other with wine we should go.

新秋夜寄諸弟

兩地俱秋夕，相望共星河。高梧一葉下，
空齋歸思多。方用憂人瘼，況且抱微痾。
無將別來近，顏鬢已蹉跎。

To my Cousins on an Early Fall Night

This autumn night falls on two places.
We watch the same Milky Way.
A leaf drops from a tall firmiana.
In my empty study, homesick thoughts mostly stay.
I worry about the sickness of other people,
But then I am also ill in a small way.
My homecoming date is nowhere near.
With my hair and face already in decay.

寄楊協律

吏散門閣掩，鳥鳴山郡中。遠念長江別，
俯覺座隅空。舟泊南池雨，簞卷北樓風。
併罷芳樽燕，為愴昨時同。

To Secretary Yang

After my staff has gone and the door closed,
In this hillside town, birdsongs last.
I notice an empty seat beside me
After our parting on River Yangzi in the distant past.

Boats on South Lake are moored in the rain.
Mats of North Tower roll up in the blast.
Feasts with fragrant wine with you are no more.
Over our former togetherness, I feel downcast.

遊龍門香山泉

山水本自佳，遊人已忘慮。碧泉更幽絕，
賞愛不能去。潺湲寫幽磴，繚繞帶嘉樹。
激轉忽殊流，歸泓又同注。羽觴自成玩，
永日亦延趣。靈草有時香，仙源不知處。
還當候圓月，攜手重遊寓。

Touring Xiangshan Springs at Longmen

The landscape is superb,
Making tourists cast their worries away.
The jade-like spring is mostly secluded,
Making us fall in love with it and stay.
From shady stone steps comes water overflowing.
Like cords, vines entwine trees in relay.
Fast, churning waves suddenly split off,
With a huge reflux draining in the same way.
Casually we drink from cups with wings of birds as
    handles
And amuse ourselves continually all day.
Magic herbs emit fragrance at times.
Where the source of fairies is, none can say.
I shall wait until there is a full moon.
A return visit here with friends I shall pay.

春遊南亭

川明氣已變， 巘寒雲尚擁。 南亭草心綠，
春塘泉脈動。 景煦聽禽響， 雨餘看柳垂。
逍遙池舘華， 益媿專城寵。

Visiting South Pavilion in Spring

Streams brighten; the air feels different.
On cold crags, clouds have already lain.
Water moves in veins to form a spring above the
　　pool.
At South Pavilion, a hint of green grasses gain.
I hear birdsongs in mild weather.
Willows look heavy after a rain.
My leisure in a grand poolside inn shames me more,
Due to the privileges as a magistrate that I obtain.

假中對雨呈縣中僚友

卻足堪為笑， 閑居夢杜陵。 殘鶯知夏淺，
社雨報年登。 流麥非關忘， 收書獨不能。
自然憂曠職， 緘此謝良朋。

Watching Rain in my Leave of Absence: To my Colleagues in the County Government

On leave, I dream of my hometown at Duling,
At my deformed feet like Que's, people jeer.
The last oriole scarcely knows about summer.

Spring rain heralds a bumper year.
Like one who read and forgot to cover his grains
    from rain,
I lost my job, but putting away books I cannot bear.
Naturally I worry about losing my post.
I write this to thank good friends that I hold dear.

廣德中洛陽作

生長太平日，不知太平歌。今還洛陽中，
感此方苦酸。飲葯本攻病，毒腸翻自殘。
王師涉河洛，玉石俱不完。時節屢遷
斥，山河長鬱盤。蕭條孤煙絕，日入空
城寒。蹇劣乏高步，緝遺守微官。西懷
咸陽道，躑躅心不安。

Written in Luoyang during
the Guangde Period

I grew up on days of peace,
Oblivious to peace-time delight.
Returning to Luoyang now,
I feel the acrid bitterness of this site.
The use of An Lushan was to curb tribal invasions,
But his revolt, like poison, put the state in blight.
Our army reached the basin between two rivers.
Spoilage of everything, including jade and stone,
    reached its height.
Winding rivers and luxuriant hills always stay the
    same.

Seasons often get engaged in changes and fight.
Bleakly, long wisps of smoke vanish to the sky
The cold, deserted city lets in sunlight.
The bad, lame people in power lack brilliant steps.
Minor officers hold the rein of justice tight.
From the west on Xianyang Road, I recall the past,
Stumbling along with my heart not feeling alright.

ZHANG JI (c766-830)
張藉

牧童詞

遠牧牛，繞村四面禾黍稠。陂中飢烏啄
牛背，令我不得戲隴頭。入陂草多牛散
行，白犢時向蘆中鳴。隔堤吹葉應同
伴，還鼓長鞭三四聲。牛牛食草莫相
觸，官家截爾頭上角。

The Cowherd

To herd buffaloes, far away I go.
All around the village, lush crops grow.
I cannot play on the ridge.
On the bank, pecking their backs are many a crow.
My herd scatters on the rich meadow.
Often towards reeds, white calves bellow.
On a leaf to a mate across the dike, I blow.

He replies with a few cracks of his long whip.
"My buffaloes, eat grass but do not fight.
Officers can hack your horns off outright".

野老歌

老農家貧在山住，耕種山田三四畝。苗蔬
稅多不得食，輸入官倉化爲土。歲暮鋤犁
傍空室，呼兒登山收橡實。西江賈客珠百
斗，船中養犬長食肉。

The Old Peasant

A poor old peasant of the hills
Farms his small plot on a hilly terrain.
He goes hungry after big taxes and small harvests.
Rotten in the state granaries is each levied grain.
At the year's end, he sends his son uphill for acorns.
In his bare hut, only a plough and a hoe remain.
In the boats of rich merchants of West River,
Plenty pearls and meat for dogs have always lain.

沒番故人

前年戍月支，城下沒全師。番漢斷消息，
死生長別離。無人收廢帳，歸馬識殘旗。
欲祭疑君在，天涯哭此時。

To an Old Friend Missing in Tibet

The year before last, at war in Tibet,
In the city, with total failure your army met.
News ended between our empire and their land.
The parting of the living and the dead was long set.
Returning horses might recognize your tattered flag.
None was collecting your wrecked tents yet.
I doubt your death in making a sacrifice for you,
Teary over the wide separation to you I now get.

HAN YU (768-824)
韓愈

謁衡岳廟遂宿岳寺題門樓

五岳祭秩皆三公，四方環鎮嵩當中。火維
地荒足妖怪，天假神柄專其雄。噴雲泄霧
藏半腹，雖有絕頂誰能窮？我來正逢秋雨
節，陰風晦昧無清風。

潛心默禱若有應，豈非正直能感通。須臾
靜掃衆峰出，仰見突兀撐青空。紫蓋連延
接天柱，石廩騰擲堆祝融。森然魄動下馬
拜，松柏一徑趨靈宮。

粉牆丹柱動光彩，鬼物圖畫填青紅。升階
傴僂薦脯酒，欲以菲薄明其衷。廟令老人

識神意，睢盱偵伺能鞠躬。手持杯玟導我
擲，云此最吉餘難同。

竄逐蠻方幸不死，衣食才足甘長終。侯王
將相望久絕，神縱欲福難爲功。夜投佛寺
上高閣，星月掩映雲朣朧。猿鳴鐘動不知
曙，杲杲寒日生於東。

Inscribed on the Gate Tower of the Temple for the Deity of the Mountains at Hengshan where I Paid a Visit and Stayed Overnight

For the five mountains, three dukes planned the
    sacrificial rite.
Many devils crowded the fire-hot, abandoned site.
A ring of four mountains surround Mount Song.
Heaven empowered a chief deity to show its might.
Half of the mountain hides under cloud and mist.
Who can reach its extreme height?
I have come right in the season of fall rain,
Without a cool breeze, clarity and sunlight.

If my earnest, silent prayers are answered,
Empathy can be bestowed on pleas that are upright.
Very soon, ridges appear as if quietly swept clean.
Jagged peaks prop the blue sky if I see aright.
Zigai joins Tianzhu; Shilin is linked to Zhurong.
The linkage can be gradual or abrupt, left and right.
On the path lined by pine and cypress to the temple,
Solemn and moved, I bow after I alight.

Ghosts and objects on murals are in green and red.
Painted walls and scarlet pillars emit dazzling light.
Walking up, I humbly offer dried fruits and wine
And a meager sum for the deity's insight.
Gazing with wide eyes, the old priest knows his will,
Being a hard worker without oversight.
Holding cups, he teaches me how to throw them,
Praising their luck-divining power, best within sight.

"By luck, you survived an exile on barbaric soil,
For a long life of plenty with satisfaction and delight.
Hopes for titles and power will in time end.
Seeking fairies and blessings is a fruitless fight."
Clouds obscure the moon and stars,
In my stay in the temple's high pavilion overnight.
At dawn, I miss gibbons calling, bells ringing
And the cold, bright sun from the east, for sleeping
    tight.

LIU YUXI (772-842)
劉禹錫

酬樂天楊州初逢席上見贈

巴山楚水淒涼地，二十三年棄置身。懷舊
空吟聞笛賦，到鄉翻似爛柯人。沉舟側畔
千帆過，病樹前頭萬木春。今日聽君歌一
曲，暫憑杯酒長精神。

In Reply to the Poem of Letian at our First Meeting in Yangzhou

By cheerless hills of Ba and waters of Chu,
In exile for twenty-three years I remain.
I feel like the wood-cutter returning after a hundred
    years.
Homesick, I was chanting nostalgic poems in vain.
A thousand sails go past my sinking boat.
Before sick trees, there is hope for renewal to gain.
Sir, as I hear your song today,
Through this cup of wine, a shot of energy I obtain.

西塞山懷古

王濬樓船下益州，金陵王氣黯然收。千尋
鐵鎖沉江底，一片降旛出石頭。人世幾回
傷往事，山形依舊枕寒流。從今四海為家
日，故壘蕭蕭蘆荻秋。

Recalling the Past at Xisai Hill

From Yizhou, Wang Jun's warships sailed away.
Sullenly, Nanjing's mandate suffered decay.
A surrender flag surfaced from the capital.
At the river's bottom, countless iron chains lay.
How often do we grieve over the past in life?
Hills pillow on cold streams in the same way.
The country is united as one today.
Bleakly among fall reeds, old forts stay.

LIU ZHONGYUAN (773-819)
柳宗元

登柳州城樓寄漳汀封連四刺史

城上高樓接大荒，海天愁思正茫茫。驚風亂颭芙蓉水，密雨斜侵薜荔牆。嶺樹重遮千里目，江流曲次九回腸。共來百粵文身地，猶是音書滯一鄉。

To Four Prefects: Zhang, Ting, Feng and Lian, from the City Tower in Liuzhou

The tall city tower joins the wilderness, to my eyes.
My sorrow is like the endless seas and skies.
A fearful wind randomly stirs the lotus pond.
At the vine-clad wall, an oblique, heavy rain plies.
In hairpin turns, rivers wind as they flow.
Layered trees on the ridge block my view due to
    their size.
We came together to the south, known for their
    tattooed natives.
Stuck in towns without mail, each of us still lies.

YUAN ZHEN (779-831)
元稹

連昌宮詞

I

連昌宮中滿宮竹，歲久無人森似束。又有
牆頭千葉桃，風動落花紅蔌蔌。

宮邊老人為予泣，小年進食曾因入。上皇
正在望仙樓，太真同憑闌干立。樓上樓前
盡珠翠，炫轉熒煌照天地。歸來如夢復如
痴，何暇備言宮裡事？

初屆寒食一百六，店舍無煙宮樹綠。夜半
月高弦索鳴，賀老琵琶定場屋。力士傳呼
覓念奴，念奴潛伴諸郎宿。須臾覓得又連
催，特敕街中許蠟燭。

春嬌滿眼睡紅綃，掠削雲鬟旋裝束。飛上
九天歌一聲，二十五郎吹管逐。逡巡大遍
涼州徹，色色龜茲轟錄續。李謨壓笛傍宮
牆，偷得新翻數般曲。

平明大駕發行宮，萬人歌舞途路中。百官
仗隊避歧薛。楊氏諸姨車斗風。

II

明年十月東都破，禦路猶存祿山過。驅令
供頓不敢藏，萬姓無聲淚潛墮。兩京定後
六七年，卻尋家舍行宮前。莊園燒盡有枯
井，行宮門閉樹宛然。

爾後相傳六皇帝，不到離宮門久閉。往來
年少說長安，玄武樓成花萼廢。去年敕使
因斫竹，偶值門開暫相逐。荊榛櫛比塞池
塘，狐兔嬌痴緣樹木。

舞榭欹傾基尚在，文窗窈窕紗猶綠。塵埋
粉壁舊花鈿，烏啄風箏碎珠玉。上皇偏愛
臨砌花，依然禦榻臨階斜。蛇出燕巢盤斗
拱，菌生香案正當衙。

寢殿相連端正樓，太真疏洗樓上頭。晨光
蔚動廉影動，至今反掛珊瑚鈎。自從此後
還閉門，夜夜狐狸上門屋。

III

我聞此語心骨悲，太平誰致亂者誰？翁言
野父何分別？耳聞眼見為君說。姚崇宋景
作相公，勸諫上皇言語切。燮理陰陽禾
黍豐，調和中外無兵戎。長官清平太守
好，揀選皆言由至公。

開元之末姚宋死，朝廷漸漸由妃子。祿山
宮裡養作兒，虢國門前鬧如市。弄權宰相

不記名，依稀記得楊與李。廟謨顛倒四海
搖，五十年來作瘡痏。

今皇神聖丞相明，詔書才下吳蜀平。官軍
又取淮西賊，此賊亦除天下寧。

年年耕種宮前道，今年不遣子孫耕。老翁
此意深望幸，努力廟謨休用兵。

Lianchang Palace

I

For years, none appears in Lianchang Palace at all.
Like bundles, palace bamboos everywhere stand tall.
Leafy peach trees grow by the wall.
The wind makes red petals fall.

An elder by the palace wept before me and said:
"As a child, I went in for food.
His Highness was in Fairy Watching Tower.
By the rails, Taizhen joined him and stood.
Pearl and jade that piled up all over
Lit the universe with moving, dazzling beams.
Dreamy and mindless on return,
How did the king find time for court affairs?

About a hundred and sixty days into winter, on Cold
    Food Day,
Palace trees looked green, with no cooking smoke in
    sight.

Old Mister He played the pipa to full applause,
Under a high moon, with a tuned string instrument,
    at midnight.
For a singer, Lishi relayed the king's wish on
Niannu
Who had a secret plan with her boyfriend overnight.
Soon, when found, she was hurried repeatedly.
A special decree made candle-burning alright.

The young charmer slept under a red gauze coverlet.
With her hair in a puff, she got dressed.
The pitch of her song reached the zenith of the sky.
The twenty-fifth prince played the flute with no rest.
The tune "Liangzhou" could be heard all over,
Followed by loud Tartar music from the west.
Li Mo, who heard the flute by the palace wall,
Performed a few times, with stolen rhythms newly
    possessed.

For the palace, big carriages set out at dawn.
Countless people line the streets in dance and song.
The absent brothers of the king let big bands move
headlong.
Like wind, the Yang sisters sped off all along.

II

Next November, in ruins the east capital lay.
The rebel, An Lushan, used the royal highway.
People dared not hide provisions to be confiscated.
Weeping quietly, all subjects had nothing to say.

Six to seven years after restoring the capital that fell,
Farms were burned down with many a dry well.
I was seeking a house before the palace.
On the shut palace with trees intact, no harm befell.

Thereafter, six kings in succession reigned.
From visiting the traveling palace, they all abstained.
Young passers-by talked about Changan.
Xuanwu Tower stood; Huae Tower waned.
The king sent workers to cut bamboos last year.
I got footloose when by chance doors lay bare.
Overgrown brambles clogged ponds.
Proudly clinging to trees were many a mindless fox
    and hare.

The king's bed still lay near a slope.
His Highness liked flower-lined steps the best.
Facing the front hall, herbs grew on an incense table.
A snake coiled round a wine bowl, emerging from a
    swallow's nest.

Duanzheng Tower linked the bedroom and palace.
Upstairs, Taizhen used to comb her hair and wash
    her face.
Coral hooks until now were still hung backwards.
Moving drapery shadows beat still dawn sunbeams
    in a race.
I pointed at those wailing beside me,
But outside my tears also ran free.
From then on, the palace doors were shut.

Every night, foxes tried to gain entry."

III

I got saddened by his words and asked:
"Who created peace? Who made turmoil stay?"
The old man replied: "How do you tell uncultured
    men apart?
From what I heard and saw, I have this to say.
Yao, Chong, Song and Jing, as ministers,
Counseled the king with pointed advice.
No battles took place across the borders.
Balanced Yin and Yang forces brought good
    harvests of millet and rice.
In choosing officials, we relied on the exalted man.
Incorrupt supervisors ruled; magistrates were nice.

As Kaiyuan's reign ended, Yao and Song died one
    by one.
By the concubines, the court was overrun.
Like noisy markets, corrupt deals of the queen's
    sister were actively done.
Lushan was reared as the palace's adopted son.
Prime ministers whose names I forgot abused their
    power.
In my vague memory, Yang and Li were the names
    they bore.
Religion got pushed aside, rocking our foundation.
For fifty years, the misrule was a national bed-sore.

Now, through our holy king and enlightened prime

minister,
Wu and Shu got peace once decrees came down.
Ridding the bandit chief of Huaixi brought peace,
Due to the efforts of the armies of the crown.

Every year, let us farm the land before the palace.
This year, let no young man be drafted and sent.
This old man deeply hopes for the luck of peace
And more time on prayers in temples to be spent."

SHI JIANWU (780-821)
施肩吾

仙客歸鄉詞

洞中日月洞中仙，不單離家是幾年。出郭
如知人代變，又須抛卻古時錢。

The Immortal Returns Home

The immortal in the cave, for many a night and day,
Has lost count of the years he has been away.
Passing the town walls, he knew about the
    generational change,
Again ridding his coins from a dynasty that could
    not stay.

LI HE (790-816)
李賀

春懷引

芳蹊密影成花洞，柳結濃煙花帶重。蟾蜍
碾玉褂明弓，捍撥裝金打仙鳳。寶枕垂雲
選春夢，鈿合碧寒龍腦凍。阿侯繫錦覓周
郎，憑仗東風好相送。

Ballad of Spring Longings

On the fragrant path, an arbor of dense flowers casts
a shadow.
Floral belts look heavy; mists coil fully round the
willow.
The moon rolling on jade-like clouds hangs like a
bright bow.
Beats from her golden plectrum with a carved
phoenix go.
She expects a spring dream with her cloud-like hair
on the pillow,
But the jade case for filigrees and the incense
"Dragon Brain" are chilly so.
Yearnings for her lover make her tie her brocade
belt to follow.
May the kind east wind give her longings for him a
tow!

潞州張大宅病酒遇江使寄上十四兄

秋至昭關後，　　當知趙國寒。　　繫書隨短羽，
寫恨破長箋。　　病客眠清曉，　　疏桐墜綠鮮。
城鴉啼粉堞，　　軍吹壓蘆煙。　　岸幘褰紗幌，
枯塘臥折蓮。　　木窗銀跡畫，　　石磴水痕錢。
旅酒侵愁肺，　　離歌繞懦弦。　　詩封兩條淚，
露折一枝蘭。　　莎老沙雞泣，　　松乾瓦獸殘。
覺騎燕地馬，　　夢載楚溪船。　　椒桂傾長席，
鱸魴斫玳筵。　　豈能忘舊路？　　江島滯佳年。

While Recovering from a Drinking Bout in the Elder Zhang's Mansion in Luzhou, I Met a Mail Courier on the River and Sent this Poem to my Fourteenth Cousin

After autumn has reached Zhao Pass,
You should know about Luzhou's chill.
This long letter of lament of mine
Is like an urgent dispatch tied to a quill.
Sparse firmianas shed fresh, green leaves.
The crisp dawn finds a guest in bed and ill.
City crows caw from battlements by misty reeds,
A losing match with army bugles that sound shrill.
In a dry pool, bent lotus stalks can be seen
After I raise my headdress and the gauze curtain.
Coin-shaped moss grows on flooded stone steps.
On the painted wooded windows, only silvery traces
    remain.
This sad guest with lung troubles suffers from the

effects of wine.

Weakly I chant my farewell lines with a lingering
strain.

I seal my poem with two strings of tears.

Like an orchid, the breaking weight of dew I cannot
sustain.

By old sedges, crickets chirp as if weeping.

Among tiles and dried leaves, a view of porcelain
beasts I gain.

Awake, I envision riding a fast horse from Yan

And in my dream, sailing a boat from Chu to see
you again.

Fine wine, good food and many guests

Form the style in which you entertain.

How can you forget your old, cherished way of life?

Good times for a lone islander are slower to obtain.

DU MU (803-852)
杜牧

遣懷

落魄江湖帶酒行，楚腰纖細掌中輕。十年
一覺揚州夢，贏得青樓薄幸名。

Confession

By rivers and lakes, as a dejected wino I stay.
Many games of love with slim Chu beauties I play.
From the brothels of Yangzhou, a ten-year dream I
    have won,
And the label "The Heartless Client in his Day".

獨酌

窗 外 正 風 雪 ， 擁 爐 開 酒 缸 。 何 如
釣船雨，篷底睡秋江。

Drinking Alone

I open a wine cask and huddle before a furnace,
With a snowstorm outside my window.
Better sleep in a fisherman's boat with awnings,
In the fall rain, mindless of the river's flow.

遣懷

道 泰 時 還 泰 ， 時 來 命 不 來 。 何 當
離城市，高臥博山隈。

Expressing my Mind

Good kingship brings a peaceful, prosperous state.
A good era does not give me good fate.
To lie as a recluse in the hills, away from the city,
For me, when will be the date?

贈別 ，其一

娉娉嫋嫋十三餘，豆蔻梢頭二月初。春風
十里揚州路，捲上珠簾總不如。

Given in Farewell, no.1

A thirteen-year-old girl, so slender.
A nutmeg bud of the second month, so tender.
In the spring breeze, for miles on Yangzhou Road,
She beats all courtesans in her splendor.

贈別，其二

多情卻似總無情，唯覺樽前笑不成。蠟燭
有心還惜別，替人垂淚到天明。

Given in Farewell, no.2

She is amorous, yet seems callous in the main.
Just a smile over our farewell drink, she cannot
  feign.

Only the caring candle shares our parting sorrow,
Shedding until dawn its tears of pain.

將赴宣州留題揚州禪智寺

故里溪頭松柏雙，來時盡日倚松窗。杜陵
隨苑已絕國，秋晚南遊更渡江。

Inscribed on Chanzhi Temple of Yangzhou before I Departed for Xuanzhou

My hometown's pine and cypress some time ago
Caught my eyes all day by a window.
Duling and Sui Garden are already far.
Crossing the river in late fall, southwards I go.

題齊安城樓

鳴軋江樓角一聲，微陽瀲瀲落寒汀。不用
憑欄苦回首，故鄉七十五長亭。

Inscribed on the City Tower of Qian

At the riverside tower, the blare of a bugle I hear.
The weak sunlight on the cold islet brings no cheer.
Any dogged looking back from the rails is futile.
Hometown beyond seventy five pavilions is not near.

春晚題韋家亭子

擁鼻侵襟花草香，高臺春去恨茫茫。蔫紅
半落平地池晚，曲渚飄成錦一張。

Inscribed on the Wei Family
Pavilion on a Spring Night

Wall-to-wall flowers and herbs give a sweet scent.
On the high terrace, the end of spring brings lament.
Half of the wilted red petals join the dark, level pool.
To the winding sandbar, a drifting piece of brocade
    is sent.

別家

初崴嬌兒未識爺，別爺不拜手吒叉。拊頭
一別三千里，何日迎門卻到家？

Leaving my Family

My young beloved son knew not his father.
To see me off, he paid no respects, with his arms
    crossed instead.
When will he greet me on my return?
We are myriad miles apart after I caressed his head.

池州清溪

弄溪終日到黃昏，照數秋來白髮根。何物
賴君千遍流？筆頭塵土漸無痕。

A Limpid Brook in Cizhou

In fall, I play by the brook all day
And count clearly the reflected white hair that stay.
What causes the endless flow of water?
Like earth, my writings will slowly fade away.

寓言

暖風遲遲柳初含，顧影看身又自慚。何事
明朝獨惆悵，杏花時節在江南。

A Message for Myself

In a warm wind, I linger under a sprouting willow,
Ashamed looking at myself and my shadow.
In an enlightened reign, why am I depressed?
South of the River, under apricot blooms, I wander
    as a wino.

春申君

烈士思酬國士恩、春申誰與快冤魂。三千
賓客總珠履，欲使何人殺李園？

Mister Chunshen

In history, a martyr avenged his benefactor's life.
Who would redress the wronged soul of Chunshen
   in strife?
Of the three thousand guests who got top hospitality,
Who could be sent to kill Li Yuan?

不飲贈酒

細 算 人 生 事 ， 彭 殤 共 一 籌 。 與 愁
爭底事，要爾作戈矛。

Not Accepting Wine

Count clearly all the facts of life.
Living to an old age or dying young are the same.
Why is wine related to sorrow
And used as a weapon to fight it in your name?

春盡途中

田園不事來遊宦，故國誰教爾別離？獨倚
關亭還把酒，一年春盡送春時。

On my Way at the End of Spring

Who told you to leave your hometown?
An assigned, expatriate official, I do no farming.
Leaning against Guan Pavilion alone with wine,
I see spring off at the end of spring.

奉陵宮人

相如死後五詞客，延壽亡來絕畫工。玉顏
不是黃金少，淚滴秋山入壽宮。

Palace Ladies as Attendants of Mausoleums

There were no poets after the death of Xiangru.
None could paint like Yanshou in bygone years.
Some pretty ladies who did not lack money
Were still sent to mausoleums as attendants in tears.

出宮人，其一

閑吹玉殿昭華管，醉折梨園縹蒂花。十年
一夢歸人世，絳縷猶封繫臂紗。

Palace Ladies Leaving the Palace, no.1

In leisure, she plays a jade flute in the palace
And plucks a pear flower by the theater with a tipsy
    head.
After ten years, like a dream, she returns as a
    commoner,
Still wearing a gauze armband in deep red.

書懷

滿眼青山未得過，鏡中無那鬢絲何。祇言
旋老轉無事，欲到中年事更多。

Penning my Thoughts

I have yet to pass the green hills before my eyes.
Helplessly, my white hair shows in the mirror as
    time flies.
I was saying peace would come as I turn old.
Towards middle age, more problems arise.

自貽

杜陵蕭次君，遷少去官頻。寂寞憐吾道，
依稀似古人。飾心無彩纈，到骨是風塵。
自嫌如疋素，刀尺不由身。

JADE RAINBOW

A Poem for Myself

Like Xiao Cijun of Duling,
I got no promotions but laid-offs again and again.
Almost like an ancient in loneliness,
I love the principles that I retain.
My unpainted heart stays bare and true.
My job in wind and dust gives me bone-deep pain.
I resent being a piece of white silk to be tailored,
Without the free will I should maintain.

齊安郡後地絕句

菱透浮萍綠錦池，夏鶯干囀弄薔薇。盡日
無人看微雨，鴛鴦相對浴紅衣。

A Quatrain on a Pond in the
Back of Qian County

With roses in summer, an oriole flirts with its song.
Water caltrops rise above duckweeds in a pond like
    green brocade.
The sun casts a red glow on bathing mandarin ducks.
None notices a drizzle all day long.

155

雨

連雲接塞添迢遞，灑幕侵燈送寂寥。一夜
不眠孤客耳，主人窗外有芭蕉。

Rain

Quiet emptiness came with rain on my drapes and
　　lamp.
A skywide rain made hometown seem further away.
Beyond my window, my host planted banana trees.
I got an earful the whole night as sleepless I lay.

讀韓杜詩

杜詩韓集愁來讀，似倩麻姑癢與搔。天外
鳳凰誰得髓，無人解合續弦膠。

Reading Collected Poems of
Han Yu and Du Fu

Poems of Han and Du are fit to be read in sorrow,
Like an itch that Magu, the fairy, can relieve.
Who is the genius like a phoenix beyond the skies?
Picking up where they left, none can achieve.

念昔遊，其一

十載飄然繩檢外，罇前自獻自為酬。秋山
春雨閑吟處，倚遍江南寺寺樓。

Recalling my Past, no.1

A free wanderer for ten years, I chant in leisure,
On a fall hill or under a spring shower.
Pouring wine for myself and seeking no company,
South of the River, I visit each temple and tower.

念昔遊，其二

雲門寺外逢猛雨，林黑山高雨腳長。曾奉
郊宮為近侍，分明雙雙玉林槍。

Recalling my Past, no.2

Outside Cloud Gate Temple, a heavy rain caught me.
While I climbed a tall, dark wooded hill.
A former private attendant of a traveling palace,
I found rain beating me and recalled paired spears of
    guards still.

念昔遊，其三

李白題詩水西寺，古木廻巖樓閣風，半醒
半醉遊三日，紅白花開山雨中。

Recalling my Past, no.3

Li Bai inscribed poems at Shuixi Temple.
Old trees winding crags top each windy pavilion or
    tower.
For three days, I tour in a half-drunken state.
Red and white hillside flowers open in the shower.

江南懷古

車書混混業無窮，井邑山川今古同。戊辰
年間金陵過，愁悵閑吟憶庾公。

Recalling my Past at South of the River

National unification is an endless quest.
People, hills and streams change not; time can attest.
In the year of Mouchen, I visited Jinling,
Recalling Yu Xin, chanting his poems and feeling
    depressed.

送容州中丞赴鎮

交阯同星座，龍泉似斗文。燒香翠羽帳，
看舞鬱金裙。鷁首衝瀧浪，犀渠拂嶺雲。
莫教銅柱北，空說馬將軍。

Seeing off the Assistant Censor of Rongzhou for his New Post

Your rare sword "Dragon Spring" has markings like
   the Big Dipper.
The constellations here and at Cochin are the same.
People burn incense by green kingfisher drapes.
Watch the dancing and the frocks stained with herbs
   of each dame.
Soldiers with rhino shields reached peaks of Five
   Ridges
A carved water fowl at the prow makes waves tame.
Let us in the north stop praising General Ma and his
   brazen pillar for beating Cochin,
But talk about the fair rule there and your future
   fame.

沈下賢

斯人清唱何人和？草徑苔蕪不可尋。一夕
小敷山下夢，水如環佩月如襟。

Shen Xiaxian

Who can match his refreshing poems?
I cannot seek him on a trail with moss and grass.
An overnight dream of his hut at Xiaofu Hill I got.
Like water and moon, his refined style is a class.

歎花

自恨尋芳到已遲，往年曾見未開時。如今
風擺花狼藉，綠葉成蔭子滿枝。

Sighing for Flowers

A late seeker for flowers, to my regret,
I saw flower buds last year when we met.
New fallen blossoms are in disarray in the wind.
Shady green leaves and many seeds are what we get.

醉眠

秋醪雨中熟，寒齋落葉中。幽人
本多睡，更酌一罇空。

Sleeping Drunk

In the fall rain, my unfiltered wine is ready.
To sleep more, a recluse like me feels inclined,
In a cold study, amid fallen leaves.
On a whole cask of brew, I get heartily wined.

江南春

千里鶯啼綠映紅，水村山郭酒旗風。南朝
四百八十寺，多少樓臺風雨中。

Spring in South of the River

Over endless woods in red and green comes the
    oriole's trill.
Past tavern flags of a windy river-town, walled in by
    a hill.
Of the four hundred eighty temples of the South
    Dynasties,
In the wind and rain, how many remain still.

長安秋望

樓倚霜樹外，鏡天無一毫。南山
與秋色，氣勢兩相高。

Viewing Changan in fall

This tower is beyond frosted trees,
Under a mirror-like, cloudless sky.
Mount Zhongnan and autumn colors,
In grandeur and greatness, are well nigh.

遊池州林泉寺金碧洞

袖拂霜林下石稜，潺潺聲斷滿溪冰。攜茶
臘月遊金碧，合有文章病茂陵。

Visiting Jinbi Cave of Linquan
Temple at Cizhou

I descend stone steps, brushing frosty trees around.
The gurgling brook, now full of ice, makes no sound.
In the twelve month, I tour Jinbi Cave with tea.
To be as productive as the sick poet of Maoling, I
feel bound.

兵部尚書席上作

華堂今日綺筵開，誰召分司禦史來？忽發
狂言驚滿座，兩行紅粉一時回。

Written at the Feast Hosted
by the Minister of War

In this splendid hall, a grand feast is in display.
Who invited me, Censor of the East Capital, today?
I startle the whole party with my sudden, wild talk.
At once, two rows of adorned ladies look my way.

ZHAO GU (806-852)
趙嘏

經汾陽舊宅

門前不改舊山河，破虜曾輕馬伏波。今日
獨經歌舞地，古槐疏冷夕陽多。

Passing the Former Residence
of Guo Ziyi in Fenyang

The river and hill before his door change not from a
    yesteryear.
The war merits of General Ma Fubo cannot compare.
Today I pass this place of song and dance alone.
Old locusts look sparse and cold; sunset is
    everywhere.

WEN TINGYUN (812-870)
溫庭筠

商山早行

晨起動征鐸，客行悲故鄉。雞聲茅店月，
人跡板橋霜。槲葉落山路，枳花明驛牆。
因思杜陵夢，鳧雁滿池塘。

Morning Trip at Shangshan

I rise at dawn for the departing carriage.
Sad and homesick, a traveler will be away.
The moon is above thatched stores as roosters crow.
On frosted plank bridges, human footprints stay.
Orange flowers brighten the courier station's wall.
Oak leaves fall on the hilly walkway.
Wild ducks and wild geese must be crowding ponds,
In dreams of Duling, where I lived on a former day.

過陳琳墓

曾於青史見遺文，今日飄蓬過此墳。詞客
有靈應識我，霸才無主始憐君。石麟埋沒
藏春草，銅雀荒涼　對暮雲。莫怪臨風倍惆
悵，欲將書劍學從軍。

Visiting the Grave of Chen Lin

I read your writings that history can attest,
Visiting your grave today as a wanderer without rest.
Your keen poetic soul should recognize me.
I admire your fate when my peerless talent cannot
    be addressed.
The bleak Brazen Birds Terrace faces dusk clouds.
The spring grass gets stone funerary unicorns
    suppressed.
I want to join the army, trading my books and sword.
Little wonder, facing the wind, I am more depressed.

LI SHANGYIN (813-859)
李商隱

杜司勛

高樓風雨感斯文，短翼差池不及群。刻意
傷春復傷別，人間惟有杜司勛。

Administrator Du of the Department
of Appointments

His writings stir me in a high tower, amid rain and
 blast,
From a poet with short, off-shaped wings, quite
 outclassed.
He specializes in poems of farewell to spring and
 people,
One of a kind, among earthlings, first and last.

贈司勛杜十三員外

杜牧司勛字牧之，清秋一首杜秋詩。前身
應是梁江總，名總還曾字總持。心鐵已從
干饙利，鬢絲休嘆雪霜垂。漢江遠吊西江
水，羊祜韋丹盡有碑。

For Administrator Du the Thirteenth of the Department of Appointments

You are Minister Du with a given name Muzhi.
In cool fall, you wrote a poem on Lady Autumn Du.
In your previous life, you should be Minister Jiang
Who went by the name Zhongchi.
Like sharp swords, Gan and Mo, your plots are rated
  high.
Over your frosty temple hair, you need not sigh.
From River Han to River Xi far away,
Like the memorial for Yang Hu, yours for Wei Dan
  will stay.

春風

春風雖自好，春物太昌昌。若教春有意，
惟遣一枝芳。我意殊春意，先春已斷腸。

Spring Wind

Although the spring wind is splendid,
Everything in spring grows too well without rest.
If spring had a mind of its own,
It should let one fragrant plant be the best.
My wish is against that of spring.
Before it comes, I feel heart-broken and distressed.

NIE YIZHONG (837-884)
聶夷中

田家

父耕原上田， 子斸山下荒。 六月禾未秀，官家已修倉。

A Peasant Family

On the plain, fields are for the father to till.
The son clears the wild wasteland under the hill.
The government already got the granaries ready
When, in July, rice plants are immature still.

LI YU (937-978)
李煜

一斛珠

曉妝初過，沉檀輕注些兒箇，向人微露丁香顆。一曲清歌，暫引櫻桃破。羅袖裏殘殷色可，杯深旋被香醪涴。繡床斜凭嬌無那，爛嚼紅茸，笑向檀郎唾。

Flirtation
(Tune: Yi Hu Zhu)

Right after her dawn adornment,
With sandalwood perfume ever so light,
She shows her lilac tongue ever so slight.
Singing without accompaniment,
She moves her cherry lips apart, just not quite.
The lining of her silk sleeves is worn,
But the shade of crimson looks alright.
The fragrant unstrained wine soon stains her deep
    goblet.
She leans against her embroidered bed.
What a pretty, helpless dame in sight!
Chewing the red wine pulp hard, left and right,
She spits at her lover,
Laughing and never acting uptight.

LIU KAI (947-1000)
柳開

塞上

鳴骹直上一千尺，天靜無風聲更乾。碧眼
胡兒三百騎，盡提金勒向雲看。

At the Borders

With a noise, an arrow shoots up a thousand feet,

Sounding more shrill as the windless sky is quiet.
Three hundred foreign cavalries grip their golden
   bridles.
To the clouds, their green eyes rivet.

SONG DYNASTY (960-1279)

WANG YUCHENG (954-1001)
王禹偁

泛吳松江

葦蓬疏薄漏斜陽，半日孤吟未過江。唯有
鷺鷥知我意，時時翹足對船窗。

Sailing on River Wusong

The sparse reeds give the slanting sunbeams away.
I have not set sail after chanting for half a day.
Only egrets seem to know how I feel.
Facing my window, on tiptoes they often stay.

村行

馬穿山徑菊初黃，信馬悠悠野興長。萬壑
有聲含萬籟，數峰無語立斜陽。棠梨葉落
胭脂色，蕎麥花開白雪香。何事吟餘忽惆
悵，村橋原樹似吾鄉。

A Trip to a Village

The hilly trail's first chrysanthemums look yellow.
On a slow horse, with lasting interest for the wilds,
    I go.
Several quiet peaks stand under slanting sunbeams.
In myriad valleys, sounds at night echo.
Wild pears shed their colored leaves like rouge
    powder.
Buckwheats have fragrant blooms like white snow.
Bridges and trees here resemble those at home.
That is why after chanting, I suddenly feel low.

LIU YUN (971-1031)
劉筠

漢武

漢武天臺切絳河，半涵非霧郁嵯峨。桑田
欲看他年變，瓠子先成此日歌。夏鼎幾遷
空象物，秦橋未就已沉波。相如作賦徒能
諷，卻助飄飄逸氣多。

King Wu of Han

The king built his terraces cutting the Milky Way.
Among semi-damp clouds, the tall, adorned
    structures were to stay,
To see fairies after sea and land had shifted ground.
·He composed a song to control floods in his day.
Xia's tripod was moved a few times, hardly a
    symbol for unity,
Qin's sunk bridge to find fairies caused delay.
The exposition of Xiangru to satire fairy-seeking
Just got the happy, indulged king more carried away.

YANG YI (974-1020)
楊億

漢武

蓬萊銀闕浪漫漫，弱水回風欲到難。光照
竹宮勞夜拜，露溥金掌費朝餐。力通青海
求龍種，死諱文成食馬肝。待詔先生齒編
貝，那教索米向長安。

King Wu of Han

The immortals' isle, Penglai, got blocked by waves
    in queue.
River Ruo with whirlwinds was too hard to get
    through.

In the lit Bamboo Palace, the king prayed all night.
For his breakfast, the palm of the brazen fairy got
much dew.
He sought rare horses from Qinghai for war
And killed Wencheng whose death from eating
horse liver was not true.
Dongfang Shuo, with teeth like shells, did not beg
for rice in Changan,
Only due to his meetings with the king for his view.

LIU YONG (987-1279)
柳永

望海潮

東南形勝，三吳都會，錢塘自古繁華。煙
柳畫橋，風簾翠幕，參差十萬人家。雲樹
繞堤沙。怒濤卷霜雪，天塹無涯。市列珠
璣，戶盈羅綺，競豪奢。

重湖疊巘清嘉。有三秋桂子，十里荷花。
羌管弄晴，菱歌泛夜，嬉嬉釣叟蓮娃。千
騎擁高牙。乘醉聽簫鼓，吟賞煙霞。異日
圖將好景，歸去鳳池誇。

Hangzhou
(Tune: Wang Hai Chao)

At a vantage point in the southeast,
As the metropolis of the old "Three Wu" region,
Hangzhou has prospered since ages ago,
Known for its painted bridges, many a misty willow
And jade-green drapes as winds blow,
For about a hundred thousand families or so.
Tall trees line shady banks.
Angry waves roll up like drifts of snow.
Endless River Qiantang is the moat of Heaven.
In markets, pearls and gems are in display.
Satin and gauze from houses overflow.
Competitions in extravagance follow.

Double lakes and layered hills look serene,
With the scent of the cassia in fall.
On endless waters, lotus flowers grow.
Notes of Qiang pipes flirt with sunshine,.
All night, songs of pickers of water caltrops go.
Laughing old anglers and girls among lotuses echo.
Your Honor's mounted retinue numbers a thousand,
    under a tall flag.
Drunk, you can hear flutes and drums,
Chanting to enjoy the mist and clouds.
One day, you can paint this fine scenery,
To brag, on your return to the Imperial Secretariat,
    for show.

玉蝴蝶

誤入平康小巷，畫檐深處，珠箔微褰。
羅綺叢中，偶認舊識嬋娟。翠眉開，嬌
橫遠岫，綠鬢嚲，濃染春煙。憶情牽。
粉牆曾恁，窺宋三年。

遷延。珊瑚筵上，親持犀管，旋疊香牋，
要索新詞，殢人含笑立尊前。按新聲，珠
喉漸穩，想舊意，波臉增妍。苦留連。
鳳衾鴛枕，忍負良天。

Lucky Encounter
(Tune: Yu Hu Die)

By mistake, I entered an alley in Pingkang Quarter.
Deep under painted eaves,
Behind a slightly raised pearl curtain,
Among gauze and brocade,
I recognized a lady I used to know.
Her painted, arching brows
Resembled far, wide ridges.
Her temple hairlocks hung low,
On a heavily powdered face, like spring mist.
I remembered my former attraction to her
And allowed myself to peep at her often,
Like Song Yu, who was peeped at,
For three years over the wall, long ago.

As I paced to and fro,
On the mat with coral holders,

She picked a brush with a rhino shaft
And then piled up sheets of perfumed paper,
To solicit a new song from me.
She tangled me with a smile,
Standing with a wine cup.
Plucking the new tune
And singing with her lovely voice,
She slowly steadied her pitch and tempo.
I recalled our former affection.
She looked prettier, showing cheeks with a glow.
After her relentless begging, I stayed,
Under a phoenix quilt and on her mandarin duck
    pillow.
Could I be ungrateful to Good Heaven if I chose to
    Forego?

YAN SHU (991-1055)
晏殊

寓意

油壁香車不再逢，峽雲無跡任西東。梨花
院落溶溶月，柳絮池塘淡淡風。幾日寂寥
傷酒後，一番蕭索禁煙中。魚書欲寄何由
達，水遠山長處處同。

Addressing my Mind

Her fragrant, painted carriage I cannot seek,
Like Wu Hill's clouds, traceless for me to peek.
Courtyard pear flowers face a big, round moon.
Willow fuzz by the pond floats in the wind turning
　weak.
Alone suffering for days from the effects of wine,
In the Cold Food Festival, I find the place so bleak.
How do I send her letters by a carp?
All over are many a long river and tall peak.

OUYANG XIU (1007-1072)
歐陽修

夢中作

夜涼吹笛千山月，路暗迷人百種花。棋罷
不知人換世，酒闌無奈客思家。

Composed in a Dream

Under myriad moonlit hills, I play the flute on a
　cool night.
Countless flowers charm me on a trail that is not
　bright.
Fleeting like a chess game, generations have passed.
Homesickness overwhelms a drunk wanderer
　without a fight,

唐崇徽公主手痕

故鄉飛鳥尚啁啾，何況悲笳出塞愁。青冢
埋魂知不返。翠崖遺跡為誰留？玉顏自古
為身累，肉食何人與國謀？行路至今空嘆
息，岩花野草自春秋。

The Hand-print of Princess Chonghui
of the Tang Dynasty

In my hometown, on and on birdsongs will still go.
Sad tunes from reed pipes beyond the borders add to
    my sorrow.
For whom did I leave my hand-print by the verdant
    cliff?
Concubine Wang, once buried, never returned, I
    know.
Who planned for our empire, besides eating meat?
A pretty lady can get into trouble since ages ago.
I sigh in vain as I reach this spot now.
From year to year, blooms and weeds duly grow.

和王介甫明妃曲

胡人以鞍馬為家，射獵為俗。泉甘草美
無常處，鳥驚獸駭爭馳逐。誰將漢女嫁
胡兒？風沙無情面如玉。身行不遇中國
人，馬上自作思歸曲。推手為琵卻手
琶，胡人共聽亦咨嗟。

玉顏流落死天涯，琵琶卻傳來漢家。漢宮
爭按新聲譜，遺恨已深聲更苦。纖纖女手
生洞房，學得琵琶不下堂。不識黃雲出塞
路，豈知此聲能斷腸？

In Answer to Wang Jiefu's Poem:
"Song of Concubine Ming"

Barbarians spend waking hours on saddled horses
And hunt with arrows, in a customary way.
Nomads settle where springs taste sweet and grasses
    grow,
Among frightened birds and beasts as they chase or
    break away.
Who would marry off a Han daughter to a barbarian
    son?
Sand will hit her jade-like face mercilessly as
    winds blow.
Concubine Ming never met a Chinese on her way
And on horseback wrote a song on homesickness.
Back and forth, she struck the strings of her pipa.
Even barbarians sighed in sorrow.

The pretty lady wandered afar and died.
To the Han empire, her pipa music was sent.
Palace ladies fought to try the new notes,
With bitter sadness and deep lament.
Those from the inner chambers with slender hands
Learned the pipa and from the halls never departed.
If they had never met yellow sandstorms beyond the
    borders,

How could they act the part of the broken-hearted?

黃溪夜泊

楚人自古登臨恨，暫到愁腸已九回。萬樹
蒼煙三峽暗，滿川明月一猿哀。非鄉況復
驚殘夢，慰客偏宜把酒杯。行見江山且吟
詠，不因遷謫豈能來？

Night Mooring at Yellow Creek

As an exile, I tour this place with complaint.
My extreme sadness brings me no cheer.
A gibbon whimpers by a stream under bright
　　moonlight.
With myriad misty trees, the three gorges look
　　unclear.
Holding a cup of wine especially soothes me,
Away from home, frightful at the end of the year.
I chant while walking and viewing this landscape.
Without being an exile, how could I have come here?

SU XUN (1009-1066)
蘇洵

九日和韓魏公

晚歲登門最不才，蕭蕭華髮映金罍。不堪
丞相延東閣，閑伴諸儒老曲臺。佳節久從
愁里過，壯心偶傍醉中來。暮歸沖雨寒無
睡，自把新詩百匝開。

In Answer to a Poem of Han Weigong on the Ninth Day

I am your least talented visitor at the end of the year.
Your gold wine goblet reflects my uncombed white
   hair.
A prime minister like you, fit for the palace,
Would host mere scholars like us, finding time to
   spare.
Drunk, I sometimes feel motivated.
Not being sad during fine festivals is almost rare.
Chilled and sleepless as I return in the dusk rain,
I start countless poems without a care.

ZENG GONG (1019-1083)
曾鞏

西樓

海浪如雲去卻回，北風吹起散聲雷。朱樓
四面鈎疏箔，臥看千山急雨來。

West Tower

Like clouds, successive sea waves rise and run past.
Scattered thunders come with the northern blast
Through thin drapes hung on four sides of the tower,
I lie to watch a rain on myriad hills approaching fast.

WANG ANSHI (1021-1086)
王安石

登寶公塔

倦童疲馬放松門，自把長筇倚石根。江月
轉空為白晝，嶺雲分暝與黃昏。鼠搖岑寂
聲隨起，鴉矯荒寒影對翻。當此不知誰客
主，道人忘我我忘言。

Climbing Baogong Pagoda

Near the pine and gate, I let my tired horse stay

And rest my long cane on a rock, tired in the same
    way.
Both hills and clouds darken at twilight.
The moonlit sky above the river creates a sunny day.
In the chilled wilds, crows and their shadows flap
    their wings.
Rats rattle the quietude, making noises right away.
Now I do not know if I come as a host or guest.
The monk forgot my face and I have nothing to say.

明妃曲

明妃初出漢宮時， 淚濕春風鬢腳垂。低徊
顧影無顏色， 尚得君王不自持。歸來卻怪
丹青手，入眼平生未曾有。意態由來畫不
成，當時枉殺毛延壽。

一去心知更不歸，可憐著盡漢宮衣。寄聲
欲問塞南事，只有年年鴻雁飛。家人萬里
傳消息，好在氈城莫相憶。君不見咫尺長
門閉阿嬌，人生失意無南北。

Concubine Ming

When she first left Han Palace on her way,
With her temple hair down, she wept on a breezy
    spring day.
As she lingered and looked around, pale-faced,
The king could not help but be carried away.

On return, he blamed the painter for having denied
His chance to meet a beauty so qualified.
Since forms and styles cannot be painted in detail,
Mao Yanshou's death was unjustified.

Of her little chance to return, she was aware,
So lovely in her devotion to Han palace wear.
She wrote home, asking about South of the Border,
Relying on the wild swan flying back every year.
Miles away, her family wrote to let her know,
"Do you not see
How a disfavored queen got barred from her local
    kin years ago?
Keep well in your foreign town; do not think of us.
Life has its downturns no matter where you go."

WANG ANSHI (1021-1086)
王安石

思王逢原

蓬蒿今日想紛披，冢上秋風又一吹。妙質
不為平世得，微言唯有故人知。廬山南墮
當書案，溢水東來入酒卮。陳跡可憐隨手
盡，欲歡無復似當時。

185

Thinking of Wang Fengyuan

Today, mugworts must have overgrown.
A fall wind over your grave must have blown.
Your excellence, though not recognized in life,
Just to your old friend, was known.
Mount Lu falling south was treated as our desk.
We claimed wine jugs filled by eastbound River Pen
    our own.
Our treasured memories of the past are gone easily.
The same joy we had before cannot now be shown.

WANG ANGUO (1028-1074)
王安國

題滕王閣

藤王平昔好追遊，高閣依然枕碧流。勝地
幾經興廢事，夕陽偏照古今愁。城中樹密
千家市，天際人歸一葉舟。極目滄波吟不
盡，西山重疊亂雲浮。

Inscribed on the Pavilion of Prince Teng

Prince Teng liked to hold feasts years ago.
This high pavilion still rests on the green river like a
    pillow.
Political changes affected this famed spot often.
Sunsets remind us of cases in history with sorrow.

On a small boat, a distant wanderer returns.
Dense city trees on homes and markets cast a
   shadow.
Floating clouds drift above the layered West Hill.
To the far gray waves, my endless poetic moods go.

WANG LING (1032-1059)
王令

暑旱苦熱

清風無力屠得熱，落日著翅飛上山。人固
已懼江海竭，天豈不惜河漢干。昆侖之高
有積雪，蓬萊之遠常遺寒。不能手提天下
往，何忍身去游其間。

The Bitter Heat in a Dry Spell

A cool wind fails to rid the heat.
The dusk sun on wings flies uphill.
Humans fear scorched rivers and lakes.
A dry Milky Way is against Heaven's will.
Tall Mount Kunlun accumulates snow.
The distant Island of Penglai often leaves a chill.
If I cannot bring back coolness from the world,
Let me roam there, a wish I yearn to fulfill.

SU SHI (1036-1110)
蘇軾

除夜大雪留濰州，元日早
晴，遂行，中途，雪復作

除夜雪相留，　元日晴相送。　東風吹宿酒，
瘦馬兀殘夢。　蔥籠曉光開，　旋轉餘花弄。
下馬成野酌，　佳哉誰與共。　須臾晚雲合。
亂灑無缺空。　鵝毛垂馬鬃，　自怪騎白鳳。
三年東方旱，　逃戶連敧棟。　老農釋耒嘆，
淚入饑腸痛。　春雪雖云晚，　春麥猶可種。

After Staying over at Weizhou due
to Heavy Snow on New Year's Eve,
I Resumed my Journey on New Year's
Day with Early Sunrise and Got Caught
up with Snow Falling again Midway

On New Year's eve I got detained
And set out the next day with sunshine shown.
With a broken dream, I awkwardly rode a lean horse.
After the effects of my overnight wine in the east
    wind had flown.
In the faint and soft dawn glow,
Remaining snowflakes came whirling down.
I dismounted for wine in the wilds,
Feeling good though none for company was known.
In a moment, dark clouds join again
And heavy snowing in all directions was full-blown.

Goose feathers seem to hang from my horse's mane.
I felt odd on a white phoenix, talking in a monotone.
After a drought for three years in the east,
Villagers fled in groups, not just a few alone.
An old peasant let go his plough, wept and sighed.
To constant hunger and pain, he was prone.
Although spring snow came late,
Wheat in spring could still be sown.
I dare not complain about a labored trip on duty,
That earns me my songs, rice and whatever may be.

過漣水軍贈趙晦之
蝶戀花

自古漣漪佳絕地，繞郭荷花，欲把吳興
比。倦客塵埃何處洗？真君堂下寒泉水。
左海門前魚酒市，夜半潮來，月下孤舟
起。傾蓋相逢拚一醉，雙鳧飛去人千里。

For Zhao Huizi while Passing the Lianshui Administrative District
(Tune: Die Lian Hua)

Rated the best, River Lian for ages can stay.
Lotus flowers wind city walls.
That Wuxing may compare well, I want to say.
Where can a tired traveler wash off his dust?
At the cold spring near a Daoist temple.
When the midnight tide comes,

The lone, moonlit boat will send you on your way.
In a wine shop of the fish market by East Sea,
Let two bosom friends get drunk, come what may.
After two wild ducks have parted,
One will be myriad miles away.

法惠寺橫翠閣

朝見吳山橫，暮見吳山縱。吳山故多態，
轉折為君容。幽人起朱閣，空洞更無物。
惟有千步岡，東西作窗額。

春來故國歸無期，人言秋悲春更悲。已泛
平湖思濯錦，更看橫翠憶峨嵋。彫欄能得
幾時好，不獨憑欄人易老。百年興廢更
堪哀，懸知草莽化池臺。遊人尋我舊遊
處，但覓吳山橫處來。

Hengcui Pavilion of Fa Hui Temple

Wu Hill at dawn looks flat across
And at dusk seems to rise to a height.
It shows many styles,
With changes for your delight.
A recluse built a red pavilion,
Deserted with nothing to show.
Only the ridge that takes a thousand steps to climb
Looks like the lintel of a window.

Spring comes to my old empire; I am here to stay.
Spring is sadder than autumn, people say.
I sail on the level lake and recall Brocade Washing
    Stream.
The green hill across reminds me of Mt Emei.
How long will carved rails last?
Those who lean on rails grow old fast.
From dynastic changes in a hundred years, sadness
    breeds.
Ponds and terraces will be under briers and weeds.
A traveler may not find my old footsteps here,
But in quest of Wu Hill flat across, he succeeds.

初夜直都廳，囚繫皆滿，日暮
　不得返舍，因題一詩於壁

除日當早歸，官事乃見留。執筆對之泣，
哀此繫中囚。小人營餱糧，墮網不知羞。
我亦戀薄祿，因循失歸休。不須論賢愚，
均是為食謀。誰能暫縱遣？閔默愧前修。

Inscribed on the Wall of the
City Hall where a Full Cell
of Prisoners Delayed my Returning
Home at Dusk on New Year's Eve

I should return early on New Year's eve,
But due to my official duty, I have remained.
I weep as I hold my writing brush,

191

In grief for prisoners detained.
Shameless commoners seek food for their livelihood.
They got caught by the net of justice and retained.
I also routinely hang on and miss my retirement,
Just clinging to the small salary gained.
Regardless of being wise or foolish,
All scheme for meals to be obtained.
Who can, for a moment, let go and take off?
Mute and shamed, I face past sages, sadly pained.

歸宜興留題竹西寺

此生已覺都無事，今歲仍逢大有年。山寺
歸來聞好語，野花啼鳥亦欣然。

Inscribed on Zhuxi Temple
on my Return to Yixing

Already I feel my life is, after all, trouble-free.
This is still a bumper year.
I got good news on my return to the hillside temple,
Happy with wild flowers and birdsongs everywhere.

吳中田婦嘆

今年梗稻熟苦遲，庶見霜風來幾時。風霜
來時雨如瀉，杷頭出茵鐮生衣。眼枯淚盡

雨不盡，忍見黃穗臥青泥。茅苫一月隴上
宿，天晴穫稻隨車歸。

汗流肩賴載入市，價賤乞與如糠秕。賣牛
納稅拆屋炊，慮淺不及明年飢。官今要錢
不要米，西北萬里招羌兒。龔黃滿朝人更
苦，不如卻作河伯婦。

Lament of a Peasant Woman of Wu

Sadly, rice plants ripen late this year.
Frosty winds will soon be here,
Coming with pouring rain.
Sickles get rusted; on rakes, lichens and fungus
    appear.
I hate to see golden ears of grain on green mud.
In the endless rain, our eyes can no longer tear.
Sleeping with straw quilts for a month on the mound,
We return with carts of rice as the sunlit sky is clear.

Carried to the market on our sweaty, red shoulders,
They are sold on begging; the price of chaff is near.
We sell the ox for taxes and rip the hut for firewood.
All these will not prevent next year's hunger, I fear.
Qiang tribesmen are recruited from the far
    northwest.
Officials shun crops and hold cash dear.
I would rather be sacrificed as the wife of River
    Spirit.
To us, more dignitaries in the court bring less cheer.

滿庭芳

蝸角虛名，蠅頭微利，算來著甚乾忙。事
皆前定，誰弱又誰強。且趁閑身未老，須
放我些子疏狂。百年裏，渾教是醉，三萬
六千場。　　思量。能幾許，憂愁風雨，一
半相妨。又何須抵死，說短弄長。幸對清
風皓月，苔茵展雲幕高張。江南好，千
鍾美酒，一曲滿庭芳。

My Philosophy
(Tune: Man Ting Fang)

Any slight vainglory
Or small gain
Is much ado in vain.
Everything is pre-determined,
About who is weak and who is strong.
Now that I am in exile and not old,
Let me be a tad mad and headstrong.
In a hundred years,
Thirty-six thousand times,
Into drunkenness, let me go headlong.

Think,
How much time is there for you?
In the sad wind and rain,
Half of your efforts failed, going against the grain.
Why do you fight to the death, then again,
Over who is right and who is wrong?

I am blessed with the cool breeze and a bright moon,
With moss on a wide mat and clouds through a high
   curtain.
South of the River is fine,
With a thousand flagons of wine
And "Man Ting Fang" arranged for a song.

六月二十日夜渡海

參橫斗轉欲三更，苦雨終風也解晴。雲散
月明誰點綴，天容海色本澄清。空予魯叟
乘桴意，粗識軒轅奏樂聲。九死南荒吾不
恨，茲游奇絕冠平生。

Night Sailing at Sea on the Twentieth Day of the Sixth Month

The Big Dipper has turned with its handle since
   midnight.
After a rainstorm, it will revert to sunlight.
Who decorates nature with a bright moon and no
   clouds,
With colors of the clear sky and sea matching right?
Like Confucius, I wish to take a raft skywards.
Waves make music resembling Xian Yuan's,
   however slight.
I do not complain about dying in the southern wilds.
Topping my life experience is each wonderful sight.

惠崇春江晚景，其一

竹外桃花三兩枝，春江水暖鴨先知。蔞蒿
滿地蘆芽短，正是河豚欲上時。

A Painting of the River on a Spring Night by Monk Huichong, no.1

Beyond the bamboos, a few twigs of peach flowers
  show.
As the spring river gets warm, ducks are the first to
  know.
When the land is overrun by mugworts and the
  asparagus is still short,
To the surface, globefish are about to go.

惠崇春江晚景，其二

兩兩歸鴻欲破羣，依依還是北歸人。遙知
朔漠多風雪，更得江南半月春。

A Painting of the River on a Spring Night by Monk Huichong, no.2

From the flock, some homing wild swans want to
  break away.
Any plans for the northbound returnees are in delay.
Knowing from afar the many snowstorms in the
  deserts,
For another half a month of spring in the south, they
  want to stay.

舟中夜起

微風蕭蕭吹菰蒲，開門看雨月滿湖。舟人
水鳥兩同夢，大魚驚竄如奔狐。夜深人
物不想管，我獨形影相嬉娛。暗潮生渚
吊寒蚓，落月掛柳看懸蛛。此生忽忽憂
患裏，清境過眼能須臾。雞鳴鐘動百鳥
散，船頭擊鼓還相呼。

Rising at Night in a Boat

Among reeds, a breeze starts to rustle and blow.
Through the open door, in the rain, the moonlit
    lake is fully aglow.
Boatmen and water fowls dream alike.
Like running foxes, big, startled fish go.
Human interactions cease as the night deepens.
I amuse myself with my shadow.
Like cold earthworms, dusk tides hang over a sand
    bar.
Like a suspended spider, the moon sets on a willow.
Fleeting are many occasions in quiet bliss
And a lifetime of worries and sorrow.
From the prow, boatmen shout and beat drums
When a hundred birds scatter at the rooster's crow.

冬至日獨遊吉祥寺

井底微陽回未回。蕭蕭寒雨濕枯荄。何人
更似蘇夫子，不是花時肯獨來。

Visiting Jixiang Temple alone
at the Winter Solstice

Any weak sunlight has yet to return to the bottom
    of the well.
Wilted grass gets wet in the cold rain spell.
Who is more willing to come here alone like me,
In the off season for flowers, can anyone tell?

端午遍遊諸寺

肩輿任所適，　遇勝則流連。　焚香引幽步，
酌茗開淨筵。　微雨止還作，　小窗幽更妍。
盆山不見日，　草木自蒼然。　忽登最高塔，
眼界窮大千。　卞峰照城郭，　震澤浮雲天。
深沉既可喜，　曠蕩亦所便。　幽尋未云畢，
墟落生晚煙。　歸來記所歷，　耿耿清不眠。
道人亦未寢，　孤燈同夜禪。

Visiting Temples during
the Dragon Boat Festival

On a sedan chair, I go where I please
And linger at scenic spots appealing to me.

I follow the scent of burning incense in the shade
And stop for vegetarian feasts with tea.
A drizzle starts and stops
Beyond a small window, secluded and pretty.
Hills hide the sun,
With a verdant cover of grass and tree.
At the tip of the pagoda,
I can view eternity.
The peak lends a glow to the city wall.
On the lake, the reflected sky is cloudy.
The depth is a delight.
The broad horizon offers visual facility,
I am not done with seeking secluded corners
When villagers at dusk let smoke free.
On return, I record my experiences,
Sleepless with details in clear memory.
The monk is not about to sleep,
So by a lone lamp, into zen meditation go we.

書李世南所畫秋景

野水參差漲落痕，疏木敧倒出霜根。扁舟
一櫂歸何處？家在江南黃葉村。

Written to Accompany a Painting of Autumn, Drawn by Li Shinan

Uneven tidal marks show on banks of a wild rivulet.
At the base of sparse trees aslant, frosty roots bare
  in the upset.

Where is the single-oared boat returning to?
Somewhere called home, South of the River, in
  Yellow Leaf Hamlet.

HUANG TINGJIAN (1045-1105)
黃庭堅

次元明韻寄子由

半世交親隨流水，幾人圖畫入淩煙？春風
春雨花經眼，江南江北水拍天。欲解銅章
行問道，定知石友許忘年。鶺鴒各有思歸
恨，日月相催雪滿顛。

For Ziyou, Following the Rhymes and
Rhyming Pattern Used by Yuanming

My old friends and relatives have died like flown
  water,
How many of us can have fame and gain?
North and south of the river, water hits the sky.
Flowers pass our eyes in the spring wind and rain.
I wish to resign and learn Daoism.
Despite age differences, our deep friendship shall
  remain.
In no time, I have a full head of gray hair.
About homesickness, each of us needs to complain.

好事近
太平洲小姑楊姝彈琴送酒

一弄醒心弦，情在兩山斜疊。彈到古人愁
處，有真珠承睫。　使君來去本無心，休淚
界紅顏。自恨老來憎酒，負十分蕉葉。

In Taiping District, a Singing Girl called Yang Shu,
Played the Qin and Served Wine
(Tune: Hao Shi Jin)

One stroke of the chord
And I felt waken.
Through her arched brows aslant,
She let her emotion show.
From her eyelashes hang teardrops like pearl,
Displaying ancients' sorrow.

A heartless client is a married man like me.
Let no tears stand between myself and the beauty.
At an old age, I hate wine with regret,
So I really let her down.
As she offered me a drink with plantain leaf,
That I had to forego.

題落星寺

落星開士深結屋，龍閣老翁來賦詩。小雨
藏山客坐久，長江接天帆到遲。宴寢清香

與世隔，畫圖妙絕無人知。蜂房各自開戶
牖，處處煮茶籐一枝。

Inscribed on Falling Star Temple

To write poetry, an old censor came to a hut,
Built by monks of Falling Star Temple, in a remote
   terrain.
Sails crawl on River Yangzi with a seamless
   horizon.
Guest stay long while shielded from a rain.
Fragrant bedrooms are shut off from the world.
Some private and peerless paintings remain.
Rooms resemble honeycombs, with open doors and
   windows.
We can go boil tea everywhere on a cane.

定風波

萬里黔中一漏天，屋居終日似乘船。
乃至重陽天也霽。催醉，鬼門關外蜀
江前。莫笑老翁猶氣岸，君看，幾人
黃菊上華顛？戲馬台南追兩謝。馳
射，風流獨拍古人肩。

My Philosophy
(Tune: Ding Feng Bo)

Exiled in Qianzhong, myriad miles away,
I lived in a hut like a leaking boat all day.
It is a rainless Double Ninth Festival today.
Get drunk fast.
The Gate-to-Hell Pass lies before River Shu.

Do not laugh at this proud, old man.
Sir, look.
On my white hair, who else would let yellow
　　chrysanthemums stay?
South of Horse Playing Terrace,
Two men named Xie wrote poems
In an imperial feast of yesterday.
Shooting on horseback,
Alone I pat a fairy on the shoulder,
Gallantly, my way.

虞美人
宣州見梅作

天涯也有江南信。梅破知春近。夜闌風細
得香遲。不道曉來開遍，向南枝。玉臺弄
粉花應妒。飄到眉心住。平生箇裏願杯
深。去國十年老盡，少年心。

On Seeing Plum Blossoms in Xuanzhou
(Tune: Yu Mei Ren)

On this land far away,
Spring still sends its message here.
Plum blossoms open and I know spring is near.
With tardy fragrance in the breeze, late at night,
They can all fully open overnight,
On south-facing branches.

By jade mirror stands, powdered ladies may appear.
Plums flowers should be jealous, in their right.
Let the petals hover between their brows to stay.
My lifelong wish is to drink hard before such a sight,
But a decade of exile has aged me all the way,
With my youthful energy waning from a height.

詠雪奉呈廣平公

連空春雪明如洗，忽憶江清水見沙。夜聽
疏疏還密密，曉看整整復斜斜。風回共作
婆娑舞，天巧能開頃刻花。正使盡情寒至
骨，不妨桃李用年華。

On Snow, a Poem Presented to
Minister Song of Guangping

I suddenly recall seeing sand in a limpid stream
When the sky with spring snow is clean and bright.

At dawn, it looks trim and even with flakes aslant,
Appearing sparse and then dense at night.
Snow is instant blooming from Heaven's skill,
Able to dance with whirlwinds and their might.
Why not mark the year with peach and plum flowers?
We are bone-chilled even if we get extreme delight.

松風閣詩

依山築閣見平川，夜闌箕斗插屋椽。我來
名之意適然，老松魁梧數百年。斧斤所赦
令參天，風鳴媧皇五十弦。洗耳不須菩薩
泉，嘉二三子甚好賢。力貧買酒醉此筵。
夜雨鳴廊到曉懸，相看不歸臥僧氈。泉枯
石燥復潺湲，山川光輝為我妍。野僧旱
飢不能饘，曉見寒溪有炊煙。東坡道人
已沈泉，張侯何時到眼前。釣臺驚濤可
盡眼，怡亭看篆蛟龍纏。安得此身脫拘
攣，舟載諸友長周旋。

Pine Wind Pavilion

From the hillside pavilion, the level stream comes in
    sight.
Between rafters, I can see stars late at night.
Coming to name the pavilion, I feel just right.
For some hundred years, an old pine is on site.
Spared by the axe, it reaches the sky's height.
Queen Wa's harp with fifty strings may recreate the
    wind's might.

Without washing my tears at Bodhisattari Spring, I
  listen alright.
Let me praise several friends, wise and upright.
I get drunk in their feast though their money is tight.
It is still dripping at dawn after a noisy rain since
  twilight.
We lie on felt blankets for monks and stay overnight.
A dry spring on parched rocks gurgles again.
Before me, hills and rivers look charming and bright.
Thirsty and hungry monks cannot have congee.
By cold brooks at dawn, cooking smoke from
  chimneys is found.
Sunk in Yellow Springs, Su Shi's body is to remain.
When can Zhang Lei come around?
In full view are waves of the fishing platform
  causing fright.
At Yi Pavilion, watch seal scripts like dragons
  wound.
By the restrictions of life, I wish to be unbound,
On a long voyage, enjoying with friends, round and
  round.

戲呈孔毅父

管城子無食肉相，孔方兄有絕交書。文章
功用不經世，何異絲窠綴露珠。校書著作
頻紹徐，猶能上車問何如。忽憶僧床同野
飯，夢隨秋雁到東湖。

A Playful Poem Presented to Kong Yifu

A writer like me is no flesh-eating aggressor.
I spurn money which I can care less.
My writings cannot be used to rule the kingdom,
Just like dewy, silk cobwebs, quite useless.
Assigned by the king as collator and historian,
I merely greet others with no work at all.
Suddenly I recall the monk's bed and peasant meals,
Dreaming of East Lake after wild geese in fall.

送王郎

酌君以蒲城桑落之酒，泛君以湘累秋菊
之英。贈君以黟川點漆之墨，送君以陽
關墮淚之聲。酒澆胸次之磊隗，菊制
短世之頹齡。墨以傳萬古文章之引，
歌以寫一家兄弟之情。江山千里俱頭
白，骨肉十年終眼青。

連床夜語雞戒曉，書囊無底談未了。有功
翰墨乃如此，何恨遠別音書少。炊沙作
糜終不飽，鏤冰文章費工巧。要須心地
收汗馬，孔孟行世日呆呆，有弟有弟力
持家，婦能養姑供珍鮭。兒大詩書女絲
麻，公但讀書煮春茶。

Seeing off Mister Wang,
my Brother-in-law

With the brew from fall chrysanthemum flowers of
    River Xiang
And Sangluo wine of Pu City, let me toast my guest.
Let me give you pitch-black ink sticks of Yi Chuan
And a song with heavy tears for farewell.
Wine can erase grievance from your breast.
Chrysanthemum wine can offer the old longevity.
The ink allows you to write for eternity.
Through the song, brotherly love is expressed.
A wanderer far away, I have white hair.
I hold regards among siblings dearest.

We talk until the rooster crows.
Discussions with your boundless mind cannot close.
Academic degree holders are like that.
Few letters from you afar will find me in regret and
    on tiptoes.
Cooking porridge with sand can never be done.
Flowery writings, like carving ice, waste time, if
    begun.
You should continue to cultivate your mind and
    character
And follow Confucius and Mencius, like the bright
    sun.
Your brothers support you in each household affair.
Your wife can cook and help your mother with care.
Your sons study and your daughters weave.

Just read your books and boil your tea there.

QIN GUAN (1049-1110)
秦觀

八六子

倚危亭。恨如芳草，淒淒剗盡還生。念柳
外青驄別後，水邊紅袂分時，愴然暗驚。
無端天與娉婷。夜月一簾幽夢，春風十里
柔情。怎奈向，歡娛漸隨流水，素弦聲
斷，翠綃香減，那堪片片飛花弄晚，濛濛
殘雨籠晴。正銷凝。黃鸝又啼數聲。

Parting Lament
(Tune: Ba Liu Zi)

By a tall pavilion,
My lament, like cut fragrant grass,
Sadly grows back in my heart.
In grief and fear, I recall
The young horse beyond the willow
And your red sleeves by the water,
As we part.

Through luck, Heaven sent me a beauty
Who shared quiet dreams with me,
Under moonlight, behind the bed curtain.

Like the lasting spring breeze,
Her tenderness I could gain.
Against my will, like flowing water,
Our joy slowly runs off.
Hearing her music is in vain.
The scent of her green silk dress is to wane.
How unbearable are falling petals, towards twilight,
Shrouded by weak sunlight and a misty, dying rain!
In a moment of concentration to rid my parting pain,
The oriole's trill begins now and again.

滿庭芳

山抹微雲，天黏衰草，畫角聲斷譙門。暫
停征棹，聊共引離尊。多少蓬萊舊事，空
回首，煙靄紛紛。斜陽外，寒鴉數點，流
水繞孤村。　銷魂。當此際，香囊暗解，羅
帶輕分。謾贏得，青樓薄倖名存。此去何
時見也，襟袖上，空惹啼痕。傷情處，高
城望斷，燈火已黃昏。

Parting Sorrow
(Tune: Man Ting Fang)

Thin clouds daub the hills.
Grasses at the horizon show blight.
A painted bugle turns mute at the drum tower.
Let me stop the boat for a while
And share a farewell drink with her.

Our past joyous meetings,
Like those at the Penglai Pavilion,
Become dim memories,
Behind a heavy sheet of mist and haze.
At sunset,
Several crows in the cold come in sight.
A stream flows around the lone village.

How soul-thrilling!
At that moment,
I covertly untie her perfumed sachet
And gently undo her gauze girdle.
I earn the notoriety
Of being the brothel's heartless client.
Once gone, when shall we meet again?
She tears on my robe in vain.
Feeling hurt, in a sad plight.
All over town, when viewed from a height,
Lit stoves and lamps tell it is already twilight.

好事近

春路雨添花，花動一山春色。行到小溪深
處，有黃鸝千百。飛雲當面化龍蛇，夭矯
轉空碧。醉臥古藤陰天下，了不知南北。

A Trip with Wine in Spring
(Tune: Hao Shi Jin)

In the spring rain, more roadside flowers appear,
Moving to give the hills spring colors.
As I walk far along the small stream,
The trill of countless orioles I hear.

Flying clouds resemble dragon and snake before me,
Spiraling in the blue void like many a swift arrow.
I have absolutely no idea where I am,
Lying drunk under an old vine's shadow.

ZHANG LEI (1054-1114)
張耒

夏日

長夏村墟風日清，簷牙燕雀已生成。蝶衣
曬粉花枝午，珠網添絲屋角晴。落落疏簾
邀月影，嘈嘈虛枕納溪聲。久拼兩鬢如霜
雪，直欲樵漁過此生。

Summer Days

In the village market, windy days of the long
   summer look clear.
On the rafts, mature swallows appear.
Butterflies sun their powdery dresses on floral twigs

at noon.

At sunlit corners of homes, to spider webs more silk
threads adhere.

Moonlight casts shadows through thin drapes.

The brook makes noise for the sleepless to hear.

I have white hair after long years of hard work.

Wish I could spend my life as a fisherman or
woodcutter here.

ZHOU BANGYAN (1056-1121)
周邦彥

玉樓春

桃源不作從容住。秋藕絕來無續處。當時
相候赤欄橋，今日獨尋黃葉路。煙中列岫
青無數。雁背夕陽紅欲暮。人如風後入江
雲，情似雨餘黏地絮。

Parting Sorrow
(Tune: Yu Lou Chun)

Living with her at Peach Flower Riverhead, I forego.

Like cut threads of fall lotus roots, my chance I
blow.

We used to meet by the Red Rail Bridge.

Today, alone I seek the road with leaves in yellow.

In the mist, countless green peaks come in a row.

Against the crimson dusk sun, wild geese go.
She disappears like reflected clouds after a blast.
Like fuzz stuck to the ground after rain, my firm
    love is my credo.

西河
金陵懷古

佳麗地。南朝盛事誰記。山園故國繞
清江，髻鬟對起。怒濤寂寞打孤城，
風檣遙度天際。斷崖樹，猶倒倚。莫
愁艇子曾繫。空遺舊跡鬱蒼蒼，霧沈半
壘。夜深月過女牆來，賞心東望淮水。
酒旗戲鼓甚處市。想依稀，王謝鄰里。
燕子不知何世。入尋常，巷陌人家，相
對如説興亡，斜陽裏。

Recalling the Past at Jinling
(Tune: Xi He)

On this beautiful land,
The memory of the glorious South Dynasties dies.
River Qing winds the old capital,
Walled in by a hill.
Like paired hair-knots, layered rocks rise.
Only angry waves lash at this lonely town.
Masts in the wind head towards the edge of far skies.

Trees at broken cliffs

Hang top down and aslant still.
To your shores,
Mo Chou's showboat once made its ties.
Cheerless, weathered relics remain.
Half of the fort sinks in the mist.
Late into the night,
After the moon has crossed the parapet,
In heartfelt delight,
I look east towards River Huai.

One could find many wine banners
And drums at play in the market.
I vaguely recall
Swallows left the rich neighborhoods,
After their downfall.
Ignorant of eras, human or historical,
They just joined the commoners,
One and all.
Face to face, they seemed to twitter,
As if discussing life's ups and downs,
At sunset.

LI QINGZHAO (1081-1143)
李清照

菩薩蠻

風柔日薄春猶早，夾衫乍著心情好。睡起
覺微寒，梅花鬢上殘。故鄉何處是，忘了
除非醉。沈水臥時燒，香消酒未消。

Homesickness
(Tune: Pu Sha Man)

Under a weak sun and early spring breeze,
I wear a lined robe, quite at ease.
Awake, I feel a slight chill in the air.
The plum flower has wilted on my hair.

Where may my hometown be?
Unless drunk, from homesickness I am not free.
The aloeswood incense that burned when I slept
Has waned, but the effects of wine are still kept.

攤破浣溪沙

病起蕭蕭兩鬢華，臥看殘月上窗紗。
豆蔻連梢煎熱水，莫分茶。枕上詩
書閑處好，門前風景雨來佳。終日
向人多蘊籍，木犀花。

In Sickness
(Tune: Tan Po Huan Xi Sha)

With gray temple hair, I wake up in disease,
Watching the waning moon through my drapes,
    ill at ease.
"Boil water with cardamom leaf tips for me.
No tea please."

Reading poems on the pillow goes well with leisure.
The view beyond my door looks fine with rain.
All day long, my intimate soulmates are
Flowers of cassia trees

訴衷情

夜來沉醉卸粧遲，梅萼插殘枝。酒醒熏破
春睡，夢斷不成歸。人悄悄，月依依，翠
簾垂。更挪殘蕊，更燃餘香，更得些時。

Spring Slumber
(Tune: Zu Zhong Qing)

Fully drunk after late removing of make up,
At night in bed I have lain.
On the wilted plum sprays, sepals clutch to remain.
I sober up in my spring slumber with incense gone.
A homecoming dream I fail to retain.

No human sound.
The moon sticks around.
My drapes fall down.
I rub wilted blooms again,
And light the rest of the incense again,
For more nap time to gain.

ZHU DUNRU (1081-1159)
朱敦儒

鷓鴣天
西都作

我是清都山水郎。天教懶慢帶疏狂。曾批
給露支風敕，累奏留雲借月章。詩萬首，
酒千觴。幾曾著眼看侯王。玉樓金闕慵歸
去，且插梅花醉洛陽。

Composed at West Capital
(Tune: Zhe Gu Tian)

In a land of fine hill and river, as a lad,
I am by nature lazy, slow and somewhat mad.
Through Heaven's decrees and my many petitions,
A life of wind and dew, under cloud and moon, I
    have had.

With endless cups of wine

And countless poems read,
Have I once eyed kingships and been misled?
I loathe returning to grand mansions, and instead
Stay in Luoyang with plum blooms and a tipsy head,

好事近
漁夫詞

搖首出紅塵，醒醉更無時節。活計綠簑青
笠，慣披霜衝雪。晚來風定釣綫閑，上下
是新月。千里水天一色，看孤鴻明滅。

The Fisherman's Song
(Tune: Hao Shi Jin)

With a swagger, I leave the dust of life.
No set waking hours do I need to know.
I wear a green coir cloak and a bamboo hat for work,
Used to charging through frost and snow.

My fishing line is idle, in the still wind at night.
The new moon is above and below.
For endless miles, against the seamless horizon,
A lone wild swan comes in and out of sight.

減字木蘭花
聽琵琶

劉郎已老。不管桃花依舊笑。要聽琵琶。
重院鶯啼覓謝家。曲終人醉。多似潯陽江
上淚。萬里東風。故園山河落照紅。

Listening to the Pipa
(Tune: Jian Zi Mu Lan Hua)

Like Mister Liu, I am young no more.
Peach flowers open as before.
Like the pipa-player, adrift in life still,
I seek her at the Xie's courtyard, with the oriole's
    trill.

Music stops; I have a tipsy head.
Much like those of an exile at River Xunyang, my
    tears are shed.
For endless miles, the east wind blows.
Red like sunset, my former kingdom, with its hill
    and river, glows.

LU BENZHONG (1084-1145)
呂本中

連州陽山歸路

稍離煙瘴近湖潭，疾病衰頹已不堪。兒女
不知來避地，強言風物勝江南。

On the Road in Yangshan County
of Lianzhou as I return

A bit away from miasma but closer to lakes, I gain.
Already I cannot bear seeing my health on the wane.
My children do not know about my seeking refuge.
Scenery and things here beat South of the River,
    they maintain.

CHEN YUYI (1090-1139)
陳與義

臨江仙
夜登小閣，憶洛中舊遊

憶昔午橋橋上飲，坐中多是豪英。長溝流
月去無聲。杏花疏影裏，吹笛到天明。二
十餘年如一夢，此身雖在堪驚。閑登小閣
看新晴。古今多少事，漁唱起三更。

On Recollecting my Old Friends in Luoyang, in a Small Pavilion at Night
(Tune: Lin Jiang Xian)

We used to drink on Wu Bridge,
Mostly heroes to our right.
The reflected moon of the long waterway
Flew quietly out of sight.
Under sparse shadows of apricot blooms,
Flute music went on all night.

Twenty some years have passed like a dream.
I am still alive, but in fright.
Leisurely at the small pavilion, after rain I greet
    sunlight.
Countless historical events through the ages
Make mere fishermen's shanties at midnight.

傷春

廟堂無策可平戎，坐使甘泉照夕烽。初怪
上都聞戰馬，豈知窮海看飛龍。孤臣霜髮
三千丈，每歲梅花一萬重。稍喜長沙向延
閣，疲馬敢犯犬羊鋒。

Spring Lament

The court was clueless in ending warfare.
Beacon fires shone as they sat in Ganquan Palace to

stare.
At first, the sound of war horses in the capital
surprised us.
The king retreated by sea, like a dragon in the air.
Officials left behind have very long, white hair.
Myriad plum flowers still appear each year.
It is small comfort to have Archivist Xiang at
Changsha,
With his tired, besieged soldiers resisting on a dare.

LU YOU (1125-1210)
陸游

宿城頭鋪小飲而睡

亭傳臨江滸，床敷息我勞。屋茅殘月冷，
庭樹北風鏖。虛市饒新兔，村場有濁醪。
氣衰仍病著，小飲不能豪。

At Chengtou Station, I Had a
Small Drink before Sleeping

The post station stands by the river.
After resting in bed, my tiredness has passed,
In a cold thatched hut, under a waning moon.
Courtyard trees fight with the northern blast.
There is unfiltered wine in the village square.
A good supply of fresh rabbit meat can last.

I am still sick with low energy.
A restricted quota for wine cannot be bypassed.

齋中弄筆偶書示子聿

左右琴樽靜不嘩，放翁新作老生涯。焚香
細讀斜川集，候火親烹顧渚茶。書為半酣
差近古，詩雖苦思未名家。一窗殘日呼愁
起，裊裊江城咽暮笳。

In my Study, Fiddling with a Writing Brush, I Wrote a Casual Poem for my Son Yu

With my qin and goblet nearby, it is quiet.
A new life style for an old man like me, I get.
I tend the fire and brew myself Gu Zhu Tea.
With incense burning, I pore over Su Kuo's poems
    in a set.
My calligraphy, done half-drunk, almost matches
    ancient work.
Though I think hard, I am not quite a famous poet.
The waning sun through my window worries me,
In this river town, with trailing notes of tartar reed
    pipes at sunset.

觀蔬圃

菘芥可葅芹可羹，晚風伊軋桔槔聲。白頭
孤宦成何味，悔不畦蔬過次生。

Looking at a Vegetable Garden

Besides pickled cabbage and mustard, celery stews I
 can get.
The evening wind sends the creak of the well-sweep.
What appeals to a white-haired, lonely official?
That I did not spend my life growing vegetables, I
 regret.

南堂雜興

十里城南禾黍村，白頭心事與誰論？惰偷
已墜先人訓，迂拙仍辜聖主恩。病退時時
親蠹簡，興來往往出柴門。斜陽倚杖君知
否，收點雞豚及未昏。

Mixed Inspiration at South Hall

Ten miles south of this town, in a village of rice and
 millet,
White-haired with concerns, I have none to address.
Idle and lazy, I fall short of my elders' guidance.
Pedant and clumsy, I let down my king's kindness.
The right mood sends me out of my brushwood gate

And after illness, to my worm-eaten books, I want
   access.
At sunset, propped on a cane, do you not know,
I gather and count chickens and pigs before
   darkness.

好事近

小倦帶餘醒，澹澹數櫺斜日。驅退睡魔十
萬，有雙龍蒼壁。少年莫笑老人衰，風味
似平昔。扶杖凍雲深處，探溪梅消息。

My Life Style
(Tune: Hao Shi Jin)

Slightly tired and with the lingering effects of wine,
I see through lattices the weak setting sun.
To fight Sleep Monsters, numbering ten thousand,
I have tea leaves to drive them off, one by one.

May the young stop mocking at old, frail people.
My life style is what it used to be.
With a cane, I walk far to the cold clouds,
For the signs of spring, by the stream, from the
   plum tree.

春日新賦

人生覓飯元多術，最下方為祿代耕。脫欲
朝衫猶老健，快如苦雨得春晴。鳥聲頻喚
五更夢，花氣頓醒三日醒。最喜晨興聞剝
啄，吾兒書札到柴荊。

A New Verse on a Spring Day

Instead of farming, an official stipend is the worst,
Of all the ways to earn your rice, if I try to rate.
Thrilled like seeing the spring sun after a long rain,
I rid my court robe, old but still in a healthy state.
Birdsongs often wake me from my dream at the fifth
    watch.
The floral scent quickly makes my hangover for the
    third day dissipate.
Happiest is the tapping of birds at dawn
While my son's letters reach my brushwood gate.

夜行至白鹿泉上

小雨病良已，新秋夜漸長。隔城聞鶴唳，
出戶逐螢光。荒徑穿蒙密，遙空望莽蒼。
泉聲落環佩，肝肺為清涼。

A Night Walk to the Top of White Deer Spring

In a drizzle, after my long illness,
I find longer dark hours for each early fall night.
Beyond the city wall, I hear cranes calling
And go outdoors for the fireflies' light.
I push through the dense growth of a deserted trail.
Under the far sky, the verdure of the outskirts comes
    in sight.
Coolness seeps into my body.
The spring sounds like jade pendants dropping
    from a height.

不睡

城遠不聞鐘鼓傳，孤村風雨夜騷然。但悲
綠酒欺多病，敢恨青燈笑不眠。水冷硯蟾
初薄凍，火殘香鴨尚微煌。虛窗忽報東方
白，且複繙經繡佛前。

Not Sleeping

In this city afar, I hear no drum or bell,
Save the disturbing wind and rain of the lone
    village at night.
Sadly my many ailments lose to the challenge of
    green wine.
I hate the blue lamp mocking me for not sleeping

tight.

The liquid of the toad-shaped ink-stone has just
thinly iced over.

The fragrant smoke from my waned duck censer is
slight.

Let me go over the sutras before an embroidered
image of Buddha,

As the eastern sky through my undraped window is
suddenly bright.

長歌行

人生不作安期生，醉入東海騎長鯨。猶當
出作李西平，手梟逆賊清舊京。金印煌煌
未入手，白髮種種來無情。成都古寺臥
秋晚，落日偏傍僧窗明。豈其馬上破賊
手，哦詩長作寒螿鳴。

興來買盡市橋酒，大車磊落堆長瓶。哀絲
豪竹助劇飲，如巨野受黃河傾。平時一滴
不入口，意氣頓使千人驚。國仇未報壯
士老，匣中寶劍夜有聲。何當凱還宴將
士，三更雪壓飛狐城。

The Patriot's Song

If in this life I am no An Qisheng,
Riding a long whale on East Sea, to my drunken
delight,

I should act like Li Xiping,
In the old capital, driving rebels out of sight.
My short-cropped hair has mercilessly turned white,
But my hands have not gripped the general's seal,
    golden and bright.
The monk's window at sunset gets a special glow.
In an old temple of Chengdu in fall, I stay night
    after night.
Who would expect me chanting like a cold cicada,
When I was once on horseback, subduing rebels
    with fight?

Let us empty my cartload of wine and pile up the
    tall jugs,
Bought by me by the bridge when I felt right.
Like a huge plain flooded by the Yellow River,
I down many cups with bamboo music in a sad
    plight.
I do not drink one drop of wine usually,
So my energy put many people in fright.
An able-bodied man ages as the national shame is
    not avenged.
My begrudged rare sword in the case rattles at night.
When can the victorious army I lead return for the
    celebratory feast,
As snow overwhelms Feihu City at midnight?

蔬圃絕句，其一

擬種蕪菁已是遲，晚菘早韭恰當時。老夫
要作齋盂備，乞得青秧趁雨移。

Quatrains on my Vegetable Garden, no.1

Too late now, but to grow turnips was what I meant.
Late rape green and early chives are right to plant.
This old man needs to prepare for fasting days.
The rain and free rice sprouts urge me to transplant.

夜坐小飲

零落槐花已滿溝，江湖又見一番秋。冰輪
有轍淩空上，銀漢無聲接心流。丹荔甘寒
勞遠致，玉醅醇冽喜新篘。移床坐對西南
電，好雨心知不待求。

Sitting at Night with a Short Drink

On the canal, scattered locust blooms have fully lain.
I watch fall coming to rivers and lakes again.
The moon, like an icy wheel, rises on its track.
The mute Milky Way flows on and on from our
    terrain.
Red litchis, sweet and cold, arrive with efforts over
    a long distance.
The newly filtered wine, pure like jade, is what I

gladly obtain.

I shift my chair to watch lightning from the
southwest.

That a good rain needs no begging, I know for
certain.

春遊

方舟衝破湖波綠，聯騎蹋殘花徑紅。七十
年閒人換盡，放翁依舊醉春風。

Spring Outing

Our paired boats plunge through green waves of the
lake.

Horses trample fallen blooms to make the trail red.

After seventy years, new people replace the old,

But I still hang on, in the spring wind with a tipsy
head.

FAN CHENGDA (1126-1193)
范成大

蝶戀花

春漲一篙添水面。芳草鵝兒，綠滿微風
岸。畫舫夷猶灣百轉。橫塘塔近依前遠。

江國多寒農事晚，村北村南，穀雨繞耕
徧。秀麥連岡桑葉賤。看看嘗麨收新繭。

South of the River
(Tune: Die Lian Hua)

One stroke of the oar swells the pond in spring,
With fragrant grass and baby geese.
The bank is fully green in the breeze.
My painted boat creaks on its myriad turns.
Hengtang Tower keeps in and out of focus as I go.

In riverside villages north and south,
Farming in the many cold spells are in delay,
Only starting in the micro-climate "Grain Rain".
Big wheatears span the ridges.
The need for mulberry leaves is low.
In time, they will get to taste flour
And let cocoon-harvesting follow.

眼兒媚
萍鄉道上乍晴，臥輿中困甚，小憩柳塘。

酣酣日腳紫煙浮，妍暖試輕裘。困人
天氣，醉人花底，午夢扶頭。春慵恰
是春塘水，一片縠紋愁。溶溶洩洩，
東風無力，欲皺還休。

Written in my Carriage during a Short Rest
from my Deep Fatigue by Willow Pond, on my
Way through Pingxiang County, as the Sun has
just Appeared
(Tune: Yan Er Mei)

A purplish mist floats above the bright horizon, on
    my way
As I don a light fur coat, on a warm, charming day.
What tiring weather!
Flowers that carry me away
Give me a dreamy head by midday.

Spring languor is like the rippled pond
That can frown and wrinkle all the way.
The weak east wind
Creates slight cresting and falling,
With ripples in dealy.

XIN QIJI (1140-1207)
辛棄疾

祝英台近
晚春

寶釵分，桃葉渡。煙柳暗南浦。怕上層
樓，十日九風雨。斷腸片片飛紅，都無
人管，更誰勸，流鶯聲住。鬢邊覷，試
把花卜歸期，才簪又重數。羅帳燈昏，

哽咽夢中語。是他春帶愁來，春歸何
處。卻不解，帶將愁去。

Late Spring
(Tune: Zhu Ying Tai Jin)

I split my jeweled hairpin,
With him at Peach Leaf Ferry Head.
South Shore looked dark under the misty willow.
Climbing the tower gives me fear
When nine days out of ten, there is wind and rain.
Flying petals that cause me pain
Are left to wane.
Who will urge the orioles to end their trill?

Peering sideways at my temple hair,
I use a flower to divine his returning date.
Once done, I start counting the days again.
Under a dim lamp, within my gauze bed curtain,
I choke up, talking in my dream.
Because of him, spring comes with sorrow.
Where will spring go?
It does not know
How to rid my woe.

清平樂

茅簷底小，溪上青青草。醉裏吳音
相媚好，白髮誰家翁媼。大兒鋤

豆溪東，中兒正織雞籠。最喜小兒
無賴，溪頭看剝蓮蓬。

Life in the Village
(Tune: Qing Ping Le)

My thatched eaves are small and low.
Above the stream, green grasses grow.
The finesse and seductiveness of the Wu dialect go
From an old drunk couple with white hair that I do
   not know.

East of the stream, hoeing beans is worked on by
   my eldest son.
By my middle boy, the weaving of a chicken coop
   is done.
Watching me shell lotus pods by the stream
Is the rascal of a lad, my smallest and most beloved
   one.

南鄉子
登京口北固亭有懷

何處望神州，滿眼風光北固樓。千古興亡
多少事，悠悠。不盡長江滾滾流。年少萬
兒鍪，坐斷東南戰未休。天下英雄誰敵
手？曹劉。生子當如孫仲謀。

Thoughts in Beigou Pavilion at Jingkou
(Tune: Nan Xiang Zi)

To view my country, where should I go?
Here at Beigou Pavilion, full vistas show.
Countless events caused dynasties to rise and fall,
A long time ago.
River Yangzi rolls endlessly in its flow.

Young General Sun with countless men that chose
   to follow
Held down the southeast against his foe.
In this world, who are the peers of this hero?
Cao and Liu.
We should beget a son like Sun Zhongmou, I know.

JIANG KUI (1155-1220)
姜夔

暗香

舊時月色，算幾番照我，梅邊吹笛。喚起
玉人，不管清寒與攀摘。何遜而今漸老，
都忘卻，春風詞筆。但怪得，竹外疏花，
香冷入瑤席。江國。正寂寂。歎寄與路
遙，夜雪初積。翠尊易泣。紅萼無言耿相
憶。長記曾攜手處，千樹壓，西湖寒碧。
又片片，吹盡也，幾時見得。

Plum Blossoms
(Tune: An Xiang)

Under the same moonlight,
Let me count how many times,
I have played the flute by the plum tree.
Despite the cold,
I woke my jade-like beauty
To climb and pluck some plum blossoms with me.
Like He Xun, I have grown old graduallly
And in the spring breeze,
Forgotten how to write poetry.
But strangely,
Those spotty blooms beyond bamboos
Pervade my jasper mat, with a scent so chilly.
This riverside town
Lies just quietly.
I sigh over the long distance to send her letters,
In the first drift of night snow.
Green goblets of wine let me tear easily.
Mute red blooms always remind me of her in my
    memory.
I always recall where I held her hand,
With countless snow-laden trees looking heavy.
By cold, emerald West Lake.
One by one,
All the petals are blown free.
To see them, when will the next chance be?

DAI FUGU (1167?-)
戴復古

清平樂

今朝欲去。有留人處，說與江頭楊柳樹。
繫我扁舟且住。十分酒興詩腸。誰禁冷落
秋光。借取春風一笑，狂夫到老猶狂。

An Old Wild Man
(Tune: Qing Ping Le)

I was about to leave today,
But something caused my delay.
To willows by the river, I say:
"Let my skiff be tied down; I shall stay."

Wine pushes my poetic mood to the utmost height.
Against the bleak fall scene, it is hard to fight.
Let the spring breeze come with instant blooming.
Being a wild old man is my right.

LI JUNMIN (1176-1269)
李俊民

秋江斷雁圖

不堪愁里見秋光，江北江南木葉黃。誰信
朔風猶跋扈？天涯吹斷弟兄行。

A Fall Scene of a Stray Wild
Goose over a River

I cannot bear to see autumn light in my sorrow.
North and south of the river, leaves turn yellow.
Who would believe the northern blast could still
  tyrannize?
Wild geese, like brothers, are split up as winds blow.

LIU KEZHUANG (1187-1269)
劉克庄

戊辰即事

詩人安得有青衫，今歲和戎百萬縑。從此
西湖休插柳，剩栽桑樹養吳蠶。

Current Events in the
Year of Wuchen (1208)

A poet cannot afford even a commoner's robe.
A million rolls of fine silk bought peace this year.
From now on, by West Lake, do not plant willows.
Only Wu silkworms and mulberry trees will be in
   our care.

清平樂
五月十五日夜玩月

風高浪快。萬里騎蟾背。曾識姮娥
真體態。素面原無粉黛。身遊銀
闕珠宮。俯看積氣濛濛。醉裏偶搖
桂樹，人間喚作涼風。

Enjoying the Moon on the Fifteenth Night of the Fifth Month (Tune: Qing Ping Le)

High winds and fast waves go
As I ride on the toad's back for endless miles.
About the Moon Goddess and her form,
I now get to know.
Her white face never had rouge and powder long
    ago.

On a tour of Pearl Palace, through Silver Gateway,
I gaze through layers of mist that stay.
Drunk, I give at times the cassia tree a sway.
"It is a cool breeze", mortals say.

玉樓春
戲呈林節推鄉兄

年年躍馬長安市。客舍似家家似寄。青錢
換酒日無何，紅燭呼盧宵不寐。易挑錦服
機中字。難得玉人心下事。男兒西北有神
州，莫滴水西橋畔淚。

Written in Jest for my Fellow Townsman, Prefectural Judge Lin (Tune: Yu Lou Chun)

Each year in Changan, I gallop at a fast pace.
My inn seems like home; home is a boarding place.
My bronze coins trade wine; days go idly by.

I roll dice and gamble under red candles all night.

It is easy to pick out what her woven palindromes
    embrace,
But hard to know her thoughts hidden from her face.
To a man, his homeland extends to the northwest.
Shedding tears over floozies, west of the bridge, is
    not right.

YUAN HAOWEN (1190-1257)
元好問

秋懷

涼葉蕭蕭散雨聲，虛堂浙浙掩霜清。黃花
自與西風約，白髮先從遠客生。吟似候蟲
秋更苦，夢和寒鶴夜頻驚。何時石岑關頭
路，一望家山眼暫明。

Autumn Thoughts

Cold leaves rustle in the scattering rain
That drips on a deserted hall and covers the clear
    frost lain.
A wanderer afar gets his white hair first.
Yellow blooms and the west wind make a natural
    twain.
Chanting like a seasonal insect is doubly bitter.

Like cold jays after dark, I have fearful nightmares
　　again and again.
On a road at a pass of a stony ridge,
When can I see my hometown to soothe my mental
　　strain?

癸己十月二十九日出京

塞外初捐宴賜金，當時南牧已駸駸。只知
灞上真兒戲，誰謂神州遂陸沉。華表鶴來
應有語，銅槃人去亦何心。興亡誰識天公
意？留著青城閱古今。

On the Twenty-ninth Day in the Fourth Month of the Year of Gui Ji (1233), I left the Capital

Diverting funds to cheer our border troops was just
　　done
When southbound invasions had hurriedly begun.
I only know our frontier men acted like children at
　　play.
Who would think our land was thus overrun?
The returning crane at the Grand Pillar must lament.
The departing brazen fairy was the heart-broken one.
Qing City remained to witness surrender rites for
　　two dynasties.
Heaven's will on politics is understood by none.

眼中

眼中時事益紛然，擁被寒窗夜不眠。骨肉他鄉各異縣，衣冠今日是何年？枯槐聚蟻無多地，秋水鳴蛙自一天。何處青山隔塵土，一菴吾欲送華顛。

To my Eyes

To my eyes, more chaotic current events grow.
I get sleepless hugging my quilt by a cold window.
My blood relatives got uprooted to different
　counties.
In the new regime, scholars as outcasts feel low.
Like a wilted sycamore tree with ants, my homeland
　is gone.
Like the fall croaking frog, turncoats gloat and
　bellow.
Where are green hills that block the dust of life?
To a temple to spend my old age, I want to go.

雁丘
摸魚兒

序：泰和五年乙丑歲，赴試并州，道逢捕雁者云：“今日獲一雁，殺之矣。其脫網者悲鳴不能去，竟自投于地而死”。予因買得之，葬之汾水之上，累石而識，號曰

雁丘。時同行者多為賦詩，予亦有“雁丘
詞。”舊所作無宮商，今改定之。

問世間，情爲何物，直教生死相許？天南
地北雙飛客，老翅幾回寒暑。歡樂趣，離
別苦，就中有癡兒女，

君應有語，渺萬里層雲，千山暮雪，
隻影向誰去？橫汾路，寂莫當年簫
鼓，荒煙依舊平楚。招魂楚些何
嗟及，山鬼暗啼風雨。

天也妒，未信歟，鶯兒燕子俱黃
土。千秋萬古，為留待騷人，狂
歌痛飲，來訪雁丘處。

The Tomb of Two Wild Geese
(Tune: Mo Yu E)

Preface: In the fifth year of the Reign of Tai He (1205),
I went to Bingzhou for an examination. A bird hunter
I met on my way said, "Today I caught a wild goose
and killed it. Its mate that had broken loose from
the net cried in grief, could not bear to leave and
plunged itself to the ground to die." Because of this,
I bought the pair from the owner and buried them
by River Fen. I piled rocks to form a headstone with
the words "Tomb of Two Wild Geese". At that time,
my companions composed poems for the geese and I
also did one. The old version was not set to music, so
now I have made revisions for the finalized version.

Let me ask earthlings:
"What is love
That is pledged for life as you grow old?"
Two birds flying together from south to north,
With aged wings,
Through seasons hot and cold.
Amid joyful meetings
And painful partings,
The infatuation and passion of lovers unfold.

The surviving bird must have told,
"Through layered clouds afar, for myriad miles,
And over twilight snow, on countless hills,
Where will my lone shadow go?"
On this route across River Fen,
With a familiar haze on the deserted plain of Chu,
Shrill flute notes and drumbeats are on hold.
None summons their souls with Chu songs.
In the wind and rain,
The cries of mountain spirits are not bold.

Heaven also envies the two wild geese,
In disbelief,
Of their immortality in a different mold,
As orioles and swallows all go to dust.
For myriad years,
The tomb waits for visiting poets to write about love,
With song, wine and nothing to withhold.

WU WENYING (1200?-)
吳文英

浣溪沙

門隔花深夢舊遊。夕陽無語燕歸愁。玉纖
香動小簾鉤。　落絮無聲春墮淚，行雲有影
月含羞。春風臨夜冷於秋。

Boudoir Complaint
(Tune: Huan Xi Sha)

She dreams an old dream, with dense blooms
　　outdoors aglow,
At sunset, sulking over a returning swallow.
Her slim, fragrant fingers fiddle; small drapery
　　hooks follow.

Tears fall quietly in spring under the falling fuzz.
Clouds scud to cover a shy moon and cast a shadow.
At night, it is colder than autumn as east winds blow.

風入松

聽風聽雨過清明，愁草瘞花銘。樓前綠暗
分攜路，一絲柳，一寸柔情。料峭春寒中
酒，交加曉夢啼鶯。西園日日掃林亭，依
舊賞新晴。黃蜂頻撲鞦韆索，有當時，纖
手香凝。惆悵雙鴛不到，幽階一夜苔生。

Disappointment
(Tune: Feng Ru Song)

I pass the Qingming Festival hearing wind and rain,
Sad over fallen blooms buried amid grass.
Before the tower runs a forked road under a green
    shade.
Each thread of willow.
Every inch of my tender feeling.
Under the effects of wine, in the spring chill,
My dawn dreams get crisscrossed by the oriole's
    trill.

In West Garden, I sweep in the pavilion of a grove,
Enjoying as before each new sunny day.
Yellow bees often bump against the ropes of swings,
To which the fragrance of her slim hands clings still.
I miss the footprints of her mandarin duck shoes,
On an overnight growth of moss on secluded steps,
Depressed that the chance of her return is nil.

霜葉飛

斷煙離愁。關心事，斜陽紅隱霜樹。半壺
秋水薦黃花，香潠西風雨。縱玉勒，輕飛
迅羽。淒涼誰弔荒臺古。記醉蹋南屏，綵
扇咽，寒蟬倦夢，不知蠻素。

Reflections
(Tune: ShuangYe Fei)

The mist is cleared up; I rid my parting woe,
Over something on my mind.
Behind frosted trees,
Red sunbeam aslant barely show.
With half a jug of fall water
And my offering of flowers in yellow,
Let me make a fragrant spray before her grave,
Like the wind and rain from the west.

I idle my jade rein
As a swift bird glides.
Who would mourn by this old, deserted terrace in
    sorrow?
I recall tramping Nanping with a tipsy head.
She sobbed behind a colored silk fan.
Like a cold cicada, I was tired and dreamy instead,
Unfeeling to another concubine, like Man Su, that I
    let go.

LIU CHENWENG (1232-1297)
劉辰翁

寶鼎現
春月

紅妝春騎。踏月影，竿旗穿市。望不盡，
樓臺歌舞，習習香塵蓮步底。簫聲斷，約
彩鸞歸去，未怕金吾呵醉。甚輦路，喧闐
且止。聽得念奴歌起。

父老猶記宣和事。抱銅仙，清淚如水。還
轉盼沙河麗。浣漾明光連邸第。簾影凍，
散紅光成綺。月浸葡萄十里。看往來，神
仙才子，肯把菱花撲碎。

腸斷腸斷竹馬兒童，空見說，三千樂指。
等多時，春不歸來，到春時欲睡。又說
向，燈前擁髻。暗滴鮫珠墜下。便當日親
見霓裳，天上人間夢裏。

Spring Moon
(Tune: Bao Ding Xian)

Adorned ladies ride horses in spring,
Treading shadows under moonlight,
Past markets with their flags and poles swinging.
Endlessly in towers and on terraces,
Song and dance go on.
From dance steps on lotus pads,
Dust and fragrant puffs arise.

When notes of the flute wane,
Colorful ladies are picked up to return,
All drunk but fearless of the guards' scolding.
On the imperial highway of the old capital,
As the loud, noisy hubbub dies,
The song "Niannu" begins to rise.

Aged people still recall,
Events in the reign of Xuan He, years ago.
Like the brazen fairy,
They shed tears, clear like water, for the former king.
In earnest, they cast their eyes
On the beautiful sands and rivers of a kingdom gone.
Row on row,
Mansions glitter in the glow.
Blinds cast many a frozen shadow,
That look like brocade with a patchy red glow.
The reflected moon in West Lake
Dips in a huge vat of grape wine.
To and fro,
See how charming couples get to go.
Are they willing not to keep the mirror-like war
    capital whole?

On bamboo horses, children play.
Broken-hearted, I cannot bring myself to say
Anything about the three thousand court musicians
    of a former day.
I have waited and waited,
But the return of spring is in delay.

I may want to sleep once spring is to stay.
Over anything on the lost empire, if I begin to relay,
She will bury her head by lamplight,
Shedding pearly teardrops out of sight.
Even if I had seen the grandeur of our old capital,
Like the "Dance of Rainbow Skirts",
With my own eyes,
It could only reappear in a mortal's dream,
All lost to the skies.

WANG YISUN (1240-1290)
王沂孫

蟬
齊天樂

一襟餘恨宮魂斷，年年翠陰庭樹。乍咽涼
柯，還移動暗葉，重把離愁深訴。西窗過
雨。怪瑤佩流空，玉箏調柱。鏡暗妝殘，
為誰嬌鬢尚如許。銅仙鉛淚似洗，嘆移盤
去遠，難貯零露。病翼驚秋，枯形閱世，
消得斜陽幾度。餘音更苦。甚獨抱清高，
頓成淒楚。謾想熏風，柳絲千萬縷。

The Cicada: an Elegy for the Kings of the Southern Song Dynasty
(Tune: Qi Tian Le)

Overcome by regrets, the disfavored queen died
To become a cicada of the courtyard tree.
In the green shade every year,
With abrupt sobs on a cool bough,
It moves among dark leaves
To vent again its heart-felt parting sorrow.
A rain sweeps past the west window,
Strangely resembling jasper pendants moving in the
    sky
And tuning at the plectrum of a jade zither.
Before a dusty mirror, her adorned face waned.
For whom did she still try to please,
With coy hair-puffs like cicada wings?

Like the brazen fairy with streams of leaden tears,
Sighing over the displaced pan
And difficulties to collect dew for the Han king,
We mourn the Song monarchs.
Like the fearful cicada with wrecked wings in fall,
We wilt in time as experiences go.
How many sunsets can we follow?
The trailing notes of a cicada sound sadder.
It alone holds onto high integrity
And suffers from instant grief and pain.
In vain, we recall the warm breezy days,
With myriad threads of the willow.

眉嫵
新月

漸新痕懸柳，澹彩穿花，依約破初暝。
便有團圓意，深深拜，相逢誰在香徑。
畫眉未穩，料素娥，猶帶遺恨。最堪
愛，一曲銀鉤小，寶簾掛秋冷。千古盈
虧休問。歎謾磨玉斧，難補金鏡。太
液池猶在，淒涼處，何人重賦清景。故
山夜永。試待他，窺戶端正。看雲外山
河，還老盡，桂花舊影。

The New Moon
(Tune: Mei Wu)

Gradually like a new scar,
It hangs from the willow,
With weak, petal-like translucence,
Barely breaking up the gloom right after sunset.
Hoping for a reunion,
She prays and bows low.
On the fragrant trail,
Whom would she have met?
The new moon is an undone painted brow.
I suspect the Moon Goddess
Must have left with parting regret.
Most lovely yet –
The small moon, like a silvery hook,
Holds up the star-studded sky,
Like a jeweled drape in the autumn chill.

Ask not about the countless cycles
In which the moon may wax and wane.
Just sigh over the toil of honing the jade axe in vain
And mending the gold mirror to be whole again.
Taiye Pond may still remain,
But in a pitiable state.
To write another verse,
On the quiet, moonlit pond,
Whose service can we obtain?
Nights go on over the hills of our old kingdom.
Let me wait
And peek through the door
For the full moon, symmetrically set.
Beyond the clouds, see our former kingdom
Age with endless time,
Under the same moon with cassia blooms as before.

ZHANG YAN (1248-1329?)
張炎

阮郎歸
有懷北遊

鈿車驕馬錦相連。香塵逐管弦。瞥
然飛過水秋千，清明寒食天。花貼
貼，柳懸懸。鶯房幾醉眠。醉中不信
有啼鵑，江南二十年。

In Memory of my Northern Sojourn
(Tune: Ruan Lang Gui)

Rare horses pull her jeweled carriage with linked
  brocade.
Fragrant dust rushed to follow.
Pipe and string notes were in play.
I caught a glance of her swing flying over the waters,
Near the Qing Ming Festival,
On Cold Food Day.

Here, in clumps flowers grow,
Amid many a drooping willow.
In her boudoir, I rest my tipsy head on a pillow.
Drunk, about any cuckoo's call to return, I do not
  know.
Having left for South of the River,
Twenty years ago.

满庭芳
小春

晴皎霜花，曉鎔冰羽，開簾覺道寒輕。誤
聞啼鳥，生意又園林。閑了淒涼賦筆，便
而今，不聽秋聲。銷凝處，一枝借暖，終
是未多情。陽和能幾許，尋紅探粉，也恁
忺人。笑鄰娃痴小，料理護花鈴。卻怕驚
回睡蝶，恐和他，草夢都醒。還知否，能
消幾日，風雪灞橋深。

A Short Warm Spell like Spring
(Tune: Man Ting Fang)

The frost glistens under sunlight.
Feather-like icicles melt at morn.
Through open drapes,
The chill seems to be slight.
Birdsongs, by mistake, to my ears,
Bring life to the garden, as if reborn.
I have rested my pen on themes of sorrow,
So for now, shut myself to the sounds of fall.
This temporary thaw
May warm up just some plants,
Being too weak to linger after all.

How long can this sunny spell go?
I seek flowers in shades of red,
Just to my desire and delight.
I chuckle over the warning bell,
Tied among flowers by a silly girl next door.
This would only put a sleeping butterfly in fright
And together
Get waken from a dream ever so light.
Do we know
How many days of this warm spell
Can rid the windy capital of deep snow?

高陽臺
西湖春感

接葉巢鶯，平波卷絮，斷橋斜日歸船。能
幾番游，看花又是明年。東風且伴薔薇
住，到薔薇，春已堪憐。更悽然，萬綠西
冷，一抹荒煙。當年燕子知何處，但苔深
韋曲，草暗斜川。見說新愁，如今也到鷗
邊。無心再續笙歌夢，掩重門，淺醉閑
眠。莫開簾。怕見飛花，怕聽啼鵑。

Spring Inspiration at West Lake
(Tune: Gao Yang Tai)

Heaped leaves make an oriole's nest.
Weak ripples roll up the fuzz.
By a broken bridge at sunset, returning boats steer.
How many more trips can I make?
To see flowers, it will be another year.
May the east wind keep roses company.
When roses are at their best,
A miserably waned spring will be here.
It is sadder still
When the lush, verdant growth by Xileng Bridge
Stays under cheerless mist in a smear.

Where are the swallows of a yesteryear?
Crooked fences with overgrown moss appear,
Near slanting streams with dark grass.
Let me stop talking about grief

Now that the bank with gulls is near.
I care less with more songs and dreams.
Let me close my doors,
To sleep leisurely with a tipsy head.
Do not open my drapes.
Flying flowers and calling cuckoos give me fear.

ZHAO MENGFU (1254-1322)
趙孟頫

絕句，其一

溪頭月色白如沙，近水樓臺一萬家。誰向
夜深吹玉笛？傷心莫聽後庭花。

Quatrains, no.1

Moonlight is white like sand above the river.
Near the waters, myriad towers and terraces stand.
Who is playing a jade flute late at night?
Doing the same thing, a king sadly lost his land.

絕句，其二

春寒惻惻掩重門，金鴨香殘火尚溫。燕子
不來花又落，一庭風雨自黃昏。

Quatrains, no.2

Behind shut doors, sadly the spring chill gives me
   pain.
From the lukewarm brazen duck censer, the scent is
   to wane.
Swallows do not return; flowers drop.
Evening comes to my courtyard with wind and rain.

YANG ZAI (1271-1323)
楊載

暮春游西湖北山

愁耳偏工著雨聲，好懷常恐負山行。未辭
花事駸駸盛，正喜湖光淡淡晴。倦憩客猶
勤訪寺，幽栖吾欲厭歸城。綠疇桑麥盤櫻
筍，因憶離家恰歲更。

A Trip to North Hill of
West Lake in Late Spring

Too much noisy rain gets my ears burned.
Too few hilly hikes in my good mood make me feel
   concerned.
I do not stay away from the fast flurry of flowers,
Just glad over how mild the sunlit lake has turned.
The tired traveler often visits temples to rest.
To the city from a quiet spot, I would rather not
   have returned.

By green fields of mulberries and wheat, I eat dishes
    of cherries and bamboo shoots.
I have left home for a year, from memory I learned.

LUO YUZI (Song Dynasty)
羅與之

看葉

紅紫飄零草不芳，始宜攜杖向池塘。看花
應不如看葉，綠影扶疏意味長。

Watching Leaves

Colored blooms vanish; no fragrant grass can
    remain.
Now is the time to go to the pond with a cane.
Viewing flowers should be worse than watching
    leaves.
From green leafy shadows, more spiritual interest
    one can gain.

YANG PU (Song Dynasty)
楊朴

莎衣

軟綠柔藍著腥衣，倚船吟釣正相宜。蒹葭
影里和煙臥，菡萏香中帶雨披。狂脫酒家
春醉後，亂堆漁舍晚晴時。直饒紫綬金章
貴，未肯輕輕博換伊。

My Straw Cloak

With the blue sky and green waters, my straw cloak
　　with a fishy smell,
As I chant or fish on a boat, goes well.
I lay down under the misty shadow of reeds.
Among fragrant water lilies, I wore it as a rain fell.
Drunk in a wine shop in spring, madly I tore it off,
To be thrown into a fisherman's hut at sunset for a
　　spell.
My straw cloak will not be casually traded.
I value not purple cordons and gold seals, easy to
　　tell.

6
YUAN DYNASTY
(1280-1367)

GUAN YUNSHI (1286-1324)
貫雲石

蘆花被

采得蘆花不浣塵，翠蓑聊復藉為茵。西風
刮夢秋無際，夜月生香雪滿身。毛骨即隨
天地老，聲名不讓古今貧。青綾莫為鴛鴦
妒，欸乃聲中別有春。

The Quilt of Reed Flowers

The reed flowers gathered with no dust shown
    Can make a moss-like quilt with green
straw once sewn.
In endless fall, west winds shatter my dreams.
In the moonlit night with fragrance, all over me
    snow has blown.

My body ages with heaven and earth,
But my fame in history is a peer of the well-known.
Envy not silken quilts with mandarin ducks.
With each creak of the boat, a special image of
     spring has grown.

YANG WEIZHENG (1296-1370)
楊維禎

春消息

鶴東煉師有兩復，神仙中人殊不俗。小復
解畫華光梅，大復解畫文仝竹。文同龍雲
挐破壁，華光留得春消息。大樹仙人夢正
甘，翠禽叫夢東方白。

Inscribed on a Painting
on "Signs of Spring"

At Hedong, two alchemists called the Fu's
Go through life as Daoists, with few worldly clues.
Younger Fu is a peer of Hua Guang, the famed
     painter of plum flowers.
Elder Fu can compare well with Wen Tong in
     painting bamboos,.
Plum flowers of Hua Guang stay to signal spring.
Like the magic dragon, Wen Tong's bamboos can
     break walls.

Fairies of big trees stay in a deep dream.
At dawn, for dream makers, a green kingfisher calls.

ZHANG YINING (1301-1370)
張以寧

嚴陵釣臺

故人已乘赤龍去，君獨羊裘釣月明。魯國
高名懸宇宙，漢家小吏待公卿。天回禦榻
星辰動，人去空臺山水清。我欲長竿數千
尺，坐來東海看潮生。

The Fishing Terrace of Yan Ling

Your old friend took off with the red dragon throne.
You alone fished in sheep skin when the moon was
    bright.
The great fame of Confucius of Lu pervaded the
    universe.
Of Han's ministerial ranks, you made light.
You shook the starry sky by sharing the royal bed.
By clear hills and waters, at the terrace you are out
    of sight.
Wish I could have a fishing pole of a few thousand
    feet
And see the rising tide of East Sea by sitting tight.

SONG LIAN (1310-1382)
宋廉

越歌

戀郎思郎非一朝，好似并州花剪刀。一股
在南一股北，幾時裁得合歡袍？

Song of Yue

Over time, my loving thoughts of you will not fade,
Like Bingzhou's carved scissors of the best grade.
One blade is in the south and the other north.
When can our wedding gowns be tailor-made?

GAO QI (1336-1374)
高啓

明皇秉燭夜遊圖

花萼摟頭日初墮，紫衣催上宮門鎖。大家
今夕燕西園，高爇銀盤百枝火。海棠欲睡
不得成，紅妝照見殊分明。滿庭紫焰作春
霧，不知有月空中行。

新譜霓裳試初按，内使頻呼燒燭換。知
更　宮女報銅籤，歌舞休催夜方半。共言
醉飲終此宵，明日且免群臣朝。只憂風露
漸欲冷，妃子衣薄愁成嬌。琵琶羯鼓相

追逐。白日居心歡不足。此時何暇化光
明，去照逃亡小家屋。

姑蘇臺上長夜歌，江都宮裡飛螢多。一般
行樂未知極，烽火忽至將如何？可憐蜀道
歸來客，南內淒涼頭盡白。孤燈不照返魂
人，梧桐夜雨秋蕭瑟。

The Evening Parties under
Candlelight of King Ming

Over Huae Tower, as the dusk sun goes out of sight..
The purple-robed staff hastily locks the doors tight.
On silver stands, myriad lit candles hang high.
The king is to hold a feast at West Garden tonight.
Like a begonia, Lady Yang is sleepless in bed.
Her well-lit face is vivid, adorned in red.
Purplish flames of courtyard torches flicker like
	spring mist.
None knows about the moon sailing overhead.

Dancers try out the "Rainbow Skirts" song that is
	new.
Servants often call for replacing candles in view.
Maids tell time according to the brazen pointer of
	the clepsydra.
At midnight, songs and dances are not through.
That heavy drinking is to last the whole night, they
	all say.
From the next dawn court, officials can stay away.

Lady Yang, thinly clad, frowns coyly,
Over a cold, dewy wind coming her way.

In turn, fast beats of the pipa and tartar drums run.
Merry-making is not enough under the sun.
How can the king have time to bring light and care
To wretched commoners, like refugees overrun.
Revelers who know no limits do not care.
The palace at Jiangdu released fireflies everywhere.
King Wu at Gusu Terrace had songs all night long.
How do we handle sudden beacon fires and warfare?
On return from Cichuan, what a pitiful sight,
He feels sad in his palace and his hair turned white.
His lone lamp fails to light up her returning soul.
Fall looks bleak with firmianas under rain at night.

登金陵雨花臺望大江

大江來從萬山中，山勢盡與江流東。鍾山
如龍獨西上，欲破巨浪乘長風。江山相雄
不相讓，形勝爭誇天下壯。秦皇空此瘞黃
金，佳氣蔥蔥至今王。

我懷鬱塞何由開？酒酣走上城南臺。坐覺
蒼茫萬古意，遠自荒煙落日之中來。石頭
城下濤聲怒，武騎千群誰敢渡。黃旗入洛
竟何祥，鐵鎖橫江未為固。

前三國，後六朝，草生宮闕何蕭蕭！英雄
乘時務割據，幾度戰血流寒潮。我生幸逢
聖人起南國，禍亂初平事休息。從今四海
永為家，不用長江限南北。

Looking at the Big River after Climbing Yuhua Terrace of Jinling

The big river draws from myriad hills, one and all,
Running eastwards as slopes fall..
Only Zhong Hill, like a dragon, heads west,
As if to break giant waves from winds gone tall.
With equal strength, the river and hill stay.
At vantage points, with peerless force each brags in
its own way.
To suppress future rulers, the Qin king buried gold
here in vain.
Good energy and omen for kingship thrive today.

From depression, how can I set my mind free?
Almost drunk, I climb a terrace, south of the city.
Through the distant mist, sunset appears.
As I sit, I catch gray, blurry images of history.
Below this stony city of King Wu, waves look cross.
King Wei's myriad cavaliers dared not sail across.
How auspicious was the omen that made King Wu's
son move to Luoyang!
After iron locks broke in the river, his kingdom
suffered a total loss.

Palaces of the Three Kingdoms era
And later in the Six Dynasties
Look desolate with rank grass.
Opportunistic warlords carved up the land.
Blood flew with cold waves with successive
    battles at hand.

Luckily, sage rulers are building the southern state,
With the first peace and a time of rest in wait.
From now on, my home will forever be in the Four
    Seas.
The use of River Yangzi as a north-south boundary
    will cease.

7

MING DYNASTY
(1368-1644)

LI MENGYANG (1472-1529)
李夢陽

石將軍戰場歌

I

清風店南逢父老，告我己巳年間事。店北
猶存古戰場，遺鏃尚帶勤王字。憶昔蒙塵
實慘怛，反覆勢如風雨至。紫荊關頭畫吹
角，殺氣軍聲滿幽朔。胡兒飲馬彰義門，
烽火夜照燕山雲。內有于尚書，外有石將
軍。石家官軍若雷電，天清野曠來酣戰。
朝廷既失紫荊關，吾能豈保清風店。牽爹
負子無處逃，哭聲震天風怒號。兒女床頭
伏鼓角，野人屋上看旌旄。

273

II

將軍此時挺戈出，殺敵不異草與蒿。追北
歸來血洗刀，白日不動蒼天高。萬里煙塵
一劍掃，父子英雄古來少。單于痛哭倒
馬關，羯奴半死飛孤道。處處歡聲噪鼓
旗，家家牛酒犒王師。應追漢家婕嫽姚
將，還憶唐家郭子儀。

III

沉吟此事六十春，此地經過淚滿巾。黃雲
落日古骨白，沙礫慘澹愁行人。行人來
折戰場柳，下馬坐望居庸口，卻憶千官
迎駕初，千乘萬騎下皇都。乾坤得見中
興土，殺伐重開載造圖。姓名應勒雲臺
上，如此戰功天下無。嗚呼戰功今已無，
安得再生此輩西備胡。

General Shi on the Battlefield

I

South of Qingfengdian, I met an old man
Who told me about the battlefield of a former day.
"It still stood in the north since the year of Jishi,
With arrowheads and the rescuers' designations
    where they lay.

The capture of our king was tragic.
Fickle and forceful like a rainstorm, invaders
ransacked.
Enemy bugles sounded by day at Zijing Pass.
In north Hebei, blood-thirsty troops were packed.

Barbarians watered their horses by Zhangyi Gate.
Beacon fires lit clouds of Yan Hill at night.
State Secretray Yu minded domestic affairs.
General Shi at the borders was ready to fight.

Like lightning and thunder, Shi's royal army
Fought relentlessly in the wilds under a clear sky.
The kingdom already lost Zijing Pass.
To keep Qingfengdian, we subjects could not try.

Carrying and helping my kin, I had nowhere to hide.
The angry wind howled; wails shook the sky, in like
manner.
Children hid in bed, hearing horns and bugles.
On rooftops, peasants eyed many a military banner.

II

At this time, the general stepped forward,
Killing his foes like cutting mugworts and grass,
one by one.
With blood-stained swords, he returned from the
north,
Under a gray tall sky, with a still bright sun.

He and his son made two generations of rare heroes.
His sword swept off smoke and dust so widespread.
At Daoma Pass, Chief Danyu wept bitterly.
At Feihu Trail, barbarian soldiers were half dead.

In joy, we made noise everywhere with drums and
    flags.
Every family rewarded soldiers with beef and brew.
This victory resembled that of Piaoyao of Han.
Memories of Tang's Guo Ziyi came back anew".

III

Pondering over this event sixty years ago,
I passed this land full of tears.
Sunset stained clouds yellow; old bones looked
    white.
The bleak, sandy battlefield saddened me after all
    these years.

I broke a willow twig in the battlefield,
Dismounted and sat to watch Jurong Pass.
I imagine a thousand officials receiving the king
On his return to the capital, escorted with class.

The re-empowered kingship is for all to see,
With the post-war state strengthened and remade.
His name should be engraved on the victory stele,
For the peerless war achievements made.

Alas, such victories today are laid to rest.
Wish generals like him are reborn for barbarian
    attacks from the west.

林良畫兩角鷹歌

I

百餘年來畫禽鳥，後有呂紀前邊昭。二子
工似不工意，呡筆決皆分毫毛。　林良寫意
只用墨，開縑半掃風雲黑。水禽陸禽各臻
妙，褂出滿堂皆動色。

空山古林江怒濤，兩鷹突出霜崖高。整骨
刷羽意勢動，四壁六月生秋飆。一鷹下視
睛不動，已知兩眼無秋毫。一鷹掉頭復欲
下，漸覺振翩風蕭蕭。

匹綃雖慘淡，殺氣不可滅。戴角森森爪
拳鐵，迴如愁胡皆欲裂

II

朔風吹沙秋草黃，安得臂爾騎駉鐵！草間
妖鳥盡擊死，萬里晴空灑毛血。我聞宋徽
宗，亦善貌此鷹。後來失天子，餓死五國
城。乃知圖畫小人藝，工意工似皆虛名。
校獵馳騁亦末事，外作禽荒古有經。

今王恭默罷遊宴，講經日禦文華殿。南海
西湖馳道荒，獵師虞長皆貧賤。呂紀白首
金爐邊，日暮還家無酒錢。從來上智不貴
物，淫巧豈敢陳王前。

良乎，良乎，寧使爾畫不值錢，
無令後事好畫兼好畋。

The Painting of Two Eagles with Horn-like Feathers by Lin Liang

I

Bian Zhao, followed by Lu Ji,
Famous painters of birds of a former year,
Detailed the form over the spirit,
With keen eyes on the tiniest hair.

Lin Liang, like black, wind-swept clouds,
With only ink on silk, brushed away.
His subtle paintings of land and water fowls
Moved all in halls on display.

In old groves of deserted hills, above angry waves,
Two eagles jut out from a cliff, icy and tall.
Brushing their feathers and adjusting attack postures,
All around, they make July look like windy fall.

One eagles fixes its gaze downwards.
The smallest thing cannot escape its sight.
The other turns its head and wants to descend,
Winging in time to make wind at a height.

Although the silk painting looks bleak,
The killing spirit of the eagles comes through.

With stern, horned beaks and iron claws,
They open their eyes wide, like barbarians we knew.

II

I wish to ride a carriage with four black horses,
With an eagle on my arm to kill wild birds among
   grass, until they die.
Among wind-swept sand, grass turns yellow in fall.
A spray of blood and feathers drops from the wide,
   sunlit sky.

I heard King Hui of Song
Painted eagles and earned his fame.
Later losing his monarchy,
A dead prisoner from starvation he became.

A painter of either form or spirit earns small glory.
Painting is art for petty people, we come to know.
Hunting or horsemanship, all unimportant pursuits,
Can wreck an empire, in warnings years ago.

Now at Wenhua Palace, the classics are taught daily.
The king stops feasts and trips, respectful and mute.
Horse trails for the royalty are vacant all over.
Hunters and gardeners become destitute.

The old Lu Ji, neglected as he stayed by the gold
   censer,
Came home without money for wine at sundown.
Wise rulers never favor material comfort.

Who dare bring crafts for sensual pleasure to the
  crown?

Liang, Liang:
"I would rather find your paintings worth nothing
Than future kings indulged in painting or hunting".

HE JINGMING (1483-1521)
何景明

歲晏行

舊歲已晏新歲逼，山城雪飛北風烈。徭夫
河邊行且哭，冰寒水冰凍傷骨。長官叫號
吏馳突，府帖連催築河卒。一年徵求不少
蠲，貧家賣男富賣田。百金縱遊非地產，
一兩已值千銅錢。往時人家有儲粟，今歲
人家飯不足。饑鶴翻飛不畏人，老鴉鳴噪
日近屋。生男長成聚比鄰，生女落地思嫁
人。官家私家各有務，百歲豈止療一身？

近聞狐兔亦徵及，列網持矰遍山域。野人
知田不知獵，蓬矢桑弓射不得。嗟吁今昔
豈異情？昔時新年歌滿城；明朝亦是新年
到，北舍東鄰聞哭聲。

Ballad on the End of the Year

The old year has waned; the new year is near.
Snow flies all over this hilly town; the northern
   blast is severe.
Icy water and cold sand cause deep frost bites
As forced laborers move by the river and tear.
The chief hollers; abrupt petty officials dash across.
Drafts for workers to build banks come again.
Heavy taxes are already levied each year.
The poor sell their sons; the rich sell their lots.
Taxes in silver are still on their flooded plots.
Curbing inflation on copper coins is in vain.
They used to have surplus grains to call their own.
Now there is not enough rice for everyone.
Hungry cranes flip and fly near people with no fear.
Old crows get nearer houses each day, cawing aloud.
They hope to be near their sons as they are grown.
And marry off their daughters once they are born.
Officials and commoners have duties of their own.
In life, one cannot nurture oneself alone.

Foxes and hares are also levied, of late I hear.
All over this hilly town, there are nets and arrows.
Villagers who know farming but not hunting
Cannot use ceremonial arrows and bows.
Alas, what a different set of rules that now goes!
People used to sing all over during a new year.
By tomorrow, another new year will be here,
But I hear weeping everywhere.

YANG SHEN (1488-1559)
楊慎

武侯廟

劍江春水綠渾渾，五丈原頭日又曛。舊業
未能歸後主，大星先已落前軍。南陽祠宇
空秋草，西蜀關山隔暮雲。正統不愧傳萬
古，莫將成敗論三分。

The Temple of Zhuge Liang

Green but wavy, spring waters of River Jian can get.
On the Wu Zhang Plain, it is sunset.
The heir of Liu Bei could not inherit the throne.
With death before military success, Zhuge Liang
    already met.
Fall grass gives a deserted air to this temple.
Beyond dusk clouds, quite apart are West Shu's
    hills and passes set.
Forever he will be in history by serving the Han
    Dynasty.
The success or failure of him is to be assessed yet.

柳

垂楊重柳管芳年，飛絮飛花媚遠天。金距
鬥雞寒食後，玉蛾翻雪暖風前。別離江上

還河上，拋擲橋邊與路邊。游子魂銷青塞
月，美人腸斷翠樓煙。

Willows

On the sure presence of drooping willows, each
fragrant spring relies,
With flying fuzz flirting in the distant skies.
After Cold Food Day, cock fights with golden claws
begin.
Before warm winds, rolling among snowflakes are
butterflies.
They throw willow twigs, by roads and bridges
Or on rivers and streams, when they break their ties.
The beauty gets broken-hearted in her misty, jade
tower,
At the moonlit green borders, the dead wanderer's
body lies.

XUE HUI (1489-1541)
薛蕙

昭王臺

燕昭無故國，薊野有空臺。寂莫黃金氣，
淒涼滄海隈。儒生終報主，亂世始憐才。
回首征途上，年年此地來。

The Terrace of King Zhao

The old Yan kingdom of King Zhao did not last.
The terrace in the capital now looks bare.
The custom of recruiting the talented with gold
ended.
Tucked away at a corner by the gray sea, it brings
no cheer.
Confucian scholars kept their vows to serve the king.
In troubled times, their talents were then held dear.
I recall on the road of expeditions,
Talented men came here every year.

XIE ZHEN (1495-1575)
謝榛

野興

白日霜凝地，飛飛雁渡河。孤峰依漢廻，
老樹得秋多。月曉山精伏，時清野父歌。
短笻隨我意，一徑入煙蘿。

Inspiration in the Wilds

Wild geese fly across the river.
On the sunlit frozen ground, frosty effects remain.
The lone peak looks far above River Han.
On fall colors, old trees gain.
Peasants in the wilds sing in peaceful times.

Under the dawn moon, mountain spirits have lain.
I walk as I please on a trail,
Amid misty creepers, with a short cane.

HUANGPU PANG (1498-1583)
皇浦汸

對月答子浚兄見懷諸弟之作

南北何如漢二京，迢迢吳越兩鄉情。謝家
樓上清秋月，分作關山幾處明。

Under Moonlight, in Answer to my Elder Brother, Zijun, Expressing my Concern for our Brothers

We are apart, north and south, like the two Han
capitals, at a different site.
The bond of brotherhood, over a long distance, is
tight.
Equal to the accomplished Xie brothers, like the
clear fall moon,
Our dispersed brothers shine as bright.

GAO SHUSI (1501-1537)
高叔嗣

寒食定興道上

二月鶯花少，千家雨雪霏。可憐值寒食，
猶來換征衣。積水生空霧，高城背落暉。
忍看楊柳色，從此去王畿。

On the Road in Dingxing County
on Cold Food Day

With few orioles and blooms in the second month,
Countless families meet rain and snow.
It is a pity on Cold Food Day,
I change into military uniform before I go.
Fog rises from pools of standing water.
The tall city wall bears the sunset's glow.
I have no heart for the color of the willow
When I am leaving for the capital today.

TANG SHUNZI (1507-1560)
唐順之

復官後報京師友人

姓名不復掛朝參，魚鳥由來性所耽。篋里
符經都已廢，山中藥草漸能譜。疏狂自分

三宜黜，懶病其如七不堪。深謝故人推轂
意，莫將楊羨比終南。

A Report to my Friends in the Capital after Resuming my Post in the Government

On the dawn court's roster, my name did not remain.
By nature, the freedom of bird and fish I entertain.
I have trashed academic texts from my book chest.
The gist of hillside medicinal herbs, I slowly gain.
I was unbearably lazy and sick, most of the time,
And suitably fired for being slightly insane.
Let me thank my old friends for recommending me.
From any shortcut to advancements I refrain.

HUANG JISHUI (1509-1574)
黃姬水

與友人共飲

青郊歇馬拂吳鈎，萍聚天涯共白頭，久客
新豐惟命酒，長謠故國一登樓。林殘半壑
飛寒雨，潮落空江急暮流。世路風煙悲去
往，莫辭此日醉箜篌。

Drinking Wine with Friends

I stay my horse and whip my Wu sword for a rest to
    gain.
In the green outskirts, all white-haired, we happen
    to meet again.
A homesick, unfulfilled writer wrote an exposition
    after climbing a tower.
About his fate, the detained wanderer of Xinfeng
    drank to complain.
The ebb of the deserted river runs fast at sunset.
Across groves and ravines in blight flies a cold rain.
I grieve over the past in the wind and dust of life,
And from today's wine and music, refuse to abstain.

LI PANLONG (1514-1570)
李攀龍

輓王中丞，　其一

司馬臺前列柏高，風雲猶自夾旌旄。屬鏤
不是君王意，莫作胥江萬里濤。

Mourning for Adjutant Wang, no.1

Before your grave, tall cypresses stand in file.
Banners remind us of your great military style.
Your death was not the king's intent.
Do not complain like the spirit of waves for many a
    mile.

輓王中丞， 其二

幕府高臨碣石開，薊門丹旐重徘徊。沙場
入夜多風雨，人見親提鐵騎來。

Mourning for Adjutant Wang, no.2

Your headquarters by Jieshi Hill looks tall.
By painted military banners of Ji Gate, I linger.
Battlefields at night are mostly rainy and windy.
Your soul returns with your cavalry in mail, first of
    all.

歲杪放歌

終年著書一字無，中年學道仍狂夫。勸君
高枕且自愛，勸君濁醪且自酌。何人不說
宦游樂？如君棄官復不惡。何處不說有
炎涼？如君杜門復不妨。縱然梳拙非時
調，便是悠悠亦所長，

Opening up my Mind at
the End of the Year

I write all year without an author's fame.
Despite learning Daoism at middle age, I am mad
    all the same.
May I advise you to sleep tight and take care of
    yourself.

May I advise you to drink unfiltered wine and sell it
  in your name.
Who does not talk about the joy of an expatriate
  official?
It is not bad if you let go the title you claim.
Everywhere people befriend the rich and shun the
  poor.
You might as well find peace and close your door.
Even if laziness and stupidity are unpopular,
Being leisurely is your strength, that is it, no more.

杪秋登太華山絕頂

縹緲真探白帝宮，三峰此日為誰雄？蒼龍
半挂秦川雨，石馬長嘶漢苑風。地敞中原
秋色盡，天開萬里夕陽空。平生突兀看人
意，容爾深知造化功。

Reaching the Peak of Mount
Taihua in Late Fall

The distant White Emperor Palace seems reachable.
Of the three peaks, which is the highest today?
Half of Canglong Ridge of this Qin land is rainy.
In the wind, stone funerary horses of Han neigh.
Fall colors end on the wide Central Plain.
In the endless sky, sunset does not stay.
Give yourself time to know fully the Creator's work,
If in life you only care about what other people say.

塞上曲送元美

白羽如霜出塞寒，胡峰不斷接長安。城頭
一片西山月，多少征人馬上看。

Seeing off Yuan Mei for the Pass

At the pass, cold white feathers look frost-like in a
    pack.
Beacon fires linking Changan and the borders run
    back to back.
As the moon is above West Hill from the city wall,
How many homesick soldiers will gaze at it on
    horseback?

WANG SHIZHENG (1526-1590)
王世貞

陪殷侍禦登靈岩絕頂

徑折全疑盡，峰回陡自開。蒼然萬山色，
忽擁岱宗來。碧澗傳僧梵，青天落酒杯。
雄風別有賦，不羨楚蘭臺。

Accompanying Attending Censor Yin on
a Hike to the Peak of Lingyin Hill

The crooked trail seems to end.
The receding steep hillside gives way.

Countless verdant hills look dark,
Suddenly Mount Tai comes in view right away.
The chime of temple bells pass green brooks
In my wine goblet, the blue reflected sky falls to
　　stay,
Strong winds here merit another exposition,
Beating that on Orchid Terrace of Chu of a former
　　day.

酹孫太初墓

死不必孫與子，生不必父與祖。突作湣陵
千古人，依然寂莫一抔土。道場山陰五
十秋，那能華表鶴來游。君看太華蓮花
掌，應有笙歌在上頭。

An Elegy for Sun Taichu at his Grave

In death, no mourning by son or grandson is needed.
In life, no father or grandfather must be around.
The dead, suddenly mourned in a mausoleum,
Is still left alone as a part of the soil underground.
The soul of a Daoist in the hills for fifty years
May not return to the ground as a crane.
Please watch the Lotus Peak of Mount Taihua.
There is music for your ascension as a fairy, I am
　　certain.

登太白樓

昔聞李供奉，長嘯獨登樓。此地一垂顧，
高名百代留。白雲海色曙，明月天門秋。
欲覓重來者，潺湲濟水流。

Visiting Taibai Tower

I used to hear about Li Bai
Who, after a long whistle, climbed this tower alone.
Here after he had cast his eyes downwards,
Because of his fame, this tower is forever known.
A bright fall moon hangs over Mount Tai.
In the same color, white clouds and the dawn sea are
    shown.
I want to seek the soul of Li Bai, as a returnee.
Endlessly, as then and now, River Ji has flown

ZHANG JIAYIN (1527-1588)
張佳胤

登函關城樓

樓上春雲雉堞齊，秦川芳草自萋萋。黃看
雨後河流急，青入窗中華岳低。客久獨澠
三尺劍，晴清何用一丸泥。登高遠眺鄉心
起，關樹重遮萬嶺西。

Climbing the City Tower of Hangu Pass

To the same level, battlements and spring clouds go.
Lush, sweet spring grasses of the central plain grow.
The rapid river after a rain appears yellow.
Within the window, green Mount Hua looks low.
A detained wanderer relies on his three-foot sword
    alone.
At peace, Hangu Pass needs not block any foreign
    foe.
My homesickness arises after climbing high and
    looking far.
Trees cover myriad ridges to the west, row on row.

LI LIUFANG (1575-1629)
李流芳

白門七夕

舊日維舟處，懸情獨柳條。秋風又京國，
客思正江潮。長路有時到，歡期難再邀。
徘徊望牛女，愁絕向中宵。

The Seventh Night at
the West Gate of Nanjing

Where the boat was tied before,
Our parting sentiment relied only on the willow.
In the capital as fall winds return,

The wanderer's thoughts ride on the river's billow.
A joyous date with you cannot be set again.
On a long way, I get to go.
Watching the Cowherd and Weaving Maid stars,
I linger approaching midnight, in extreme sorrow.

XU WEIHE (c1580-1637)
徐維和

酒店逢李大

偶向新豐市里過，故人尊酒共悲歌。十年
別淚知多少，不道相逢淚更多。

Meeting Old Li at a Wine Shop

By chance, Xinfeng was the city I passed.
Over wine, I sang sadly with a friend of the past.
For ten years, the countless tears we had shed,
Compared with those of reunion, were unexpectedly
    surpassed.

郵亭殘花

征途微雨動春寒，片片飛花馬上殘。試問
亭前來往客，幾人花在故園看。

Wilted Flowers of a Courier Station

In the spring chill, the rain on the road is slight.
Petals blown in the air get wilted outright.
Let me ask the travelers before this station:
In their own gardens at home, how many flower-
watchers sit tight?

QIAN QIANYI (1582-1664)
錢謙益

金陵秋興八首次草堂韻，
己亥七月初一作，其一

龍虎新軍舊羽林，八公草木氣深深。樓船
蕩日三江湧，石馬嘶風九城陰。掃穴金陵
還地肺，埋胡紫塞慰天心。長干女唱平遼
曲，萬戶秋聲息搗砧。

Eight Poems on Autumn Inspiration in Jinling,
Following the Rhymes Used by Du Fu, in a Poem
of a Similar Title, Written on the First Day of the
Seventh Month, in the Year of Jihai (1659), no. 1

Our new navy is as fierce as any on a former day.
By Bagong Hill, like plants, strict discipline is in
display.
The galleons sail on River Yangzi with its surge.
Darkly, stone horses of the royal mausoleum neigh.

Our men sweep their hideouts to restore Jinling.
Let us bury barbarians beyond the borders, to follow
Heaven's way.
May the maidens of Changgan sing of peace and
leisure.
From beating the mallet in fall for soldiers' clothing,
we can stay away.

金陵秋興八首次草堂韻，
己亥七月初一作，其二

雜虜橫戈倒載斜，依然南斗是中華。金銀
舊識秦淮氣，雲漢新通博望槎。黑水游魂
啼草地，白山新鬼哭胡笳。十年老眼重磨
洗，坐看江豚蹴浪花。

Eight Poems on Autumn Inspiration in Jinling,
Following the Rhymes Used by Du Fu, in a Poem
of a Similar Title, Written on the First Day of the
Seventh Month, in the Year of Jihai (1659), no. 2

Mixed bandits from the borders collapsed in defeat.
With China, the glow and glory of the Southern
Dipper stay.
The Qinhuai area is long known as the capital.
Our navy sailed the Yangzi, like the ancient raft for
the Milky Way.
New ghosts from Mount Changbai weep at Tartar
reed whistles.

Wandering souls from Heilongjiang wail on grass
  for being astray.
After ten years, this old man is clear of accusations.
I sit and wait for my return on a triumphal day.

西湖雜感

冬青樹老六陵秋，慟哭遺民總白頭。南渡
衣冠非故國，西湖煙水是清流。早時朔漠
翎彈怨，他日居庸宇喚休。苦恨嬉春鐵崖
叟，錦兜詩報百年愁。

Mixed Thoughts at West Lake

In fall, six Song kings' graves got moved, marked
  with a holly.
White-haired people of a lost empire wept bitterly.
The elite migrated south from the old kingdom.
Waters of misty West Lake flew clearly.
Before, they griped about dynastic changes on
  hearing northern music.
In future, beyond Jurong Pass, defeated foreign
  rulers will flee.
The Yuan poet, Tie Ya, wrote "Spring Frolic" with
  deep hatred
And revenged with the "Jin Dou" rhyming style to
  set his grief free.

迎神曲

三年蜀血肯銷沉？我所思兮在桂林。卻望
蒼梧量淚雨，湘江何似五湖深。

Receiving Spirits

Did our martyrs' blood become jade underground,
  all these years?
I think of the last Ming resisters at Guilin.
King Shen's death at Cangwu caused much grief at
  River Xiang.
At Five Lakes, Ming Dynasty's collapse brought
  more tears.

吳門春仲送李生還長干

闌風伏雨暗江城，扶病將愁起送行。煙月
揚州如夢寐，江山建業又清明。夜烏啼斷
門前柳，春鳥銜殘花外櫻。尊酒前期君莫
忘，藥囊吾欲傍餘生。

Seeing off Li Sheng in Mid-Spring on his
Return to Changgan from Wumen

The endless rainstorm keeps this river town under
  its shadow.
I shall see you off, in sickness and sorrow.
The Qingming Festival comes again to Nanjing.

Yangzhou is dreamlike with misty moonlight aglow.
Spring birds mouth spoiled cherries beyond flowers
Night crows by the gate cry and break the willow.
Do not forget about our wine date previously set.
For the rest of my life, a medicine bag is by me as I
  go.

KUANG LU (1604-1650)
鄺露

洞庭酒家

昔日洞庭霞，霞邊賣酒家。晚虹橋外市，
秋水月中槎。江白魚吹浪，灘黃雁踏沙。
相將楚漁夫，招手入蘆花。

A wine Shop of Lake Dongting

Lake Dongting's clouds resemble those years ago.
To the wine shop by the clouds we go.
A magic raft on fall waters can reach the moon.
Beyond the bridge is a market with a dusk rainbow.
Fish blow bubbles, like white waves in the river.
Wild geese step on the sandy beach in yellow.
At the beckon of a fisherman of Chu,
Onto a boat among reed flowers we follow.

CHEN ZILONG (1608-1647)
陳子龍

渡易水

并刀昨夜匣中鳴，燕趙歌歌最不平。易水
潺湲雲草碧，可憐無處送荊卿。

Crossing River Yi

My sharp sword sounded for action in the chest last
  night.
Sad songs of Yan and Zhao show fight.
Clouds and grass look green by gentle River Yi.
What a pity, Jingke is nowhere in sight.

秋日雜感，其一

滿目山川極望哀，周原禾黍重徘徊。丹楓
錦樹三秋雨，白雁黃雲萬里來。夜雨荊榛
連茂苑，夕陽麋鹿下胥臺。振衣獨上要離
墓，痛哭新亭一舉杯。

Mixed Thoughts on an
Autumn Day, no.1

A view of our entire land gives me sorrow and pain.
I linger at the Zhou capital, now millet fields, again
  and again.

From myriad miles away, white wild geese come
through yellow sandstorms.
Red maples and colorful trees face the late fall rain.
Deer descend a bleak terrace at sunset.
The glory of gardens, drenched with brambles at
Nnghtm, cannot sustain.
Like the Jin people at New Pavilion, I drink and
weep bitterly.
With respect, I visit the grave where Yaoli, the
assassin, has lain.

錢塘東望有感

清溪東望大江回，立馬層崖極望哀。曉日
四明霞氣重，春潮三折浪雲開。禹陵風雨
思王會，越國山川出霸才。依舊謝公攜屐
處，紅泉碧樹待人來。

Reflections on Looking East
from Qiantang County

Looking east at the winding river, big and limpid,
I stay my horse at a layered cliff with sorrow.
Siming Hill looks very misty under the dawn sun.
Three surges of the spring tide bring many a
cloud-like billow.
The land of Yue will produce men with hegemonic
power.
In the wind and rain at his mausoleum, I recall King
Yu long ago.

The same hill stands where Xie Lingyun hiked
with his wooden clogs.
To our fine empire, Heaven will send down our
national hero.

WU WEIYE (1609-1671)
吳偉業

阻雪

關山雖勝路難堪，才上征鞍又解驂。十丈
黃塵千尺雪，可知俱不似江南。

Delayed by Snow

Though the scenery excels, traveling is unbearably
slow.
I undo my bridle after mounting on a saddle a while
ago.
I know it is unlike South of the River,
With heaps of yellow soil and piles of snow.

過吳江有感

落日松陵道，堤長欲抱城。塔盤湖勢動，
橋引月痕生。市靜人逃賦，江寬客避兵。
廿年交舊散，把酒嘆浮名。

Feelings at Wujiang County

The sun sets on Songling Road.
Around the city, the long bank seems to go.
Reflections of the pagoda move in the lake.
Holes of the bridge make many a moon-like shadow.
To evade taxes, people left behind a quiet city.
To dodge navies on the wide river, voyagers rely on
    a different ply.
My friend of twenty years have dispersed.
Over wine and my lack of fame, I sigh.

聽女道士卞玉京彈琴歌

I

駕鵝逢天風，北向驚飛鳴。飛鳴
入夜急，側聽彈琴聲。

借問彈者誰？云是當年卞玉京。

玉京與我南中遇，家近大功坊底路。小院
青樓大道邊，對門卻是中山住。中山有女
嬌無雙，清眸皓齒垂明璫。曾因內宴直歌
舞，坐中瞥見塗鴉黃。問年十六尚未嫁，
知音識曲彈清商。歸來女伴洗紅妝，枉將
絕技矜平康，如此才足當侯王。

萬事倉皇在南渡，大家幾日能枝梧。詔
書忽下選蛾眉，細看輕車不知數。中山

好女光徘徊，一時粉黛無人顧。艷色知
為天下傳，高門愁被旁人妒。盡道當前
黃屋尊，誰知轉盼紅顏誤。南內方看起
桂宮，北兵早報臨瓜部步。聞道君王走
玉驄，犢車不用聘昭容。幸遲身入陳宮
裡，卻早名填代籍中。

II

依稀記得祁與阮，同時亦中三宮選。可憐
俱未識君王，軍府抄名被驅遣。漫詠臨
春瓊樹篇，玉顏零落委花鈿。當時錯怨
韓擒虎，張孔承恩已十年。但教一日見
天子，玉兒甘爲東昏死。羊車望幸阿誰
知，青冢凄涼竟如此。

我向花閒拂素琴，一彈三嘆為傷心。暗將
別鵠離鸞引，寫入悲風怨雨吟。碧玉班中
怕點留，樂管門外盧家泣。私更裝束出
江邊，恰遇丹陽下渚船。剪就黃絁貪入
道，攜來綠綺訴嬋娟。

此地由來盛歌舞，子弟三班十番鼓。月明
弦索更無聲，山塘寂寞遭兵苦。十年同
伴兩三人，沙董朱顏盡黃土。貴戚深閨
陌上塵，吾輩漂零何足數。坐客聞言起
嘆嗟，江山蕭瑟隱悲笳。莫將蔡女邊頭
曲，落盡吳王苑裡花。

Listening to the Music on the Qin Played by a Daoist Priestess, Bian Yujing

I

Her music reminds me of flying geese facing a blast,
Heading north and crying in fright.
With interest, I listen to the beats
That get faster into the night.

Who is the musician?
Bian Yujing of a former year.

Bian and I met in the capital.
She lived near Da Gong Fang, across a big road.
There was a grand mansion with a small courtyard,
Occupied by descendants of Prince of Zhongshan
    as their abode.

Bian sang:
"With bright pendants, white teeth and clear eyes,
Over other beauties, a daughter of Zhongshan could
    tower.
In a feast hired to play music for song and dance,
I saw she adorned her brow with yellow powder.
Upon inquiry, she said she was sixteen and single.
An expert in music, crisp fast notes she could hit.
On return, other musicians washed their faces clean
And lamented a waste of musical skill in a brothel.
To be married to the royalty, only the daughter of
    Zhongshan was fit.

In panic, the king hurriedly began his southern reign.
For how many days could his kingship continue?
Edicts suddenly called for new palace ladies,
With slender horses and light carriages in an endless
    queue.

The fair daughter of Zhongshan was bypassed.
For the moment, not a look at her was cast.
Her beauty was known all over the land.
Sadly, she was jealously treated by those outclassed,

It was stated that a royal mansion was about ready.
Who would know, in a twinkle, promises for the
    beauties were aborted.
The king's residence was to resemble Cassia Palace.
Near Guabu, the sight of northern soldiers was
    reported.

They heard the monarch had left on horseback.
Carriages for the palace ladies were not sent.
Luckily, she was late in the selection process.
Early on, to a substitute list of assignments her
    name went.

II

At the same time, the Qi and Ruan daughters
Were chosen as palace ladies, I vaguely recall.
What a pity, the military had named them as exiles
Before they all were able to see the king at all.

Do not compare them with King Chen's concubines.
They lost their filigrees and pretty forms like jade.
Han Qinhu was wrongly accused of killing Zhang
    and Kong,
Who had King Chen's favor for a decade.

If a palace lady could see the monarch for a day,
She would be willing to die for an indulgent king.
Who could know how the Jin king chose his women?
The green grave of Lady Wang was her sad ending.

I play string music for brothels.
In grief, I pluck once and sigh again and again.
My songs dwell on sorrow in parting,
In the wind and rain, for a sad person to complain.

Bamboo pipes sounded last night atop the city wall.
The urgency to recruit musicians also was kept.
I feared being picked as a court musician.
Songstresses before their doors and those married to
    the rich all wept.

By chance I could sail downstream for Danyang,
After secretly reaching the riverside in a silk dress.
With a yellow robe, I passed for a Daoist priestess
And brought a zither to sing about ladies in distress.

Here, songstresses and dancers used to be popular.
Many troupers played with ten different instruments
    in shows.

String bands now became mute on moonlit nights.
By River Shantang, it was deserted after the painful
    war came to a close.

My colleagues after ten years dwindled to two or
    three.
Pretty women like Sha and Dong went underground.
The exalted daughter of Zhongshan was like dust.
From a wanderer like me, little worth mentioning
    can be found."

As I listen in my seat, I think of my bleak kingdom
    and sigh.
By the music of barbarian reed pipes, our people get
    carried away.
Miss Cai of Han sang about hardships of life with
    the Xiongnus.
May songs like this stop, though all good things in
    life end one day.

下相極樂庵讀同年北使時詩卷

蘭若停驂灑墨成，過河持節事分明。上林
過雁無還表，頭白山僧話子卿。

Reading the Poems of my Contemporary, Written as an Envoy to the North, in Jile Temple of Xiaxiang County

After a stop in a temple, your poems were done.
Your duties as an envoy were precisely run.
Su Wu was of high integrity, like a wild goose that
did not return.
White-haired monks talk fondly of him; you are the
other one.

圓圓曲

I

鼎湖當日棄人間，破敵收京下玉關。慟哭
六軍俱縞素，沖冠一怒為紅顏。紅顏流落
非吾戀，逆賊天亡自荒宴。歸掃黃巾定黑
山，哭罷君親再相見。

相見初經田竇家，侯門歌舞出如花，許
將戚里箜篌伎。等取將軍油壁車。家本
姑蘇浣花里，圓圓小字嬌羅綺。夢向夫
差苑裏遊，宮娥擁入君王起。前身合是
採蓮人，門前一片橫塘水。橫塘雙槳去
如飛，何處豪家強載歸？此際豈知非薄
命，此時只有淚沾衣。薰天意氣連宮
掖，明眸皓齒無人惜。

奪歸永巷閉良家，教就新聲傾坐客。坐客飛觴紅日暮，一曲哀弦向誰訴？白皙通侯最少年，揀取花枝屢回顧。早攜嬌鳥出樊籠，待得銀河幾時渡。恨殺軍書抵死催，苦留後約將人誤。相約恩深相見難，一朝蟻賊滿長安。可憐思婦樓頭柳，認作天邊粉絮看。遍索綠珠圍內第，強呼絳樹出雕闌。若非壯士全師勝，爭得蛾眉匹馬還。

II

蛾眉馬上傳呼進，雲鬟不整驚魂定。蠟炬迎來在戰場，啼妝滿面殘紅印。專征簫鼓向秦川，金牛道上車千乘。斜谷雲深起畫樓，散關月落開妝鏡。傳來消息滿江鄉，烏柏紅經十度霜。教曲妓師憐尚在，浣紗女伴憶同行。舊巢共是銜泥燕，飛上枝頭作鳳凰。長向尊前悲老大，有人夫婿擅侯王。當時只受聲名累，貴戚名豪競延致。一斛明珠萬斛愁，關山漂泊腰肢細。錯怨狂風揚落葉，無邊春色來天地。嘗聞傾國與傾城，翻使周郎受重名。妻子豈應關大計，英雄無奈是多情。全家白骨成灰土，一代紅妝照汗青。

君不見舘娃初起鴛鴦宿，越女如花看不足。香徑塵生烏自啼，屧廊人去苔空綠。換羽移宮萬里愁，珠歌翠舞古梁州。為君別唱吳宮曲，漢水東南日夜流。

Yuanyuan

I

The Ming king killed himself on a fateful day.
Through Shanhai Pass to the capital, General Wu
    fought his way.
The defeated army wept bitterly, all dressed in white.
The raging general reclaimed his beauty, come what
    may.
"I did not come only for my kidnapped beauty.
Against Heaven's will, the rebels acted in absurdity.
After my return to clear the foes and their bases,
I cried and mourned for the king and my father
    before seeing my lady."

They first met through Tian, a nobleman's relative,
    in his home.
When she was a musician of his, like a floral spray.
The young performer was a gift to the general,
In wait for his painted carriage on a later day.
From a brothel in Gusu, Yuanyuan came,
Tender like gauze and brocade, with a casual name.
She dreamed of touring gardens like those of Fucha,
Where the title of a palace lady she cold claim.
She must be a lotus picker in her previous life,
With a door facing a pool, like that of Xi Shi.
Shipped quickly to the capital as if in flight,
Which rich family would own her, she could not
    foresee.

At this moment, over her unlucky fate,
She could only let her tears run.
A favored, overbearing lady was ruling the harem.
Her pretty face was favored by none.
On return to the Tian family behind closed doors,
Her new voice got her audience impressed.
Her clients drank as she sang until sunset,
But to whom could her sorrow be expressed?
General Wu was young, elegant and fair-skinned.
His loyalty to a chosen lady he could sustain.
He wanted to free her, like a caged bird, without
    delay.
Waiting to cross the Milky Way was uncertain.
Hateful war dispatches were urgent and pressing.
She missed joining the general with a reunion date
    in delay.
Meeting again was hard despite the deep love and
    trust.
Bandits like ants filled Changan one day.
Pity the lovesick man, like a willow by a tower,
Transformed into powdery fuzz in the sky sailing,
Seeking his beauty, like Lady Green Pearl, in the
    inner chambers
And shouting for her presence, like Miss Red Tree,
    by a carved railing.

If it were not for the full victory the strong man
    earned,
His lady on horseback could not have returned.

II

On horseback, Yuanyuan was escorted back,
With uncombed hair but calmness maintained.
General Wu welcomed her in a lavish style.
On her teary face, her rouge powder waned.
He led his troops west with flute and drum,
With myriad chariots by way to Shu, in display of
    his power.
At moonless Dashan Pass, she adorned herself.
In a distant, sloping valley was her painted tower.
News about her reached her riverside village,
After her absence for a decade.
Her music teachers were still alive,
The memory of her fellow silk-washers did not
    fade.
She alone became a phoenix at the tip of a twig.
Before, they were all swallows in an old nest.
They drank often and griped about aging.
In marrying up, someone among them got her best.
Her fame became her liability.
The rich and powerful competed to be her lover.
The small gain for her came with sorrow,
As a frail wanderer all over.

Blame not the gale that swept off flowers.
In turn, endless spring finally came.
In history, I heard of a peerless charmer and empire-
    wrecker.
Zhou Yu, to the contrary, earned great fame.
General Wu was by nature amorous.
How could his wife and children have schemed to
    deserve the malady?
The whole family became white bones in the soil.
A shiny spot in history was given to the lady.

Do you not see
The new Guanwa Palace and the joy King Wu could
    get?
He could not see enough of the flower-like Yue lady
    yet.
Now the fragrant path is dusty under cawing crows.
Full of green moss, the deserted sound-making
    corridor is quiet.
Endless grief follows each change of dynasty.
General Wu reveled in Hangzhou, or Liangzhou
    in the past.
Let us not sing in memory of the Wu Palace.
Unlike the river always flowing east, good times
    never last.

FANG YIZHI (1611-1671)
方以智
獨往

同伴都分手，麻鞋獨入林。一年三變姓，
十字九椎心。聽慣干戈信，愁因風雨深。
死生容易事，所痛為知音

My Exile Alone

My companions have all scattered.
I have become a monk alone.
Three times a year, I changed my name.
With gut-wrenching pain, my short poems are done.
I believe in any news of war through habit.
In a big rainstorm, my sadness has overgrown.
Death can be easily dealt with and less painful
Than the different values my comrades-in-spirit
    have shown.

HUANG ZHOUXING (1611-1689)
黃周星

秋日與杜子過高座寺登雨花臺

披髮何時下大荒，河山舉月共淒涼。客來
古寺談秋雨，天為幽人駐夕陽。去國屈原
終婞直，無家李百只伴狂。百年多少凴高
淚，每到西風灑幾行。

Visiting Guozuo Temple and Climbing Yuhua Terrace with Mister Du on a Fall Day

With loosened hair, we tour this land of blight.
A pathetic state of the empire comes in sight.
As guests to this old temple, we talk about fall rain.
For recluses, Heaven lengthened hours of twilight.
Li Bai, a poet without a family, feigned madness.
Qu Yuan left his state and forever acted upright.
We tend to weep over our land, in the west wind,
For the past hundred years, as we reach a height.

QIAN BINGDENG (1612-1693)
錢秉鐙

揚州訪汪辰初，其一

關橋乍泊旋相訪，問遍揚州識者疏。市井
草深尋巷入，江城花滿閉門居。僮驚客到
饒蠻語，篋付几收只漢書。我過七旬君逾
八，笑啼同是再生予。

Visiting Wang Chenchu at
Yangzhou, no.1

Once moored by Guan Bridge, I tried to visit you.
To tell me about you in Yangzhou, few were able.
Your secluded home in this river town of many
　　flowers was found
After I passed the market place, rank grass and
　　many a lane.
Your house boy was taken aback by my southern
　　dialect.
Only books on South Ming Dynasty lie in your
　　chest and on the table.
I am over seventy and you are over eighty.
Between tears and laughter, as survivors, let us
　　discuss being born again.

揚州訪汪辰初，其二

猶憶城隅方舊年，孤蹤早上漢陽船。一家
局促三間屋，廿載崎嶇萬里天。筆墨資生
何處賣，艱危紀事異地傳。白頭相見留深
坐，又損瓶中糴米錢。

Visiting Wang Chenchu at Yangzhou, no.2

I recall our meeting in Yangzhou on a former day.
Early on, to Hanyang your lone returning steps can
  be traced.
Your family lived in a cramped, shared space of a
  house,
For twenty years of hardship, myriad miles away.
Where could you have sold your books for a living?
Afar, your history of embroiled South Ming
  Dynasty gets embraced.
Both white-haired, you detained me for a long visit.
This can also deplete your grocery money in a way.

GU YANWU (1613-1682)
顧炎武

白下

白下西風落葉侵，重來此地一登臨。清笳
皓月秋依壘，野燒寒星夜出林。萬古河山

319

應有主，頻年戈甲苦相尋。從教一掬新亭
淚，江水平添十丈深。

Nanjing

Fallen leaves in the west wind take over Nanjing to
  my sight.
In my return trip here, I climb to a height.
From ramparts come tunes on reed pipes under a
  bright moon.
Cold stars and wild fires appear beyond the forest
  at night.
This land for millennia should have its rightful king.
For years relentlessly we are engaged in fight.
Let us weep like the Jin people at New Pavilion,
With tears swelling the river greatly, over our
  territorial right.

海上

滿地關河一望哀，徹天烽火照胥臺。名王
白馬江東去，故國降幡海上來。秦望雲空
陽鳥散，冶山天遠朔風回。遙聞 一下親征
詔，夢想猶虛授鉞才。

On the Sea

Sadly, war effects on our land fully lie.
South of the River, beacon fires light up the whole
  sky.

Like the usurper on a white horse, our foes charge.
For the Qing forces at sea, our surrender flags fly.
Our men at cloudless Qinwang Hill scatter like birds.
Invaders, like a northern blast, close in at Ye Hill.
From afar, I hear of the king leading the army.
My dream of offering my talent cannot apply.

汾州祭吳炎，潘檉章二節士

露下空林百草殘，臨風有慟奠椒蘭。韭溪
血化幽泉碧，蒿里魂歸白日寒。一代文章
亡左馬，千秋仁義在吳潘。巫招虞殯俱露
落，欲訪遺書遠道難。

A Sacrificial Poem for Two Men of Integrity in Fenzhou: Wu Yan and Pan Chengzhang

In the dewy wind, grasses of the empty grove wane.
I offer libation to men of integrity in grief and pain.
From Haoli, your souls returned under a cold, bright
  sun.
Your blood became jade at Jiu Brook where your
  bodies had lain.
Exalted men like Wu Kui and Pan Zhong are in
  Song history.
Essays of Zuo Qiuming and Sima Qian still remain.
Sorcerers summon souls with the dirge "Yu Bin",
  all wet with dew.
A visit to access your writings afar is hard to gain.

GONG DINGZHI (1615-1673)
龔鼎孳

上巳將過金陵

倚檻春愁玉樹飄，空江鐵鎖野煙消。興懷
何恨蘭亭感，流水青山送六朝。

On a Forthcoming Visit to Jinling on the Third Day of the Third Month

Sadly, I lean on a railing with music on a spring day.
Iron locks will not stop Qing navies on their way.
I regret the loss of my country, like those at Orchid
  Pavilion.
The Six Dynasties are gone; flowing waters and
  green hills remain.

WU JIAJI (1618-1684)
吳嘉紀

一錢行贈林茂之

先生春秋八十五，芒鞋重踏揚州土。故
交但有丘塋存，白楊摧盡留枯根。昔遊
倏過五十載，江山宛然人代改。滿地干
戈杜老貧，囊底徒餘一錢在。桃花李花
三月天，同君扶杖上漁船。杯深顏熱城

市遠，卻展空囊碧水前。酒人一見皆垂
淚，乃是先朝萬曆錢。

For Lin Maozi at a Farewell Feast

At the age of eighty-five, in shoes worn by monks,
Sir, you step on the soil of Yangzhou again.
Your old friends are here but under grave mounds.
White poplars all wilt and their roots wane.
Time went fast; you were here fifty years ago.
Human conditions change; hills and rivers remain.
Like Du Fu, you are poor with wars everywhere.
On only one coin in your pocket, you sustain.
Under peach and pear flowers in early spring,
You board a fishing boat with me and your cane.
Before green waters, you show your empty purse.
Far from the city, with much wine, a hot flushed
   look you gain.
Customers at the wine shop weep on seeing you
And your coin from a former dynasty, in the
   Wanli's reign.

ZHANG HUANGYAN (1620-1664)
張煌言

甲辰八月辭故里，其一

國亡家破欲何人，西子湖頭有我師。日月
雙懸于氏墓，乾坤半壁岳家祠。愧將赤子
分三席，擬為丹心借一枝。他日素車東浙
路，怒濤豈必屬鴟夷。

Leaving my Hometown in the Eighth Month of the Year of Jiachen (1664)

Where shall I go with a broken home and a fallen
  country?
By West Lake, the bodies of my teachers lay.
Like the sun and moon, Yu Qian shines in his grave.
For holding up half of our empire, the shrine of Yue
  Fei will stay.
Ashamed to be one of the three patriots,
I claim to win a spot with sincerity, in my own way.
For his loyalty, Wu Zixu may not be the "Spirit of
  the Waves" alone.
Let me be judged in my hearse on Dongzhi Road,
  on my funeral day.

FEI MI (1625-1701)
費密

朝天峽

一過朝天峽，巴山斷入秦。大江流漢水，
孤艇接殘春。暮色愁過客，風光惑榜人。
明年在何處？杯酒慰艱辛。

Chaotian Gorge

Right after Chaotian Gorge,
Ba Hill enters Shanxi province with its incline.
River Han joins the Yangzi.
My lone boat sails in waning spring.
The scenery enchants the oarsman.
Twilight saddens a traveler in passing.
Where shall I be next year?
Let me reward myself in hardship with wine.

MOU TONG (1627-1697)
繆彤

渡江

涼月漾中流，金山隱隱浮。尚餘
殘醉在，和夢到揚州。

Crossing the River

Among ripples, the cold, reflected moon flows.
The floating Gold Hill Isle vaguely shows.
I still have a tipsy head.
To Yangzhou, my dream goes.

ZHU YIZHUN (1629-1709)
朱彝尊

玉帶生歌

I

玉帶生，吾語汝：

汝產自端州，汝來自橫浦。幸免事降表。
僉名謝道清。亦不識大都，承旨趙孟頫。

能令信公喜。辟汝置幕府。
當年文墨賓，代汝一一數：
參軍誰？謝皐羽
寮佐誰？鄧中甫
弟子誰？王炎午

獨汝形軀短小，風貌樸古，步不能趨，口
不能語。既無鸜之鵒之活眼睛，兼少犀紋
彪紋好眉嫵。賴有忠信存，波濤孰敢侮？

II

是時丞相氣尚豪，可憐一舟之外無尺土，
共汝草檄飛書意良苦。四十四字銘厥
背，愛汝心堅剛不吐。

自從轉戰屢喪師，天之所壞不可支。驚
心柴市日，慷慨且誦臨終詩，疾風蓬勃
揚沙時。傳有十義士，表以石塔藏公
屍。生也亡命何所之？

或云西臺上，晞髮一叟涕漣洏，手擊
竹如意，生時亦相隨。冬青成陰陵骨
朽，百年蹤跡人莫知。

會稽張思廉，逢生賦長句。抱遺老人閣筆
看，七客寮中敢吞怒。

III

如今遇汝滄浪亭，漆匣初開紫衣露。洗汝
池上之寒泉，漂汝林端之霏霧。俾汝留傳
天地間，墨花恣灑鵝毛素。海桑陵谷又經
三百秋，以手摩挲尚如故。

註：‘玉帶生’乃南宋丞相文天祥之
藏硯，因硯上藏帶狀，生玉色石紋，
且硯銘有‘玉子帶兮磷磷’之語，
故元人命名‘玉帶生’

327

Mister Jade Belt

Mister Jade Belt,
Let me tell you:
A product of Duanzhou,
You came here through Hengpu Pass.
By luck, you took no part on the surrender papers,
Signed by Xie Daoqing
And in the Yuan capital,
The edicts copied by Zhao Mengfu.

You could make Wen Tianxiang happy,
And by his order, were kept in his headquarters.
Who were his secretaries?
Let me count for you, one by one:
Who was his adjutant?
Xie Gaoyu.
Who was his assistant?
Deng Zhongfu.
Who was his disciple?
Wang Yanwu.

Only you are short and small,
With a plain, old face.
You cannot walk.
You cannot talk.
Unlike mynas' eyes, your grains cannot be as bright.
Your lines cannot match the pretty brow-like stripes
    of rhinos and tigers.
However, relying on your loyalty and faith,

Against the odds of life, you can fight.

II

At that time, the high-spirited prime minister,
With piteously scant land to administer,
Wrote with you urgent dispatches with temerity.
The forty-four words engraved on your back
Expressed his love for your strength in adversity.

In succession, Wen suffered defeat,
A scheme of Heaven hard to beat.
On that fearful day of execution in Chaishi,
He chanted his last poem with noble generosity.
In the big sandstorm,
It was said ten righteous men
Buried his corpse inside a stone stupa.
Mister Jade Belt, where did you go as a refugee?

Others say, on West Fishing Terrace,
A man with loosened hair wept bitterly,
Hitting a bamboo ruyi to summon Wen's soul.
At that time, with your master you must be.
The bones of kings of Song Dynasty decayed.
A holly marking the graves became a shady tree.
For a hundred years, where did you flee?
Zhang Silian of Huixi
Came across you and wrote a seven-word poem.
Yang Weizheng, an old collector of Yuan,
Rested his writing brush and eyed you carefully.
Among other collected gems in his hut,

Named "Seven Guests", including himself,
Only you shone forth, like a rage, with much energy.

III

Now in Canglang Pavilion, we meet.
From the open lacquered box,
Your purple robe shows.
Three hundred years of upheaval have passed.
Touching you, I can feel your untarnished quality.
Let me wash you in a cold spring above a pond
And cleanse you with misty rain,
From the tips of many a tree.
Between Heaven and Earth will remain your legacy.
From a white goose-feathered brush,
Let your ink be sprayed heartily.
After another three hundred years of changes,

Note: "Mister Jade Belt" is an ink-stone owned by Prime Minister Wen Tianxiang (1236-1283) of the Southern Song Dynasty. Because of the stripes looking like jade and an engraved inscription with the phrase "The Phosphorescent Jade Belt", a person in the Yuan Dynasty named it "Mister Jade Belt".

XIA WANCHUN (1631-1647)
夏完淳

舟中憶邵景說寄子退

登臨澤國半荊榛，戰伐年年鬼哭新。一水
晴波青翰舫，孤燈暮雨白綸巾。何時壯志
酬明主，幾時浮生哭故人。萬里飛騰仍有
路，莫愁四海正風塵。

For Zitui, Recalling Shao Jingshuo on a Boat

New war casualties, as ghosts, weep every year.
On half of this swampy land, brambles have lain.
In my boat like a blue bird, I sail amid sunlit waves,
With a white headdress, by a lamp in the dusk rain.
When can I repay the kindness of my sage king
And in this uprooted life, weep for a dead friend?
Worry not about the turmoil everywhere.
On the distant road ahead, there is no dead-end.

精衛

北風蕩天地，有鳥鳴空林。志長羽翼短，
銜石隨浮沉。崇山日以高，滄海日以深。
愧非補天匹，延頸振哀音。辛苦徒自力，
慷慨誰為心？滔滔東逝波，勞勞成古今。

Jing Wei: the Legendary Bird that Carried Pebbles to Fill the Sea

A northern blast shook the earth and sky.
As a bird chirped in a grove that looked bare.
With a strong will and short wings,
It mouthed pebbles and floated in the air.
Lofty hills rose taller; gray seas ran deeper.
The bird went on, day to day and year to year.
It stretched its neck for a sad note in shame.
With the sky-mending feat, it failed to compare.
It toiled alone in vain.
Of its noble generosity, who was aware?
Like the big endless waves flowing east,
We all make history with no efforts to spare.

WANG SHIZHEN (1634-1711)
王士禎

悼亡詩

鋪首經秋澀綠苔，承塵蛛網任成灰。只餘
金縷裙猶在，爭忍無情報施來。

Mourning for my Wife

Green moss hides door rings since your dying day.
Cobwebs collecting dust go to ashes.
Only your frocks with gold threads still stay.
How can I bear to callously give them away?

曉雨重登燕子磯絕頂作

岷濤萬里望中收，振策危磯最上頭。吳楚
青蒼分極浦，江山平遠入新秋。永嘉南渡
人皆盡，建業西風水自流。灑淚重悲天塹
險，浴鳧飛燕滿汀洲。

Written on a Re-visit at the Peak of Swallow Ridge in a Dawn Rain

I see the waves of River Yangzi in its endless flow,
Propped on a cane at the ridge, as high as I can go.
Early fall comes to the flat, distant landscape,
With green waters and gray shores afar, as my eyes
    follow.
In the reign of Yongjia, the defeated moved south
    and all perished.
The river still runs in Nanjing, as west winds blow.
I weep in deep grief at this natural barrier.
The shoal is full of bathing wild ducks and many a
    flying swallow.

WANG YANHONG (?-1642)
王彥泓

無題

幾層芳樹幾層樓，只隔歡娛不隔愁。花外
遷延惟見影，月中尋覓略聞謳。吳歌淒斷

偏相入，楚夢微茫不易留。時節落花人病
酒，睡魂經雨思悠悠。

Untitled

Despite the heights of fragrant trees or towers that I
　　may attain,
I get no joy, just worries and pain.
I lingered beyond flowers to see only her shadow.
Searching under moonlight, her songs I could barely
　　ascertain.
Sad love tunes of Wu easily come into my heart.
It is hard to let vague, erotic dreams remain.
In late spring, I am lovesick and drunk,
For thinking of her in sleep, endlessly in the rain.

HAN QIA (1644-?)
韓洽

關山月

曉 角 數 聲 哀 ， 邊 風 卷 地 來 。 十 年
征 戍 客 ， 不 上 望 鄉 臺 。

Moonlit Passes and Hills

Sadly the morning bugles sound.
Border winds come sweeping the ground.

After ten years, drafted soldiers at the borders,
On the Home Watching Tower, cannot be found.

MENG YANG (Ming Dynasty)
孟洋

登岳陽樓

此地昔曾過，危樓今始攀。日銜天際樹，
雲動水中山。津驛趨三楚，江關控八蠻。
亂帆何處去，風浪未知還。

Climbing Yueyang Tower I start to climb this tall
tower today
Although I visited this area in the past.
Scudding clouds seem to move reflected hills.
Sunlight on trees in the horizon is steadfast.
Watchtowers of the stream control the eight
　　barbarian areas.
Past the riverside courier stations, access to the
　　Three Chus is fast.
Where are those boats with upset sails heading?
They are not returning yet on waves in the blast.

ZHANG MEIZHONG (Ming Dynasty)
章美中

仲春虎丘

孤閣生殘照，平臺下夕陰。疏鐘不知處，
人影在花林。古剎雲光杳，空山劍氣深。
依依池上月，猶復照登臨。

Tiger Mound in Mid-spring

The waning sunset falls on a lone pavilion,
With the flat terrace in the shade by twilight.
Human shadows appear in the groves with blooms,
With scant chimes of bells, from an unknown site.
An old temple is shaded at times by clouds.
On this deserted mound, the legendary sword is
    still bright,
The faint moon above the pond
Still shines on tourists with its light.

YUAN KAI (Ming Dynasty)
袁凱

白燕

故國飄零事已非，舊時王謝見應稀。月明
漢水初無影，雪滿梁園尚未歸。柳絮池塘

香入夢，梨花庭院冷侵衣。趙家姊妹多相
忌，莫向昭陽殿裡飛。

The White Swallow

In unstable times, things are not what they were
    yesterday.
Former rich neighborhoods are mostly in decay.
Your bright, moonlit body on waters is shadowless.
When it snowed in the royal garden, you were away.
With willow fuzz on the pond, I dream amid wafts
    of fragrance.
By courtyard pear blooms, through my robe, the
    chill makes headway.
Palace ladies, like the Zhao sisters of Han, are
    mainly jealous.
Fly not into mansions of the elite, like Zhaoyang
    Palace, I pray.

8
QING DYNASTY (1644-1911)

LI E (1692-1752)
厲鶚

湖樓題壁

水 落 山 寒 處 ， 盈 盈 記 踏 春 。 朱 闌
今已朽，何況倚闌人。

Inscribed on the wall of a Lake Tower

A brook drops from the cool hillside.
I fully recall an earlier spring outing here.
The red rails have already worn down,
Let alone the travelers of a yesteryear.

YAN SUICHENG (1694-?)
嚴遂成

龍泉關

燕晉分疆處，雄關控上游。地寒峰障日，
天近鶚橫秋。虎護千年樹，人披六月裘。
夜來風不止，嚴鼓出譙樓。

Dragon Spring Pass

At the boundary of Hebei and Shanxi,
Upstream, strong controlling forces of the pass lie.
Peaks block the sun to chill the earth.
In fall, water hawks cross the sky.
Tigers protect thousand-year-old trees.
People wear fur coats in July.
Rapid drumbeats emerge from watch towers.
At night, the wind does not die.

QIAN ZHAI (1708-1793)
錢載

出東林六七里望廬山

連峰出雲雲半開，奔渠卷雪響春雷。雲中
屈曲明如玉，都是天池頂瀉來。

Viewing Mount Lu about Six to Seven Miles from Donglin Temple

In spring, the waterfall thunders and sprints like
  rolling snow.
From linked peaks rise clouds spread halfway.
The twisted bulk among clouds, bright like jade,
Comes from the Pond of Heaven and its overflow.

YUAN MEI (1716-1798)
袁枚

澶淵

路出澶河水最清，當年照影見東征。滿朝
白面三遷議，一角黃旗萬歲聲。金幣無多
民已困，燕雲不取禍終生。行人立馬秋風
里，懊惱孱王早罷兵。

Chan Yuan

River Chan is most limpid, as I compare.
Armies heading east got reflections in a former year.
All the faint-hearted proposed moving the capital.
The imperial flag and cheering for the king gave
  barbarians a scare.
Giving up the Yan capital resulted in calamity.
The national spirit and economy were in disrepair.
In the fall wind, I stay my horse,
Irked by the coward king's early withdrawal in
  warfare.

一卷

一卷書開引睡遲，洞房屢問夜何其。高堂
憐惜小妻惱，垂老還如上學時。

One Scroll

One open book keeps my sleeping on hold.
On my bedtime hours at night, my wife often told.
My parents pity my young, frowning wife
And adjust my study hours when I am already old.

夜坐

夜坐西窗雨一齋，眼前物理苦難猜。燭光
案已猛如火，偏有飛蛾陣陣來。

Sitting at Night

I sit at night by the west window, with rain in excess.
The laws of nature before me are very hard to guess.
The candle on the stand is already glowing like fire,
But swarms of moths fly towards it nonetheless.

同金十一沛恩遊棲霞寺望桂林諸山

I

奇山不入中原界，走入窮邊才逞怪。桂林天小青山大，山山都立青天外。我來六月遊棲霞，天風拂面吹霜花。一輪白日忽不見，高空都被芙蓉遮。

山腰有洞五里許，秉火直入沖烏鴉。怪石形成千百種，見人欲動爭谽谺。萬古不知風雨色，一群仙鼠依為家。出穴登高望眾山，茫茫雲海墜眼前。

疑是盤古死後不肯化，頭目手足骨節相鈎連。又疑是女媧氏一日七十有二變，青紅隱現隨雲煙。蚩尤噴妖霧，屍羅袒右肩。猛士植竿髮，鬼母戲青蓮。

II

我知混沌以前乾坤毀，水沙激蕩風輪顛。山川人物熔在一爐內，精靈騰踔有萬千，彼此遊戲相愛憐。

忽然剛風一吹化爲石，清氣既散濁氣堅。至今欲活不得，欲去不能。只得奇形詭狀蹲人間。不然造化縱有千手眼，亦難一一施雕鐫。而況唐突真宰豈無罪，何以耿耿群飛卻衝天？

金臺公子酌我酒，聽我狂言呼否否。更指
奇峰印證之，出入白雲亂招手。幾陣南風
吹落日，騎馬同歸醉兀兀。我本天涯萬里
人，愁心忽掛西斜月。

Watching the Hills of Guilin on a Trip to Xixia Temple with Jin Peien, the Eleventh

These hills look peculiar at the far borders.
On the central plain, such strange hills do not lie.
The sky of Guilin is small; green hills are big.
Every hill stands beyond the blue sky.

In the sixth month, I visited Xixia Temple.
The wind from a height hit my face with frost.
Then the bright sun suddenly could not be seen.
Lotus-like hills barred my view; the tall sky was lost.

Into a hillside cave of a very good size,
I rushed with a torch thrusted at the crows.
Looking alive and active in the deep, wide valley,
In myriad shapes, each stony formation shows.

For ages, these pillars, unaware of wind and rain,
Made home for a pack of rats from the skies.
Outside the cave, I climbed to watch the hills.
A vast sea of clouds appeared before my eyes.

They could be the undecomposed body of Pangu,
With his head, eyes, limbs and bones hooked to stay,

Or in weak red and green, following cloud and mist,
The seventy-two changes of Nu Wa in a day.

They resemble Buddha baring his right shoulder
Or Chiyou letting off the devil's mist in a spray,
Or angry, fierce warriors with their pole-like hair,
Or the ghost mother engaging a lotus bloom in play.

II

I know the chaotic, primordial world was destroyed,
With the wheel of wind upside down
And water and sand in violent agitation.
Nature, people and things were fused in a cauldron.
Myriad goblins sprang upwards in motion,
For play with mutual care and loving emotion.

A sudden gale turned the goblins into rocks.
Their spirituality waned; the foul energy was strong.
Now they could neither live nor move,
Crouching in the human world.
With their weird looks, they had to get along.
Even if the Creator had a thousand hands and eyes,
It would be hard for him to sculpture every one.
To be rude to the Creator is not free of crime.
Why do the peaks all faithfully aim at the skies?

My elite friend, Jintai, served me wine.
In my babbles, he did not believe.
Again I pointed at the strange peaks as my proof.
Among white clouds, they could beckon and weave.

Puffs of the southern wind blew at sunset.
On horseback, we returned, feeling drunk.
Basically a wanderer afar, I suddenly found
With the west moon aslant, my sad heart had sunk.

JIANG SHIQUAN (1725-1785)
蔣士銓

響屧廊

不重雄封重艷情，遺蹤猶自慕傾城。憐伊
幾兩平生屐，踏碎山河是此聲。

The Corridor with the Sound of Clogs

King Wu preferred sensuous love to heroic fame.
From his bent on female charm, this relic came.
Through the sounds of these light, common clogs,
What a pity, the wreckage of his empire came.

LI JIAN (1747-1799)
黎簡

小園

水影動深樹，　山光窺短牆。秋村黃葉滿，
一半入斜陽。幽竹如人靜，　寒花為我芳。
小園宜小立，新月似新霜。

A Small Garden

Water ripples the tree's dark shadow.
Over a short wall, peep at hills that are still bright.
Yellow leaves fill the village in fall,
With one half under slanting sunlight.
Chilled flowers give me fragrance.
Quiet like us, secluded bamboos stay out of sight.
The new moon shines like early frost.
To me, a short stay in s small garden feels right.

HUANG JINGREN (1749-1783)
黃景仁

都門秋思，其一

四年書劍滯燕京，　更值秋來百感并。臺上
何人延郭隗？市中無處訪荊卿。雲浮萬里

傷心色，風送千秋變徵聲。我自欲歌歌不
得，好尋驕卒話平生。

Autumn Thoughts in the Capital, no 1

Stuck in the capital, four years of studies I spent.
The coming of autumn brings much lament.
A host like that of Jingke cannot be found.
Unlike Guo Kui, I am not sought for my talent.
Clouds scud for myriad miles in cheerless colors.
Sad sounds through wind-swept swings are sent.
I want to sing, but cannot.
To discuss life ambitions with caddies, I readily
    went.

都門秋思，其二

五劇車聲隱若雷，北邙惟見冢千堆。夕陽
勸客登樓去，山色將秋繞郭來。寒甚更無
修竹倚，愁多思買白楊栽。全家都在風聲
裡，九月衣裳未剪裁。

Autumn Thoughts in the Capital, no 2

Like hidden thunders, the rumble of carriages is
    slight.
Only countless graves on North Hill come in sight.
Towards fall, hill colors appear above the city wall.
I climb a tower, certain that sunset will have passed.

To look prim and proper in the chill,
I have no slender bamboo to lean on,
With a wish to plant white poplars, feeling downcast.
Warm clothing for fall has yet to be tailored.
I watch my whole family trapped in a blast.

後觀潮行

海風捲盡江頭葉，沙岸千人萬人立。怪底
山川忽變容，又報天邊海潮入。鷗飛艇亂
行雲停，江亦作勢如相迎。鵝毛一白尚天
際，傾耳已是風霆聲。

江流不合幾回折，欲折濤頭如折鐵。一折
平添百丈飛，浩浩長空舞晴雪。星馳電激
望已遙，江塘十里隨低高。此時萬戶同屏
息，想見窗櫺齊動搖。

潮頭障天天亦暮，蒼茫卻望潮來處。前陣
方平羅剎磯，後來又沒西興樹。獨客弔
影行自愁，大地與身同一浮。乘槎未許
到星闕，採藥何年傍祖州。賦罷觀潮長
太息，我尚輸潮歸即得。回首重城鼓角
哀，半空純作魚龍色。

Ballad on Watching Tidal Bores, a Successive Piece

A sea wind fully sweeps off the estuary's leaves.
Oddly, the river and hill look different from before.
Countless people stand on the sandbanks.
From the sky's verge starts the incoming tidal bore..
With still clouds, jumbled boats and gulls in flight,
The river plays host and gets ready to look right.
The crest is a white goose feather at the horizon,
Roaring like a thunderous gale as we listen tight.

It bends a few times to suit the river's regular flow.
Bending iron is as hard as breaking the first billow.
Once broken, it shoots up to a great height,
In the vast sky, as sunlit dancing snow.
Like sharp electricity or swift stars, it gets far away.
For ten miles, it changes the height it wants to stay.
Ten thousand families hold their breaths right now.
I can imagine lattices of windows all rock and sway.

The crests form a blockade and darken the sky,
Creating a wide span of grayness as they ply.
First tidal bores have flooded Luosha Ji,
With more coming, drowning trees of Xixing where
    they lie.
A wanderer mourns his shadow when walking alone.
To the same impermanence, Heaven and I am prone.
I cannot reach palaces among stars on a raft.
When can I find Zhuzhou's herbs of longevity, as
    known?

I sigh and sigh after writing about tidal bores,
Being worse off for not returning when due.
Drum and bugle in the capital sound sad as I recall.
Half of the sky looks like a fish-dragon in hue.

少年行

男兒作健向沙場，自愛登臺不望鄉。太白
高高天尺五，寶刀明月共輝光。

Ballad on Youth

A man for the battlefields, showing fight,
Loves to climb terraces but avoid his hometown's
  sight.
Close to the king like Venus at a height,
He holds a rare sword that shines like moonlight.

笥河先生偕宴太白樓醉中作歌

紅霞一片海上來，照我樓上華筵開。傾觴
綠酒忽復盡，樓上謫仙安在哉！謫仙之樓
樓百尺，笥河夫子文章伯。風流仿佛樓中
人，千一百年來此客。

是日江上同雲開，天門淡掃雙蛾眉。江從
慈母磯邊轉，潮到然犀亭下回。青山對面
客起舞，彼此青蓮一抔土。若論七尺歸

蓬蒿，此樓作客山是主。若論醉月來江
濱，此樓作主山作賓。

長星動搖若無色，未必常作人間魂。身後
蒼涼盡如此，俯仰悲歌亦徒爾。杯底空餘
今古愁，眼前忽盡東南美。高會題詩最
上頭，姓名未死重山丘。請將詩卷擲江
水，定不與江東向流。

Written while Drunk in a Feast at Taibai Tower, Hosted by Mister Sihe

Red clouds from the sea shine.
In a grand feast at the tower, we dine.
Where is Li Bai, a poet and an immortal?
Suddenly we have emptied many jugs of wine.
This tower, named after Li Bai, is tall.
Mister Xi He, as a writer, has no peer.
Gallant like Li Bai, you are his incarnate,
After a thousand years coming here.

Mount Tianmen looks like paired, faint antennae of
    a moth.
Over the river, snow looks like clouds of one color
    today.
By Cimu Cliff, the river starts to turn,
With a reflux at Yanxi Pavilion on its way.
Facing the green hill, guests dance.
Like Li Bai, in dust we shall all rest.
If our bodies should perish in the wilderness,

The hill would be a host and this tower a guest.
If he came for the river's moon with a tipsy head,
This tower would be a host and the hill a guest
   instead.

If Li Bai, the Changgeng Star, twinkled without
   color,
He would not always stay in our hearts.
Bleakness is common to all after death,
Despite sad songs delivered high and low.
Empty cups of wine and eternal grief will follow.
Here are the best poets of the southeast that I know.
Hills may crumble but forever their names will go.
Please throw my poems in the river and let me vow.
My fame will not be lost in the eastward flow.

SHU WEI (1765-1815)
舒位

花生日詩，魏塘道中作

啼鶯如夢送歸艎，日子平分夜未央。願取
鴛鴦湖里水，釀成春酒寄花嘗。

The Birthday of Flowers, Written on the Way to Weitang

To return amid the dreamy oriole's trill, I am due.
The sun and moon make equal time; the night is not
through.
From my boat, I wish to take some water of Lake
Mandarin Duck,
So flowers can taste my spring brew.

空谷

空谷佳人絕世姿，鳩媒一去苦相思。天寒
修竹娟娟靜，翠袖蒼茫獨立時。

Empty Valley

This beautiful lady in the empty valley is peerless.
With the libel off, she yearns for her husband,
feeling cheerless.
Leaning quietly against a slender bamboo, on a cold
day,
On this vast land, she is independent and fearless.

雪夜雜詩

秋老關山唱采薇，刀鐶無恙遠人歸。舊時
楊柳芳菲盡，一朵瑤花繡鐵衣。

A Random Poem on a Snowy Night

Homesick border soldiers sing "Pluck Vetches" in
 late fall.
My man returned from afar with no wounds at all.
Like willows of the old days, I am plain and pale.
Let me stitch a jade flower onto his coat of mail.

玉屏山看晚霞

水上屏山山下池，暮雲樓閣映參差。中間
一抹紅霞影，小李丹青小謝詩。

Watching Evening Clouds on Yuping Hill

Yuping Hill towers a pool below.
Reflected dark clouds and pavilions vaguely show.
A daub of red clouds appears in the middle,
Reminding me of Li's paintings and Xie's poems
 years ago.

楊花詩

歌殘楊柳武昌城，撲面飛花管送迎。三月
水流春太老，六朝人去雪無聲。較量妄命
誰當薄，吹落鄰家爾許輕。我住天涯最飄
蕩，看渠如此不勝情。

Willow Flowers

At Wuchang City, endless songs of farewell flow.
The fuzz hits the face as you come and go.
The river runs in the third month in late spring.
A lady in the Six Dynasties thought of them as snow.
How do my life's wanderings compare with theirs?
Who lands more softly elsewhere as winds blow?
I am adrift furthermost at the sky's verge.
Enflessly, willow flowers make me feel low.

題柳

一絲楊柳一梭鶯，費許天工織得成。已是
春愁無片斷，峭風猶作剪刀聲。

Willows

Each strand of willow leaf or every swift oriole
Takes much effort from Heaven to be made.
Spring sorrow is already endless.
Sharp winds still sound like the scissor-blade.

永州

一水如衣帶，風吹入永州。朝陽岩上日，
遙見瀟湘樓。庵塔草書好，谿山小記幽。
榜人問前路，未解意勾留。

Yongzhou

The river flows like the belt of my robe.
Into Yongzhou, the wind is well on its way.
Under the sun, on Chaoyang Ridge,
I can see Xiaoxiang Tower far away.
Xi Hill gives me a fleeting moment of peace.
On the temple's pagoda, a fine inscription is in
    display.
The boatman asks about my route ahead,
Failing to sense my wish to stay.

CHEN WENSHU (1771-1843)
陳文述

夏日雜詩

水窗低傍畫欄開。枕簟蕭疏玉漏催。一夜
雨聲涼到夢，萬荷葉上送秋來。

Summer Days

By the painted rail is my low waterside window.
Time flies as I lie on my thin mat and pillow.
I get chilled in my dream during the overnight,
    noisy rain.
Fall is here as myriad lotus leaves sway to and fro.

CHENG ENZHE (1785-1837)
程恩澤

渡淮即事

汝穎沙渦競短長，還收瞧澮五文章。遂磨
洪澤而東鏡，似築深紅以外牆。天際數峰
眉嫵翠，中流一畫墨痕蒼。即看歌舞雄都
會，何處風雲古戰場。

Current Events on Crossing River Huai

In length, four tributaries, Ru, Ying, Sha and Guo,
  vie.
Five colors of riverlets, Qiao and Hui, neatly lie.
It drains east to form Lake Hongze, like a honed
  mirror.
To be a dark red wall on River Yangzi, it seems to
  try.
The mid-stream is a painting, done in dark black ink.
Like brows, green, charming peaks stand at the edge
  of the sky.
Where are the famed battlefields of the past?
In the grand metropolis, see the singers and dancers
  that ply.

GONG ZHIZHEN (1792-1841)
龔自珍

西郊落花歌

西郊落花天下奇，古來但賦傷春詩。西郊
車馬一朝盡，定庵先生沽酒來賞之。先生
探春人不覺，先生送春人又嗤。呼朋亦得
三四子，出城失色神皆痴。

如錢塘潮夜澎湃，如昆陽戰晨披靡，如八
萬四千天女洗臉罷，齊向此地傾胭脂。奇
龍怪鳳愛漂泊，琴高之鯉何反欲上天為？

玉皇宮中空若洗，三十六界無一青娥
眉。又如先生平生之憂患，恍惚怪
誕百出難絕期。先生讀書畫之藏，
最喜維摩卷裡多清詞。

又聞淨土落花深四寸，瞑目觀想尤神
馳。西方淨國未可到，下筆綺語何漓
漓。安得樹有不盡之花更雨新好者，三
百六十日長是落花時。

Falling Blooms at the West Outskirts

Falling blooms of the west outskirts are wonderful
   and transcendent.
Since the old days, poems are only on spring lament.
When carriages stop going to the west outskirts,
I arrive with wine for enjoyment.

People jeer at me for my saying goodbye to spring.
They would not notice me when I came and went.
I call up three to four friends.
Outside the city, we look mesmerized and shocked
    in merriment.

They remind me of the night tidal bores of Qiantang,
The dawn defeat of the battle at Kunyang,
And the face-washing of countless fairies.
To this land, all their rouge is sent.
They resemble strange dragons and phoenixes in
    wanderlust,
Or for whatever reason, the carp of Qingao on its
    ascent.

The Jade Emperor's palace is cleaned out.
In the thirty-six layers of the sky,
All ladies with black moth-like brows are absent.
I also recall the vicissitudes of my life
With uncommon absurdities, numerous and ever-
    present.
I read only Buddhist classics.
On the fresh ideas in the vimalakirti sutra, I am bent.

I heard about Buddha's land
And its four-inch thick fallen blooms.
With closed eyes, I quickly visualize the scene with
    longings and intent.
I have yet to reach the Nirvana in the west.
From streams of sensual writings, I cannot relent.

I wish trees could flower on and on,
Raining down new pretty ones, on their descent.
Then for three hundred and sixty days,
The time for falling blooms would be omnipresent.

秋心

秋心如海復如潮，但有秋魂不可招。漠漠
鬱金香在臂，亭亭古玉佩當腰。氣寒西北
何人劍？聲滿東南幾處簫？斗大明星爛無
數，長天一月墜林梢。

My Autumn Mood

My mood in autumn is like sea waves at a height.
Her soul in fall cannot be summoned for my sight.
The fragrance of her tulips still remains on my arm.
Her old, long jade pendants from her waist looks
    right.
Who responds to flute notes of complaint in the
    southeast?
Against invaders from the cold northwest, who will
    fight?
The moon falls from tree tops of the tall sky.
Countless big stars are shining bright.

WEI YUAN (1794-1857)
魏源

高郵州署秋日偶題

傳舍官如住寺僧，半年暫住此荒城。湖邊
無處看山色，但愛千家帶雨耕。

A Casual Verse on a Fall Day at
my Office in Gaoyouzhou

As the courier station's short-term staff, like a monk
I appear.
I live in this deserted town for half a year.
By the lake, in the rain, I find no hill colors,
But the sight of countless families tilling the soil can
endear.

HE SHAOJI (1799-1873)
何紹基

寧羌川

回首終南尚郁蒼，鞭絲帽影已新霜。郵亭
尚記金牛峽，部落空傳白馬羌。漾水兩源
偏共嶺，蜀山萬點此分疆。近城復見平川
景，衰柳晴懸落日黃。

River Ningqiang

As I look back, the lush greeneries of Mount
    Zhongnan still remain.
A new coat of frost is for my whip and hat to gain.
I can recall Golden Ox Road with courier stations,
But the tale of the White Horse group of the Qiang
    tribe is not certain.
This is our border with Shu of countless hills.
From one hill, River Ningqiang and River Han drain.
Under bright sunset, waning willows all look yellow.
Near the city, plains and streams are in sight again.

LU YITONG (1805-1863)
魯一同

明月

明月非春水，如何滿地流？離離出海嶠，
盈盈注金溝。花露時翻鵲，風江有去舟。
多愁伴看汝，扶影傍南樓。

Bright Moon

The bright moon is not spring water.
Fully on the ground, how can it flow?
Brightly it rises from a tall hill by the sea,
Filling rivers to the brim with a golden glow.
Magpies flip often among floral dew.

On the windy stream, a departing boat is to go.
It accompanies you in intense sorrow,
Supporting you by South Tower with your shadow.

重有感

披髮何人訴上蒼，孤舟百戰久低昂。前軍
力盡宵泅水，幕府謀深坐裹糧。握節魂歸
雲冉冉，揚灰風疾海茫茫。神光金甲分明
見，濺血銜鬚下大荒。

More Reflections

Who would petition Heaven so help could be sent?
The naval chief fought alone, often in lament.
The exhausted vanguard swam at night for safety.
From the scheming commander, no support was lent.
A dusty blast sweeps across the vast sea under slow
    clouds.
Your soul will return with a tally and the power to
    represent.
Your golden armor with spiritual light will shine.
By giving your life and blood, you make history,
    past and present.

YAO XIE (1805-1844)
姚燮

哭張廉際亮

伉爽平生意氣多，短車塵巷喜頻過。更番
雪我愁中涕，強忍聽君醉里歌。白髮未能
留歲月，夕陽誰使滿山河。不如宣武門前
柳，尚有荒枝照逝波。

Weeping for the Incorruptible Zhang Jiliang

Energetic in life, you were upright, open and fair.
You loved to befriend commoners in neighborhoods,
    plain and bare.
Once again, you wiped off my snivels in sorrow.
With your songs while drunk, I forced myself to
    bear.
Hills and rivers are fully and naturally under sunset.
I fail to stop time and my gray hair.
Willows by Xuanwu Gate will shine through time.
With them, humans cannot compare.

ZHENG ZHEN (1806-1864)
鄭珍

雲門礓

牢江驅白雲，　流入蒼龍門。　門高一千仞，
柱天氣何尊！　蕩蕩百步中，　水石互吐吞。
阿房廣樂作，　巨窖洪牛奔。　餘波噴青壁，
震怒不可馴。　眉水若處女，　春風吹綠裙。
迎門卻挽去，　碧入千花村。

我行始兩日，　異境壯旅魂。　扶懸自何年？
信有真宰存。　夕陽一反射，　倒樹明蒼根。
老蝠抱石花，　紅暈雙車輪。　仰嘆山水奇，
俯躓造化跟。　想見混成日，　待與見者論。

Stone Steps of Gateway-to-the-Clouds

Like a gray dragon riding white clouds,
Between steep, door-like cliffs, River Lao flows.
How majestic the pillars look against the sky!
For myriad feet high, each cliff goes.
In a hundred steps, the torrent runs off in spits
And seems to devour the steps as it swallows.
The roar is heavenly music from Qin Palace
Or in a huge cellar, the noise of big running cows
      with echoes.
Onto the green walls, the angry breakers
Look untamable and make a spray.
Like virgins, calm surfaces are as level as brows,

Displaying a green frock in spring as a wind blows.
Approaching the cliffs, the winding flow is seen,
Entering Qianhua Village, in a reflux of green.

This unusual place perks my spirit in traveling
After two days of my trip have just gone through.
Where did cliffs start to hang along the waters?
That a real Creator exists, I find it to be true.
Gray roots of fallen trees bare
In the sunset with its reflected glow.
An old bat holds onto a rock with lichens
Forming another wheel-like sun with a red hue.
I look up and sigh, admiring the wonderful sight,
And in the Creator's footsteps, bow and follow.
I shall wait to discuss, with another eye-witness,
The imagined work out of chaos. on the First Day
    long ago.

WANG KAIYUN (1833-1916)
王闓運

圓明園詞

I

宜春苑中螢火飛，建章長樂柳十圍。離宮
從來奉遊豫，皇宮那復在郊圻？舊池澄綠

流燕薊，洗馬高粱遊牧地。北藩本鎮故元
都，西山自擁興王氣。

九衢塵起暗連天，辰極星移北斗邊。溝洫
填淤成斥鹵，宮廷映帶覓泉源。淳泓稍見
丹棱沜，陂陀先起暢春園。暢春風光秀
南苑，霓旌鳳蓋長遊宴。地靈不惜邑山
湖，天題更創圓明殿。

II

圓明始賜在潛龍，因旧邸第作郊宮。十八
籬門隨曲澗，七楹正殿倚喬松。軒堂四十
皆依水，山石參差盡亞風。甘泉避暑因留
蹕，長楊扈從且弢弓。

純皇纘業當全盛，江海無波待遊幸。行所
留連賞四園，畫師寫放開雙境。誰道江南
風景佳，移天縮地在君懷。當時只擬成
靈囿，小費何曾數露臺。殷勤毋佚箴驕
念，豈意元皇失恭儉！

III

秋獮俄聞罷木蘭，妖氛暗已轉離坎。吏
治陵遲民困腐，長鯨跋浪海波枯。始驚
計吏憂財賦，欲賣行宮助轉輸。沈吟五
十年前事，厝火薪邊然已至。揭竿敢欲
犯阿房，探丸早見誅文吏。此時先帝見
憂危，詔選三臣出視師。宣室無人侍前

席，郊壇有恨哭遺黎。年年輦路看春草，處處傷心對花鳥。

玉女投壺強笑歌，金杯擲酒連昏曉。四時景物愛郊居，玄冬入內望春初。裊裊四春隨鳳輦，沈沈五夜遞銅魚。內裝頗學崔家髻，諷諫頻除姜后珥。玉路旋悲車轂鳴，金鑾莫問殘燈事。鼎湖弓箭恨空還，郊壘風煙一炬間。

IV

玉泉悲咽昆明塞，惟有銅犀守荊棘。青芝岫裡狐夜啼，繡漪橋下魚空泣。何人老監福園門，曾綴朝班奉至尊。昔日喧闐厭朝貴，於今寂寞喜遊人。遊人朝貴殊喧寂，偶來無復金閨客。賢良門閉有殘磚，光明殿毀尋頹壁。文宗新構清輝堂，為近前湖納曉光。

妖夢林神辭二品，佛城舍衛散諸方。湖中蒲稗依依長，階前蒿艾蕭蕭響。枯樹重抽盜作薪，遊鱗暫躍驚逢網。別有開雲鏤月臺，太平三聖昔同來。寧知亂竹侵苔落，不見春風泣露開。平湖西去軒亭在，題壁銀鈎連倒薤。金梯步步度蓮花，綠窗處處留贏黛。

V

當時倉猝動鈴駝，守宮上直餘嬪娥。蘆笳
短吹隨秋月，豆粥長飢望熱河。上東門
開胡雛過，正有王公班道左。敵兵未爇
雍門萩，牧童已見驪山火。應憐蓬島一
孤臣，欲持高潔比靈均。丞相避兵生取
節，徒人拒寇死當門。

即今福海冤如海，誰信神州尚有神！百年
成毀何匆促，四海荒殘如在目。丹城紫禁
猶可歸，豈聞江燕巢林木？廢宇傾基君好
看，艱危始識中興難。

VI

已懲禦史言修復，休遣中官織錦紈。錦
紈竭枉江南賦，鴛文龍爪新還故。總饒
結彩大宮門，何如舊日西湖路！西湖地
薄比郇瑕，武清暫住已傾家。惟應魚稻
資民利，莫教鶯柳鬥宮花。詞臣詎解論
都賦，挽輅難移幸雒車。相如徒有上林
頌，不遇良時空自嗟！

Yuanming Garden

I

Fireflies flew in the Yichun Garden.
By Jianzhang and Changle palaces stood many a
   willow.

The traveling palace was always built in Henan.
Why they put one in the outskirts of the capital we
　　do not know.
Beijing, the old capital of Yan, with a limpid green
　　lake,
And rivers, Xima and Gaoliang, used to be the royal
　　hunting ground.
As the former capital of Yuan, it was a frontier town.
On West Hill, the roused energy of kings was found.

The Polar Star moved near the Big Dipper.
Dust from a dynastic change darkened all the sky.
After a landfill of the salty, alkaline soil, a spring
　　was sought
For a sharp belt of waterways for palaces nearby.
In the style of Danling Pond like a half moon,
Changchun Garden was built from a man-made
　　incline.
It could compare well with South Garden
Where in regal style, the king had feasts and wine.

Earth Spirit let the lake water from Yi Hill flow to
　　this site.
The Son of Heaven named the garden "Round" and
　　"Bright".

II

First used by the king's fourth son, Hidden Dragon,
The study became expanded as a country retreat.
Eighteen gates with fences followed a winding river.
A tall pine overtopped the seven-pillared main hall.
Forty grand parlors flanked the waters.
Jagged rocks made wind-breakers, one and all.
With attendants and arrows in quivers for hunting,
The king was escorted here often to escape the heat.

On inspection tours in a peaceful reign,
King Qianlong's inherited power reached its height.
An artist drew pictures of two architectural styles
And four gardens of traveling palaces, to his delight.
When alerted to fine scenes in South of the River,
He had them transported and reduced for his easy
    place of call.
At that time, he wanted a zoo like "Ling You" of a
    Zhou king.
How high the cost, like that for a Han king's terrace,
    was thought small.

A hard-working king should heed vanity.
Who would think he lacked frugality and humility?

III

Just before fall hunting at Mulan stopped,
Eight Trigram Sect had sacked the palace in vain.
Corrupt officials impoverished the people.

Two opium wars, like long whales, bled them again.
The Head of Treasury began to worry about funds,
Hoping to sell the retreat for a relief from the gain.
Let me chant about this history of fifty years.
Like lying on just lit firewood, the crisis was hidden
    but certain.
The Taiping rebels pressed towards the capital.
Already, officials were commoners' targets of
    assassination.
At this point, King Xianfeng saw the danger
And sent three ministers as heads of suppression.
He sighed for the lack of wise counsel
And wept in the outskirts for survivors in confession.
He watched spring grass in his carriage each year.
Before flowers and birds, he was sad everywhere.

With palace ladies in games, he forced himself to
    smile.
Wine parties went on night after night.
The king loved to live in a country retreat,
Only staying in the capital in winter until spring.
Four ladies also rode in the imperial carriage.
Through the five periods at night, the brazen fish
    charm was passed.
The king followed Han culture, like the Han milk
    mother in his hire.
And often got subtle hints against excesses.
On rattling carriages, he soon fled in sorrow.
In the palace, about wars he did not inquire.
Regrettably, he died in his retreat in Yehol.

When forts in the outskirts fell, to Yuanming
    Garden, foreigners set fire.

IV

Now Jade Spring chokes in sad tears, draining into
    clogged Lake Kunming.

Guarding brambles is only a brazen rhino on site.
Among green rocks, foxes cry at night.
Under Xiuyi Bridge, fish weep in vain.
An old servant, quartered by the gate of Fu Garden,
Through several dynasties, served the royalty.
In loneliness, he enjoys visitors and their company.
He loathes the din of those with power and might.
Compared to the court elite, other visitors are quiet.
The rare guest of the court is no longer in sight.
At the shut Xianliang Gate, some broken bricks lie.
In Guangming Palace, fallen walls are in blight.
The new Qinghui Hall of King Xianfeng burned,
Near the front lake, built for accessing dawn light.

It was rumored that a forest spirit left the garden.
Statues of Buddha, like those in Sravasti, were
    looted outright.
Moxas before the steps rustle on and on.
Rushes in the lake grow to a great height.
New shoots from wilted trees become stolen
    firewood.
Jumping fish meeting nets move with fright.
In peaceful times, the Cloud-Moon Terrace of a

favored consort
Was visited by three kings, year to year.
Bamboos have overtaken it, with overgrown moss.
Of spring breeze and dewdrops, we are not aware,
Save inscriptions in strong brush strokes on walls.
West Lake is no longer in the garden; just tall
　　pavilions stand there.
Ladies stepped on gold lotus pads of the adorned
　　stair,
With bluish-black painted brows by green windows
　　everywhere.

V

At that time, the sudden retreat began without delay.
Guards and maids were left to stay.
Towards Jehol, they hungrily ate soy milk and gruel,
Under the fall moon, with tunes from reed pipes in
　　play.
Foreigners, called "Barbarian Chicks", entered
　　Dongbian Gate.
For negotiators, pacifists lined the pathway.
No sooner had the enemy troops broken in
Than a fire, like that at Li Shan, started right away.
The only minister who resisted should be valued,
Who, like lofty Qu Yuan, drowned himself unarmed.
A resister faced death guarding the door.
The spineless prime minister dodged and lived
　　unharmed.

Injustice lies deep like the waters of Lake Fu.
Who would believe in God on this land?
How fast was the destruction of centennial buildings?
How sharp was the image of the full-scale ravage at
    hand!
The king could still go back to the Forbidden City.
Displaced citizens missed their nests on return.
Look hard at wrecked structures and foundations.
Through hardship and danger, about national revival
    we first learn.

VI

If they punished the censor for discussing a plan of
    restoration,
Why did they not cancel costly wedding gowns in
    brocade?
When taxes from South of the River were exhausted,
Robes with stitched mandarin ducks and dragons
    got newly made.
Already decorations for the palace gate were of the
    top grade,
In no comparison to the old Yuanming Garden.
Like Xunxia, the land near the garden is poor.
The temporary retreat bankrupted us with taxes paid.
The garden let palace ladies vie with orioles and
    willows.
To commoners, rice fields and fish ponds should
    have come to their aid.
It was hard to change the mind of the king,
Although a proposal to move the capital to Xian was
    sent.

Xiangru failed to warn the Han king at Shanglin
   Garden.
Over unlucky periods of misrule, I sigh in lament.

SHEN ZENGZHI (1850-1922)
沈曾植

西湖雜詩

湖上波光罨雪光，張祠清絕勝劉庄，仙人
自愛樓居好，六面山屏曉鏡妝。

A Random Poem at West Lake

The glare of snow pales under the gleam of the lake.
The most serene Zhang shrine does not let the Liu
   mansion overtake.
By a mirror-like lake, the hills form a six-sided
   screen.
The shrine is fit for a fairy on her toilet at daybreak.

KANG YOUWEI (1858-1927)
康有爲

秋登越王臺

秋風立馬越王臺，混混蛇龍最可哀。十七史從何説起，三千劫幾歷輪回。腐儒心事呼天問，大地山河跨海來。臨睨飛雲橫八表，豈無倚劍歎雄才。

Climbing Yue King Terrace in Fall

I stay my horse at Yue King Terrace as fall winds
    blow.
Mixing good and bad people is the greatest sorrow.
The history of China is too complex to talk about.
Like kalpas, dynasties come and go.
A rotten scholar like me asks of the sky,
About the fate of this big, seaboard land that I know.
Glancing sideways at clouds flying to infinity,
Leaning with my sword, I sigh for the lack of a
    talented hero.

蘇村臥病寫懷，其一

少年心事本拏雲，南望樵山日又曛。賣畚何慚王景略？畫虀故是范希文。擬經制禮吾何敢？蠟屐持籌事未分。稷契許身空笑爾，稻梁不及鶩鵝群。

Expressing my Mind while Sick
in Bed in Su Village, no.1

Youthful aspirations are sky high in the main.
South of Xiqiao Hill, it is sunset again.
Wang Meng, the strategist, once proudly sold dust
    baskets.
Fan Zhongyan, the statesman, diced pickles for more
    meals to gain.
How do I dare plan for the country with the classics
    and rites?
A leaning towards being hired or retired, I have yet
    to ascertain.
Jeer at me for hoping to be another top minster
    like Ji and Qi.
I am not a duck or goose, after each morsel or grain.

蘇村臥病寫懷，其二

縱橫宙合一微塵，偶到人間閱廿春。世界
開新逢進化，賢師受道愧傳薪。名山渺莽
千秋業，大地蒼茫七尺身！南望九江北京
國，拊心辜負總酸辛。

Expressing my Mind while Sick
in Bed in Su Village, no.2

Like dust in the universe, I am just another fellow.
I happened to have been born twenty years ago.

With shame I fail to share what I learned from my
  teachers.
Through progress, new world orders go.
The prospect is hazy in revitalizing China, a project
  for the millennia.
As an adult in this vast, boundless land, I feel low.
I have let down my compatriots in Beijing and
  teachers in Jiujiang,
Feeling sour over labor lost on the republican cause,
  now in limbo.

出都留別諸公，其一

滄海驚波百怪橫，唐衢痛哭萬人驚。高峰
突出諸山妒，上帝無言百鬼獰。豈有漢廷
思賈誼？拼教江夏殺禰衡！陸沉預為中原
嘆，他日應思魯二生。

Farewell to my Friends as I
Leave the Capital, no.1

Myriad weird foreigners came from fearful waves of
  the deep sea.
In fright, countless nationals wept bitterly.
Many feel jealous of my uncommon, pointed views.
The silenced king let the Dowager and her men
  misrule freely.
Like Ni Heng, I brave death to be true to my
  character.

How come I am ignored by the court like Jia Yi?
I sigh for the future collapse of our empire.
The grit of two patriots of Lu and mine will be in
    history.

出都留別諸公，其二

天龍作騎萬靈從，獨立飛來縹緲峰。懷抱
芳馨蘭一握，縱橫宙霧千重。眼中戰國成
爭鹿，海內人才孰臥龍？撫劍長號歸去
也，千山風雨嘯青鋒。

Farewell to my Friends as I Leave the Capital, No.2

Let me ride the Heavenly Dragon followed by
    countless spirits
And fly to the far dim peaks alone.
I embrace the highest ideals, like fragrant orchids,
In this universe with fog overgrown.
I see China being partitioned just as the Warring
    States.
Who among us is the secluded man of talent, left
unknown?
As I leave, I touch my sword and let out a long howl,
In a rainstorm on myriad hills, with my sharp blade
    in tone.

TAN SITONG (1865-1898)
譚嗣同

題宋徽宗畫鷹

落日平原拍手呼，畫中神俊世非無。當年
狐兔縱橫甚，只少台臣似郅都。

Inscribed on a Painting of Eagles
by Huizhong of Song

The eagles in the painting, at the end of the day,
Show spiritual charm and common obedience skills
    in play.
A censor like Zhi Du, called "The Gray Eagle",
    was absent.
Traitors, like foxes and hares, controlled the court
    all the way.

獄中題壁

望門投止思張儉，忍死須臾待杜根。我自
橫刀向天笑，去留肝膽兩昆侖。

Inscribed on the Wall of my Prison

All doors opened to a Tang official wrongly
    imprisoned.
A Han executioner let a just counselor feign death
    and run free.

I hold a sword across my chest and laugh to the sky.
In life and death, these two lofty men embolden me.

潼關

終古高雲簇此城，秋風吹散馬蹄聲。河流
大野猶嫌束，山入潼關未解平。

Tong Pass

High clouds wind this town as in the past.
Galloping horses sound noiseless in the fall blast.
Rivers in the big wilderness already mind the banks.
The height of hills into Yong Pass will last.

ZHANG BINGLIN (1868-1936)
章炳麟

獄中贈鄒容

鄒容吾小弟，被髮下瀛洲。快剪刀除辮，
乾牛肉作餱。英雄一入獄，天地亦悲秋。
臨命須摻手，乾坤只兩頭。

For Zhou Rong in Prison

Zhou Rong, my little brother with disheveled hair,
Left for Japan to seek something new.
He ate beef jerky for food
And with scissors, quickly cut off his hair queue.
Once this hero was jailed,
Heaven and Earth grieve for justice undue.
Facing death, we should join hands,
In this universe, just me and you.

時危四首，其一

時危挺劍入長安，流血先爭五步看。誰道
江南徐騎省，不容臥榻有人鼾。

Four Poems on Dangerous Times, no.1

At this dangerous time, to the capital I wish to go,
With my sword for a bloody battle against the
    republic's foe.
Xu sought help for South Tang from a neighboring
    king,
Who said, "I do not accept a snoring bed-fellow".

時危四首，其二

威儀已嘆漢宮消，繡緷諸于足自聊。明鏡
不煩相曉照，阿龍行步故超超。

Four Poems on Dangerous Times, no 2

Over the end of the grand republic, I sigh.
To prop it up for looks and comfort, we try.
Like a bright mirror, the intent of Yuan for kingship
　is clear.
The integrity of a minister of Jin, A Long, is what
　I go by.

JIN TIANYU (1874-1947)
金天羽

黃鶴樓

平楚山河一掌收，謫仙人去我登樓。英雄
王霸思江表，戰鬥風煙急上游。手酌鸕鶿
傾漢水，腳翻鸚鵡戲滄州。浮雲劫火衆頭
換，幾輩生兒似仲謀。

Yellow Crane Tower

This area with flat treetops is small, from a height.
I climb the tower after Li Bai had left the site.
Heroes and hegemonic kings ruled South of the
　River.

Upstream at the Red Cliffs, wind and smoke quickly
 aided the fight.
Hand each other cormorant cups of wine from River
 Han.
Kick off parrot goblets to tease Parrot Isle for our
 delight.
Dynasties and people change, like floating clouds
 and kalpas with fire.
When can we beget a son like Zhongmou as bright?

QIU JIN (1875-1907)
秋瑾

對酒

不惜千金賣寶刀，貂裘換酒也堪豪。一腔
熱血勤珍重，灑去猶能化碧濤.

Before Wine

To sell my jeweled sword, my decision is made.
Bartering furs for wine is a grandiose trade.
Let me treasure often the patriotism in me.
My splashed blood in sacrifice will be waves in jade.

秋海棠

栽植思深雨露同，一叢淺淡一叢濃。平生
不借春光力，幾度開來鬥晚風。

Begonias

I give them the same amount of water and heartfelt
  care.
The color of one bunch is deep and the other fair.
Never in their lives do they need spring-like weather.
Fighting the fall wind, they flower several times a
  year.

感憤

莽莽神州嘆陸沉，救時無計愧偷生。摶沙
有願興亡楚，博浪無椎擊暴秦。國破方知
人種賤，義高不礙客囊貧。經營恨未酬同
志，把劍悲歌涕淚橫。

Feeling Angry

Our big country is sinking on a nose dive.
Clueless to help, I feel ashamed to be alive.
At Bolangsha, an assassin missed killing the brute
  Qin king.
To unite our people like loose sand, I want to strive.
A poor person can keep his lofty ideals.

An inferior people cannot let their country survive.
Sword in hand, I sing and weep, sniffing on and on.
I regret letting my compatriots down, hard as I
    connive.

日人石開索和即用原韻

漫云女子不英雄，萬里乘風獨向東，詩思
一帆海空濶，夢魂三島月玲瓏。銅駝已陷
悲回首，汗馬終慚未有功。如許傷心家國
恨，那堪客里度春風。

In Response to a Poem Written by Mister Ishii, a Japanese, Using his Rhymes

Do not say a woman is no hero.
Alone towards east, on countless windy miles I go.
I dream of Japan with a lovely moon.
Under the broad sky at sea, my poetic thoughts flow.
Like a rare horse, I am ashamed of my fruitless
    efforts.
Like a brazen camel, I look back at my fallen
    empire in sorrow.
So broken-hearted over the sufferings of my land,
How can I be an indulged guest as spring winds
    blow?

詠燕

飛向花間兩翅翔，燕兒何用苦奔忙？謝王
不是無茅屋，偏向盧家玳瑁梁。

Swallows

They flap their wings toward many a flower.
What makes swallows toil, going higher or lower?
Straw huts of the poor are everywhere,
But they nest on turquoise beams of those in power.

CHEN ZENGSHOU (1878-1949)
陳曾壽

湖上雜詩，其一

殘夢鈞天付混茫，瓜廬仍占水雲鄉。荷聲
忽滿三千界，成就南軒一榻涼。

Miscellaneous Poems on the Lake, no.1

I vaguely recall my post in the Qing court before
   its downfall.
Now a gourd-like hut is my secluded port of call.
The sudden wind that brings noise to lotuses and the
   universe
Succeeds in cooling my mat in South Hall.

湖上雜詩，其三

海棠花畔叫秋蟲，枕簟星光螢影中。長夜
通明了無睡，虛堂流轉只荷風。

Miscellaneous Poems on the Lake, no.3

Autumn insects chirp by plots of crabapples.
Pillows and mats lie under fireflies and starlight.
I feel sleepless in the well-lit, endless night.
The air in the hall smells of lotus blooms with none
  in sight.

觀瀑亭

百丈飛泉掛一亭，岩欄危坐俯冥冥。松身
獨表諸天白，石氣寒噓太古青。洞草無心
來鳥啄，梵潮如夢起龍腥。元壇真宰愁何
事，瀸湧爐香會百靈。

Waterfall-Watching Pavilion

By a hanging pavilion, the high flying waters go.
Sitting on a high stone rail, I watch the dark void
  below.
A lone pine stands against the bright, broad sky.
In the chill, misty rocks look green from eons ago.
Birds come to peck aimlessly at the grass by caves.
Dream-like Buddhist chants make fishy dragons rise
  to follow.

A hundred spirits gather by censers with fragrant,
puffing smoke.
How can the supreme, true master of the universe be
in sorrow?

SU MANSHU (1884-1918)
蘇曼殊

憩平原別邸贈玄玄

狂歌走馬遍天涯，斗酒黃雞處士家。逢君
別有傷心在，且看寒梅未落花。

For Xuanxuan at our Stay
in a Villa of Pingyuan

In this villa of a recluse, we wine and dine.
All over, you have galloped and sung as you please.
In our meeting, I sense you are broken-hearted.
Let us watch chilled plum flowers still on trees.

以詩并畫留別湯國頓，其一

蹈海魯連不帝秦，茫茫海水著浮聲。國民
孤憤英雄淚，灑上鮫絹贈故人。

An Inscription on a Painting to Say Goodbye to Tang Guodun, no.1

Like Lu Zhonglian against Qin, you resisted Qing,
Willing to die for your cause at the end.
Lonely and angry, like other nationals, I tear for a
    hero,
On a silk handkerchief, as a gift for an old friend.

以詩并畫留別湯國頓，其二

海天龍戰血玄黃，披髮長歌覽大荒。易水
蕭蕭人去也，一天明月白如霜。

An Inscription on a Painting to Say Goodbye to Tang Guodun, no.2

Our navy fought like dragons with blood in black
    and yellow.
I sing in the wilds with loosened hair in sorrow.
With a bright moon, the sky is white like frost.
Like Jingke at River Yi, against tyranny I want to go.

莫愁湖寓坐

清涼如美人，莫愁如月鏡。終日
對凝妝，掩映萬荷柄。

Sitting Indoors by Lake Mochou

Qingliang Hill is a beauty.
Lake Mo Chou is a mirror, moon-like and bright.
I face lotus pickers, all dolled up through the day,
Amid myriad lotus stalks, in and out of sight.

本事詩十首，其一

春雨樓頭尺八簫，何時歸看浙江潮？芒鞋
破鉢無人識，踏過櫻花第幾橋？

Ten Poems of my Activities, no.1

At a tower, I play my Japanese flute on "Spring
   Rain".
For Zhejiang's tidal bore, when can I return again?
None knows me with my straw sandals and a broken
   bowl.
On how many bridges with cherry blossoms have
   my feet lain?

LIN WEN (1885-1911)
林文

春望

殘雪猶留樹，春聲已滿樓。睡醒鄉夢小，
起視大江流。別後愁多少，群山簇古丘。
獨來數歸雁，到處總悠悠。

Spring Prospect

The sounds of spring have already filled the tower,
With trees retaining the waning snow.
I wake from a dream with a hint of homesickness
And rise to watch the big river in its flow.
Ancient hillocks crowd to form the ranges.
Since we parted, how deep is my sorrow?
I count returning wild geese alone.
Everywhere, things go leisurely and slow.

JIANG SHI (Qing Dynasty)
江湜

由江山至浦城，雪後渡越諸嶺，
輿中得絕句九首，其一

連宵雨霰苦紛紛，今上籃輿盼夕曛。萬竹
無聲方受雪，亂山如夢不離雲。

From Jiangshan to Pucheng, I Passed Several Hills after Snow and Wrote Nine Quatrains in my Sedan Chair, no.1

It is painful to have snowflakes overnight.
On a bamboo sedan chair, I long for twilight.
Countless bamboos get muffled by new snow.
With clouds, the jagged hills look dreamy and right.

玉虹

陳鈞洪譯